THE
EARTH
CHRONICLES
HANDBOOK

THE
EARTH CHRONICLES HANDBOOK

*A Comprehensive Guide
to the Seven Books of
The Earth Chronicles*

ZECHARIA SITCHIN

Bear & Company
Rochester, Vermont

Bear & Company
One Park Street
Rochester, Vermont 05767
www.BearandCompanyBooks.com

Bear & Company is a division of Inner Traditions International

Copyright © 2009 by Zecharia Sitchin

Library of Congress Cataloging-in-Publication Data

Sitchin, Zecharia.
   The Earth chronicles handbook : a comprehensive guide to the seven books of the Earth chronicles / Zecharia Sitchin.
      p. cm.
   Summary: "An encyclopedic compendium of the myths and actual events from humanity's ancient civilizations that reveal the influence of visitors from the 12th planet—the Anunnaki"—Provided by publisher.
   ISBN 978-1-59143-101-5 (hardcover)
   1. Sitchin, Zecharia. Earth chronicles. 2. Civilization, Ancient—Extraterrestrial influences. 3. Interplanetary voyages. 4. Immortality. 5. Middle East— History—To 622. 6. Central America—Antiquities. 7. Stonehenge (England) 8. Mythology, Sumerian. 9. Armageddon. 10. Prophecies. I. Title.
   CB156.S5726 2009
   930.1—dc22

                                                                2009000315

Printed and bound in the United States by Lake Book Manufacturing

10 9 8 7 6 5 4 3 2 1

Text design and layout by Priscilla Baker
This book was typeset in Garamond Premier Pro

To send correspondence to the author of this book, mail a first-class letter to the author c/o Inner Traditions • Bear & Company, One Park Street, Rochester, VT 05767, and we will forward the communication.

Dedicated to the memory
of my beloved wife
FRIEDA RINA SITCHIN

INTRODUCTION

Wisdom hath built her house;
She hath hewn out her seven pillars.

PROVERBS 9:1

The seven books that comprise *The Earth Chronicles* began neither as a pre-conceived series nor even as a book. As an oak tree with seven branches, its acorn seed was a schoolboy's query why a word in the Hebrew Bible—*Nefilim*—that derives from the verb meaning To Fall, To Come Down, was translated 'Giants'. The schoolboy was I; the word is in Genesis chapter 6; the search for an explanation lasted a lifetime; the answer required—as the Bible itself does—going back to the Beginning.

The quest for the biblical Beginning opened a Pandora's Box filled with countless more questions. Why does the Bible describe the *Nefilim* as "sons of the gods" who chose wives from among the "daughters of the Adam"? Who were the *Elohim* who had fashioned The Adam in their image? Was there a Garden of Eden, and if yes, where and what was it? Was there a Deluge, was there a Noah, and if yes, who was he? How did Mankind learn how the Heavens, the Earth, and Man himself had been created? What scientific knowledge had existed in antiquity—indeed, how did Civilization itself begin? Was there a kingdom in a land called (in the Bible) Shine'ar that preceded ancient Babylon, Assyria, Egypt? And how did other civilizations arise around the world with uncanny similarities to the olden ones?

Unavoidably, the quest spread from Bible to archaeology. There was indeed a Cradle of Civilization in the ancient Near East; its monuments, artifacts, and written records unfolded a vivid history of lands and peoples whose tales of gods of heaven and Earth led through mythology to religion, from astronomy to genetics. Before long, what began as a simple question mushroomed to embrace virtually every scholarly discipline, ranging from the depths of Earth to the Solar System and Outer Space, from the Past to the Future, from the Beginning to the End of Days.

As one book followed another, spanning the continents, diverse cultures and even different religions, it became evident that these were all branches of the same one tree. A Global Theory emerged, and the tales of gods and men were rendered in my books as a unified history of Earth and Mankind. The pantheons of Greece and Rome, of Aztecs and Hindus are identified as those of Sumer and Babylon; the Mayan and Olmec calendars are compared to those of Assyria and Egypt; Inca tales of creation or a day the sun stood still echo the Hebrew Bible; pyramids and massive stone circles in varied lands reveal a basic kinship. It all makes sense because it explains the otherwise inexplicable, by my unique assertion that there is one more planet in our solar system which periodically nears our vicinity, whose astronauts had come to Earth, fashioned Mankind, were its gods, and when they left promised to return.

The result of decades of research, study, and writing is thus daunting in its scope. The seven books of *The Earth Chronicles* total more than 2,300 pages; and I have often been asked by readers: How does one 'keep a handle' on all that mass of information? Guided by readers' queries, this Handbook is the answer; alphabetically arranged, its hundreds of entries provide the relevant data about gods and demigods, kings and kingdoms, patriarchs and priests, archaeological sites and mythical places. Entries indicate links to related entries, and—when appropriate—add the particular or innovative 'take' of "ZS" on the subject. By applying a Uniform Answer to the diverse civilizations and periods, this Handbook serves as the first attempt ever to globalize ancient knowledge.

This Uniform Answer has stood the test of time: Every discovery, every technological advance, that have taken place in the past decades have invariably corroborated, without fail, the ancient evidence that others ignore or dismiss as Myth but that I consider Truth. In a way—in a significant way—the seven volumes of *The Earth Chronicles* have emerged as a depository of global Ancient Knowledge, the precious treasure that the Bible calls Wisdom.

They are, in a way, the Seven Pillars of Ancient Wisdom.

ZECHARIA SITCHIN

HANDBOOK KEY

The following key has been employed for the handbook entries:

- **Bold** = Sumerian

- *Italics* = Akkadian, Canaanite or (H) Biblical Hebrew

- CAPITAL letters = Egyptian

- The letter or sign for *ḥeth,* pronounced as 'ch' in German/Scottish lo<u>ch</u>, is transcribed as an underlined <u>h</u>.

- Words in double quotation marks are direct quotes from Sumerian and Akkadian clay-tablet texts, the Bible, or other ancient texts and inscriptions.

- ZS = Zecharia Sitchin

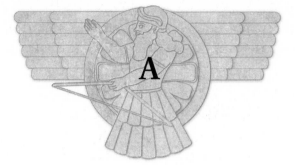

▸ Aaron: The brother of Moses who started the Jewish priestly line at the time of the Exodus.

▸ Abel (H *Hevel*): The second son of Adam and Eve, "a keeper of herds," who was killed by his brother Cain. For a Sumerian take on the subject, see Agriculture, Cain, Domestication.

▸ Abraham (According to the Bible, changed from his original name **Abram** = 'Beloved Father' or 'Father's Beloved'): The first Hebrew Patriarch, credited with the start of Monotheism, the belief in a sole God—identified in the Bible as '*Yahweh*'. According to Genesis, God made a covenant with Abram to grant to his descendants the lands between the Brook of Egypt (a winter stream in the Sinai peninsula) and the Euphrates river in northern Mesopotamia, rewarding him for his unwavering fealty to the sole God, and for carrying out an assignment known from Genesis chapter 14 as The War of the Kings. In *The Wars of Gods and Men* ZS linked those events to ones described in tablets known as the Khedorlamoer Texts, and synchronized the timing and movements of Abram with the chronologies of Mesopotamia and Egypt, leading to the conclusions that Abram was born in 2123 B.C. in Sumer's religious center *Nippur* (**Ne.Ibru**), from which came his identification as *Ibri*—"A Nippurian"—in the Hebrew Bible, and per ZS, his name **Ib.ru.um** in Sumerian. He moved with his father Tera<u>h</u>, a priest, to Ur, Sumer's capital, then to <u>H</u>arran (a site now in Turkey), and finally to Canaan (now Israel) on divine orders. ZS has shown that those migrations coincided with events recorded in Sumerian and later Babylonian texts, including the War of the Kings when he defended the Spaceport in the Sinai peninsula. After the destruction of that spaceport with nuclear weapons (recorded in the Bible as the upheavaling of Sodom and Gomorrah) and the resulting demise of Sumer, Abram's name was changed to the Semitic *Abraham*; his spouse's was changed from Sarai to *Sarah*, and they had a son, Isaac. They were both buried in Hebron. *See* H̲arran, Khedorla'omer Texts, Nippur, Patriarchs, Spaceport, Ur, War of the Kings.

▸ **Ab.Sin** ("Her father is Sin"): The Sumerian name for the zodiacal constellation honoring Inanna/Ishtar, the daughter of the god Sin. Our name for it, Virgo (= 'The Maiden') goes back to the beginning of the zodiacal system, when the constellation honored the goddess Ninharsag who never married. The pictorial depiction of the constellation remained unchanged, to this day—that of a beautiful woman. *See* Inanna.

▸ Abydos: An ancient Egyptian site where a tablet ascribed to the Pharaoh Seti I (and depicting him and his son Ramses II) was discovered. Inscribed in hieroglyphics, it listed the ancient Egyptian royal dynasties, starting with the Pharaoh MEN (Menes in Greek).

▸ **Ab.zu,** *Absu* ("The Primeval Source/Depth," from which 'Abyss'). The gold mining land of the Anunnaki in Southeast Africa, "where great waters rapidly flow." Ea/Enki's domain. According to Sumerian Creation texts, it was at Enki's abode there that he fashioned, together with Ninharsag, a 'Primitive Worker'—Man—mixing the "essence" of a young Anunnaki with "clay of the Abzu." *See* Anunnaki, DNA, Gold.

▸ Achaemenids: A tribal dynasty in Anshan, a province in Elam east of Sumer, whose kings laid the foundations of the Persian empire. They included Cyrus, who captured Babylon in 539 B.C. and decreed the rebuilding of the Temple in Jerusalem, Darius I and Xerxes I who invaded Greece in the 5th century B.C., and Darius III who fought the invading Greek army of Alexander the Great in the 4th century B.C. *See* Alexander the Great, Elam, Persia/Persians, Susa, Xerxes.

▶ Acropolis: The hilltop complex of ancient temples in the Greek capital, Athens.

▶ **Adab:** An early Sumerian city.

▶ Adad (also *Hadad*): Enlil's youngest son (the Sumerian **Ishkur**) whose main domain was mountainous Anatolia (today's Turkey)—the land of the Hittites, who called him 'Teshub' (= 'Wind Stormer') and depicted him with his weapon, a lightning bolt, standing upon a bull (his 'cult animal'). After the Deluge he was sent to supervise the mining of gold and tin in South America, where his presence was recorded by his carved image on the 'Gate of the Sun' in Tiahuanacu (now in Bolivia) and of his emblem on a mountainside in the Bay of Paracas (now in Peru). Canaanite texts called him simply *Ba'al* (= Lord), master of the 'Landing Place' in the Lebanon mountains. *See* Ba'albek, Hittites, Storm God.

▶ *Adam*: (From H *Adamah* = Earth), so literally (H) 'He of the Earth'—Earthling. The creation tale in Genesis refers to him as *The* Adam, a new species of intelligent being fashioned by the *Elohim* (a plural term) who said "let us fashion the Adam in our image and after our likeness" (Genesis 1:26). Sumerian creation tales attributed the feat to the god Enki and the birth-goddess Ninharsag following a decision of the Anunnaki to create a 'Primitive Worker' (*Lulu amelu*) by genetic engineering—combining their genes with those of a hominid that had already existed on Earth. The Bible then uses 'Adam' as the personal name of the progenitor, with his wife Eve, of the line of Mankind's antediluvial patriarchs. ZS has suggested that the biblical tale, and more so its Sumerian antecedents, provide the 'Missing Link' in human evolution.

▶ **Adapa:** "The wisest of men," a son of Enki by an Earthling woman who was the first human to be given knowledge—writing, mathematics and astronomy. According to a text known as 'The Epic of Adapa', he was the first Earthling to journey to Nibiru, to be presented to Anu. Enki made sure Adapa would return to Earth without the longevity of the Anunnaki.

▶ *Adda-Guppi*: The High Priestess in the temple of the god Sin in H̱arran (now in southeastern Turkey) who (in 555 B.C.) persuaded the god to make her son Nabuna'id king of Babylon. She witnessed the departure of Sin from Earth and his eventual return—miraculous events that were recorded by Adda-Guppi and Nabuna'id on four stone columns erected in the god's temple. (Nabuna'id turned out to be the last king of Babylon). *See* Ehulhul, H̱arran, Nabunaid, Sin.

▸ Aditi, Adityas: In the Hindu tales of the gods, the initial seven great gods of the Hindu pantheon, sons of the god Kasyapa and the goddess Aditi— among them Vishnu, Varuna, Rudra and Indra. In time, as in the Greek tales of the gods, they were joined by five more to form the twelve members of the divine clan that became dominant after several generations of competing and warring gods. In those wars, magical weapons were used in aerial battles. *See* Aerial Battles, God/gods.

▸ Admonitions of IPU-WER: The name given to an ancient Egyptian papyrus whose long hieroglyphic text contains prophetic sections about a coming time of troubles and tribulations, a kind of messianic birth pangs leading to the appearance of a Redeemer who will usher an idyllic era. The title given to this text comes from the fact that it includes a series of admonitions to those who have abandoned religious practices, including a call for them to repent and be baptized. The papyrus purports to prophecy in the 26th century B.C. about events in the 22nd century B.C.; some scholars believe that it was in fact written after the described events.

▸ Aerial Battles: Various ancient texts describe aerial battles of the gods, the oldest of them being the Sumerian 'Tale of Zu' in which a god called **Zu** (or **An.Zu** according to recently discovered text fragments) betrayed the trust of Enlil and stole the 'Tablets of Destinies' that were essential to the operation of Mission Control Center in Nippur. The tablets were eventually retrieved after Zu was defeated in an aerial battle with the god Ninurta. An Egyptian text known as 'The Contending of Horus and Seth' asserts that the prolonged conflict between these two gods ended only after Horus defeated Seth in an aerial battle over the Sinai peninsula. In Greek tales of the gods, the fierce battles between Zeus and the monstrous giant Thyphoeus (Typhon) culminated when Zeus, in his Winged Chariot, shot a thunderbolt at the magical aerial contraption of his adversary. Detailed descriptions of aerial battles between the gods— flying in "cloud-borne chariots"—are found in the Hindu Sanskrit texts, such as the Vedas, the Puranas and the Mahabharata.

▶ Aerial Chariots: Besides references to and descriptions of aerial chariots in texts dealing with aerial battles (see previous entry), 'Aerial Chariot' (Sumerian **Mar.gid.da**, Akkadian *Tiyaritu*), 'Sky Chamber' (Sumerian **Mu**), 'Boat of Heaven', 'Divine Black Bird' (**Im.du.gud**) and similar terms are used in ancient Near Eastern texts to describe the personal aircraft—as distinct from spacecraft or rocketships (**Gir**)—of various gods, among them the Mesopotamian Ninurta, Marduk, and Inanna/Ishtar, the Egyptian gods Ra and Thoth, the Canaanite Ba'al and Anat, the Hindu god Indra and his 'Vimana'. The Assyrian version of the Atra-Hasis tale of the Deluge uses the term *rukub ilani* (= 'Divine Chariots') for the aerial vehicles in which the gods took off to escape the avalanche of water. The Bible, in the tale of the Prophet Elijah's ascent to heaven uses a term commonly translated 'Whirlwind', and in the vision of the Prophet Ezekiel a *Merkava* = literally 'chariot'. *See also* Rocketships, Shem.

▶ Africa: The continent that was, "after the Earth was divided," the domain of **Enki** and his six sons. *See also* Lower World.

▶ Afterlife: The ancient Egyptian Pharaohs believed that they would attain immortality in an Afterlife—that they would journey, after dying and found worthy when their hearts would be weighed, to the 'Planet of Millions of Years' to live happily ever after among the gods. The Journey To The Afterlife was described and illustrated in texts such as the Book Of The Dead and Pyramid Texts. *See* Journey to the Afterlife.

▶ *Agade*: *See* Akkad.

▶ Ages: The divisions of the past and its events into defined periods, whether of uniform duration or not. While modern scholars speak of an Ice Age (defined by climate) or the Stone, Copper, Bronze and Iron Ages (defined by the predominant tools' materials), ancient peoples had already divided their historic and legendary past into Ages. The Sumerians, followed by the Babylonians and Assyrians, attached particular significance to Zodiacal Ages (that mathematically lasted 2,160 years each, or 25,960 years in a complete cycle); these numbers co-related with the 432,000 years (120 **Sars** of 3,600 years each) that—according to the Sumerian King Lists and Berossus—passed from the arrival of the Anunnaki to the Deluge (per ZS, 3,600 years was the mathematical orbital period of **Nibiru**). The Egyptians divided prehistory and history by dynastic rulers—first divine, then semi-divine, and finally Pharaonic; the priest Manetho stated that the "duration of the world" was 2,160,000 years— exactly (per ZS) 1,000 times the 2,160 years of a zodiacal age. The Mesoamerican Ages consisted of 'Suns' of varying lengths, four past and a fifth 'Sun' of the Present. Hindu traditions defined the Ages experienced by Earth and Mankind as 'Yugas' that were precise multiples of the number 432,000 (thus linked to the Sumerian Ages). *See* Apocalypse, Berossus, History/Cyclical, Manetho, Yugas, Zodiacal Ages.

▸ **Agga**: A king of Kish, a city in Sumer, who was a rival of the famed **Gilgamesh**, king of Uruk.

▸ Agni: A Hindu god, brother of Indra, whose weapon was fiery thunderbolts.

▸ Agriculture: Scientific data determined that the cultivation of cereals and then other food crops began circa 10500 B.C. in the ancient Near East, in an area embracing today's western Syria, eastern Lebanon and northern Israel. ZS has pointed out that the modern scientific findings corroborate the Sumerian tales of how the gods Enlil and Enki, needing to feed the gods and the remnants of Mankind after the Deluge, used a mountain base as a seed laboratory for the cultivation of crops and animal husbandry; he identified the place as the Baalbek platform in Lebanon. In the Americas, legends also attributed to the gods the introduction of maize (corn). *See* Domestication.

▸ *Aḥaz*: An 8th century B.C. Judean king whose sun clock in Jerusalem, known as (H) *Ma'alot Ahaz* (= 'stairs/degrees of Ahaz') provided a prophetic miracle described by the Bible in II Kings 20 and Isaiah 38.

▸ *Ahiram* (English: Hiram): King of the Phoenician city Tyre who assisted his ally King Solomon in building the Temple in Jerusalem (10th century B.C.).

▸ AH-MOSE (Ahmosis, Amosis in Greek): The founder of ancient Egypt's 18th dynasty (1570–1352 B.C.) that included the famed Pharaohs Thothmose (THOTH-MES, also written Thothmosis, Tutmosis) I, II, III and IV, the female Pharaoh Hatshepsut, as well as Akhen-Aten and Tut-Ankh-Amen. The royal names were theophoric, the first part being the name of a god (AH, THOTH, etc.) and the second part, MSS (read Mes/Mose/Mosis) meaning 'issue of, born of' that god. ZS has suggested that Hatshepsut was the "Pharaoh's daughter" who raised the biblical *Moses*, giving him a name ending with MSS (= Mose, *Moshe*) as was typical of her dynasty. *See* Hatshepsut, Moses, Sphinx, Thothmes.

▸ Akapana: One of the main archaeological features of the ancient site of Tiahuanacu (also spelled Tiwanaku) near the shores of Lake Titicaca in Bolivia. A hill-like structure that some suggest is the remains of a pyramid. Excavations revealed in its interior a series of channels and chambers connected by conduits that suggested to ZS it was a facility for metallurgical processing. *See* Tiahuanacu.

▸ AKHEN-ATEN: The Pharaoh Amenhotep/Amenophus IV who, circa 1379 B.C., introduced in Egypt the worship of the celestial disc called 'Aten'—a form of monotheism according to some scholars; per ZS, it was a new name, denoting a Cross, for Nibiru, in line with expectations of its Return into view. In his inscriptions the Pharaoh claimed that he was a god-son, heralding a messianic time. *See* Aten, Winged Disc.

▸ A.ki.ti (= 'Build [on] Earth Life'): The Sumerian New Year festival whose ceremonies required the reigning city god to leave, disappear, and return in a procession whose seven stations emulated the original space journey from Nibiru to the Seventh Planet (Earth). Celebrated as the *Akitu* festival in Babylon, it assumed a central role in the elevation of its god

Marduk to supremacy; there, the New Year ceremonies included 'Passion Plays' that re-enacted Marduk's Resurrection, having been buried alive to die inside the Great Pyramid, then emerging alive and triumphant. *See* Nabu, Pyramid Wars.

▸ *Akkad, Akkadian*: The Mesopotamian land adjoining Sumer on the north-west, settled by people whose language—"Akkadian"—is considered the Mother Tongue of all Semitic languages (including Hebrew, Canaanite, Phoenician, Aramaic, Arabic, etc.). A text known as 'The Legend of Sargon' relates that, at a time of turmoil in Sumer, the airborne god-dess Inanna/Ishtar, landing in a field, had sex with its gardener, and recommended him to the Anunnaki leadership to be the next king. Titled *Sharru-kin* (= 'Trustworthy King'—from which '*Sargon*')—he established circa 2370 B.C. a new capital, *Agade* ('Union, United'—from which *Akkad)*, and the united realm was henceforth known as Sumer & Akkad. The Akkadian dynasty, especially during the reign of Sargon's grandson Naram-Sin, engaged in conquest and warfare at the behest of Inanna/Ishtar, angering the other gods; in 2230 B.C. they terminated the dynasty and obliterated Agade. *See* Naram-Sin, Sargon of Akkad.

▸ Akkadian Prophecies: A group of pro-Marduk cuneiform texts written in Old Babylonian and thus dated to the 22nd century B.C. that describe in apocalyptic terms what is to befall Mankind and even its gods. Listing a variety of wrongs, they predict a time of troubles and tribulations of unheard-of magnitude—divine judgments and punishments coming as natural calamities, overwhelming devastations, wars, toppling of kings and kingdoms, killing of officials and priests, desecration of temples, hunger and mass suffering—leading to the appearance of a Redeemer who will right the wrongs, comfort the people, and bring salvation to all. Underlying this sequence was the view that Past, Present and Future are part of a continuous flow of events manifesting a pre-ordained Destiny; in this particular case, the inevitability of Marduk's triumph over less worthy gods. *See* Admonitions of Ipu-Wer, Marduk, Nabu.

▸ **Alalu**: A ruler of the planet Nibiru who was deposed by Anu and escaped to Earth. Per ZS, it was he who discovered the availability of gold on

Earth, leading to the coming of the Anunnaki to Earth to obtain the metal. During one of Anu's visits to Earth, the two wrestled and Alalu bit off Anu's 'manhood'.

▶ Ale-woman: Called *Siduri* in the Epic of Gilgamesh, she was the innkeeper who gave succor and advice to Gilgamesh when he reached the "Sea of the waters of death" on his way to Tilmun (= 'Land of the Missiles'). ZS has identified the place as the outskirts of Jericho, near the shores of the Dead Sea, and pointed out the parallels to the later biblical tale of the safe haven given the Israelite spies by the 'Innkeeper-woman' Rahab in Jericho.

▶ Alexander (the Great): The son of the Macedonian king Philip II and queen Olympias who (in 334 B.C) led an army across the Hellespont (now called the Dardanelles) strait separating Europe and Asia Minor, and in a series of battles defeated the army of the Persian king Darius. He conquered Asia from the Mediterranean Sea all the way to India, and Egypt in Africa. Historians consider Alexander's invasion of Asia a response to previous Persian attacks on Greece; ZS has additionally highlighted the personal motivations of Alexander, stemming from court rumors that his real father was the Egyptian god Amon—making him a demigod and worthy of immortality. This explains why Alexander, after the first inconclusive battle with the Persians, set his course to the oasis of Siwa in Egypt, the site of a famed oracle, seeking confirmation of his divinity. He then proceeded to Babylon, where he paid homage to Amon/Ra/Marduk by entering the great god's tomb within the Esagil ziggurat. Alexander himself died in Babylon, at age 32, in 323 B.C.

▶ Alexandria: A city in Egypt on the Mediterranean coast, built for burying Alexander the Great after his death. It was famed in antiquity as a center of learning, linked to its great library (which was destroyed, together with its invaluable manuscripts, when it was set on fire by Moslem conquerors in A.D. 642). The city was famous in antiquity for its harbor.

▶ Allah: The sole Great God worshipped by Moslems, symbolically represented by the sign of the Crescent.

▸ *Allat*: The later name of the goddess *Elat*, a consort of the Canaanite god *El*, who was worshipped in the Near East, especially in the Sinai peninsula and northern Arabia.

▸ Al Mamoon: The Moslem ruler ('Caliph') of Egypt who, in A.D. 830 employed masons, blacksmiths and engineers to tunnel his way into the Great Pyramid in Giza in search of hidden treasure. Slightly missing the original entranceway in the pyramid's north face, he reached the descending corridor that had been a familiar feature of other pyramids. Then, due to a chance drop of a stone block, his men discovered the unique features in this pyramid's upper parts—the 'King's' and 'Queen's' chambers and the horizontal and ascending passages leading to them, including the magnificent Grand Gallery.

▸ Alphabet, Alphabetic Writing: The first writing system, in Sumer, advanced from pictographs denoting objects or actions to the use of wedgelike ('cuneiform') signs to denote syllabic pronunciation. Egyptian writing progressed similarly, but continued to use pictographs ('hieroglyphs') throughout. As a result, both systems required the use by scribes of hundreds of signs. Alphabetic writing, that appeared for the first time in the Sinai peninsula in the mid–second millennium B.C., was the achievement of a genius who switched to a vocal system, choosing the simplified pictograph of an object, such as an oxhead (*Aluf* in Semitic Hebrew) to denote the sound "A," of a house (*Bayit*) to denote the sound "B," and so on. The result was the reduction of the script to an 'alpha-bet' of just twenty-two signs. ZS has seen in the timing and location of the alphabet's invention possible answers to the question: In what language and script did Moses, on Mount Sinai at the time of the Exodus, write down the divine dictation (on just two stone tablets)? (Re the Hebrew Alphabet, *see also* DNA.)

▸ Amalekites: A tribe that blocked the Israelite entry into the Sinai during the Exodus, leading to a fierce battle.

▸ **Amar.Pal**: Another possible reading of the name **Amar.Sin**. ZS has suggested that Amar.Sin/Amar.Pal was the *"Amraphel, king of Shine'ar"* (i.e., of Sumer) who, according to Genesis 14, led an alliance of "kings of the East" against an alliance of "kings of the West"—a war in which Abraham played an important role. ZS pinpointed the date of that attack as 2041 B.C., equating it with Ur III royal annals ('Date Formulas') about Amar-Sin's military expedition against "rebel lands" in the west. The real target, according to ZS, was the Spaceport in the Sinai, and the principal mission of Abraham was to defend the Spaceport. *See* Amar.Sin, Spaceport, Tilmun.

▸ **Amar.Sin** (= 'Seen by Sin'): The third ruler (2047–2039 B.C.) of Sumer's Third Dynasty of Ur, son of Shulgi, who tried to defend Sumer by military offensives in the north and the west. He led a punitive military expedition against an alliance of pro-Marduk Canaanite kings, possibly attempting to seize control of the Spaceport in the Sinai. *See* Amar.Pal, En.shag, Tilmun.

▸ Amazon: South America's immense river, running with its numerous tributaries from the Andes mountains in the west to the Atlantic Ocean in the east, mostly through a great rain forest—a distance of more than 2,000 miles. Unnavigable in its deeper jungle parts, the River became a source of reports of lost cities, such as a legendary 'Akakor'.

▸ AMON (Ammon, Amen): An epithet-name, meaning 'The Unseen', for the Egyptian god RA. Per ZS, Ra was the Egyptian name of the god whom the Babylonians called Marduk, and the epithet (often in the combined form Ra-Amon), came into usage when Ra/Marduk was exiled from Egypt. ZS has linked the events to the chaotic period in Egypt known as the First Intermediate Period that began circa 2160 B.C. and separated the Old Kingdom from the Middle Kingdom in Egyptian history.

▸ Amorites (*Amurru*, **Martu**): A Semitic people inhabiting the lands west of the Euphrates River, now mostly Syria. Culturally and religiously part of Sumer & Akkad, in time their chieftains qualified to reign in Sumer and in Babylon. Their best known center, Mari, was extensively excavated.

▸ *Amos*: One of the Prophets of the Hebrew Bible who conveyed to the people of Israel and other nations the Word of God. Chronologically, he was the first of them, having begun to prophesy circa 760 B.C. He correctly predicted the future assaults by Assyria, and dwelt on the coming 'Day of the Lord', a "day when the Earth shall darken in the midst of daytime"—per ZS, the return of Nibiru to Earth's vicinity. *See* Day of the Lord.

▶ **An** (= 'Heaven'); **An.** *Anu* (= 'The Heavenly One'): The ruler on the planet Nibiru when its astronauts came to Earth. Father by his official spouse Antu of Enlil, and by other wives of Ea/Enki and Ninharsag. Though scion of a long line of Nibiruan royalty, he seized the throne by deposing the reigning king Alalu; their enmity reverberated through the ensuing generations. As head of the pantheon, his numerical rank was 60. Per ZS, Anu made at least three recorded visits to Earth—one when it became necessary to launch a full fledged Earth Mission; another after a mutiny of the Anunnaki, when it was decided to create a "Primitive Worker;" and a state visit with Antu circa 4000 B.C. when civilization was granted to Mankind.

▶ AN, Annu (Called *On* in the Bible): The original name of the Egyptian city later known as Heliopolis that was ancient Egypt's first religious center. Hieroglyphic inscriptions tell that Pharaohs were allowed to enter the Holy of Holies of the city's great temple once a year to view the "celestial barque" in which the god RA, the son of Ptah, had arrived on Earth from the "Planet of millions of years." According to Genesis 41, when Joseph was appointed Overseer Over Egypt, the Pharaoh "gave him Assenath, the daughter of Potiphera, the Priest of On, for a wife." *See* Ben-Ben.

▶ *Anakim* (H): Commonly translated 'Giants'; *see* Anunnaki *and Nefilim.*

▶ *Anat* (= 'She who responds'): A goddess who in Canaanite lore was the playmate of the god Ba'al; many of those tales ascribe to her the lovemaking and sky-roaming adventures attributed in Sumerian/Akkadian texts to Ishtar.

▶ Anatolia: Asia Minor, today's Turkey.

▶ Angels: In the Bible, the term is used to translate the Hebrew word *Mal'achim*, which literally means 'emissaries'. Though it was used in the Bible to denote even a king's ambassadors, the translation "angels" is taken to mean divine emissaries, commonly depicted as winged beings. In the Bible, a class of angels called *Seraphim* are described in Isaiah 6 as having six wings each; the two golden *Cherubim* atop the Ark of the Covenant had four wings each (similar to divine entities protecting the coffin of the Pharaoh Tut-Ankh-Amen). In Mesopotamia, both gods and their emissaries were depicted wearing uniforms with attached wings— per ZS, to indicate their status as astronauts. *See* Cherubim, Eaglemen, Winged Beings.

▶ ANKH: The ancient Egyptian pictographic hieroglyph that looks like a plumbline instrument and means 'Life'.

▶ **An.na** (= 'Heavenly stone'): The Sumerian term for Tin—*Anaku* in Akkadian, from which in Hebrew *Anak* = necklace and *Anakh* = a plumbline instrument. *See also* Ankh.

▶ Anshan: A Persian province that was a stronghold of the Achaemeans, who made their mark on the ancient world when Cyrus became king in 549 B.C.

▶ **An.shar** (= 'Foremost of the Heavens'): Per ZS, the planet we call Saturn. Its role in the formation of the Solar System is described in the Mesopotamian 'Epic of Creation'. *See also* Ki.shar.

▶ Antarctica: The icebound southernmost continent, where the Earth's south pole is located. Though unknown to Europeans before its discovery in 1820, the existence of maps from earlier dates that correctly show the continent, indicates that it was already known in prior eras. ZS has suggested that the Sumerian geographic name **Erkallum**, usually translated 'the Great Below', referred to Antarctica, and was the biblical "Great Deep" where the Deluge or Great Flood began; it was caused, per ZS, by the slippage of the ice shelf off the Antarctic continent, creating an immense tidal wave, a rise in sea levels, and climate change. *See also* Nibiru Orbit.

▸ Antikythera Mechanism: An incredible device of bronze geared wheels within geared wheels, tightly arranged in a wooden box, that was discovered by Greek divers in a shipwreck off the Mediterranean island of Antikythera in A.D. 1900. Other artifacts in the shipwreck dated to as early as the 4th century B.C.; the ship itself has been dated to circa 200 B.C. Early Greek writing inside the box and on some of the wheels indicated that this was a complex device to compute celestial motions of the Sun, Moon and planets in relation to zodiacal time. The closest geared astronomical or horological devices appeared in Europe only some 1700 years later. The device, now in the National Archaeological Museum in Athens, has been x-rayed, MRI'd and otherwise studied; but with all that the experts have no answer to the questions, Who had the astronomical knowledge and the technical capability needed for this device, who was there to use it, in 400/200 B.C., and what was it for? For the explanation by ZS, see *Journeys to the Mythical Past*.

▸ **Antu**: An/Anu's official spouse. Because she was his half-sister (same father, different mother), her son Enlil became Anu's Legal Heir though he was not Anu's Firstborn son. She accompanied Anu on his state visits to Earth.

▸ **Anunnaki** (= 'Those who from Heaven to Earth came'), sometimes shortened to **Anunna** (= 'The heavenly ones'): The Nibiruans who had come to Earth to mine its gold. The first group of fifty was led by Ea. More came after the arrival of Enlil and the establishment of seven settlements, each with a specific function, in the **E.Din** (= 'Home/Abode of the Righteous Ones'), later known as Sumer. At the peak of their presence on Earth they numbered 600, joined by 300 **Igi.gi** with special tasks. They were the "gods of Heaven and Earth" whom the ancient peoples worshipped. ZS has suggested in his writings that the biblical term *Anakim*, commonly translated 'giants', is in fact the Hebrew rendering of **Anunnaki**; they were termed *Ilu* (= 'Lofty Ones') in Akkadian—the biblical *Elohim*. According to the Sumerian King List, the Anunnaki reigned on Earth for 120 Sars (= 432,000 Earth years) from their arrival until the Deluge; ZS has concluded that they departed from Earth in the 6th century B.C. *See* An (Anu), Ea/Enki, El, Elohim, Enlil, Nazca, Nefilim, Nibiru, King/Kingship.

▸ **An.zu** (= 'Knower of Heaven'): An antagonist of Enlil who managed to steal the 'Tablets of Destinies' and disrupt the 'Bond Heaven-Earth'. The Sumerian text describing the events and the ultimate defeat of the evil god by Enlil's son Ninurta has been known as *The Myth of Zu*; but a recent discovery of a missing fragment of the text revealed that the offender's name, thought to be just Zu, was in fact An.Zu. *See* Aerial Battles, Zu.

▸ Aphrodite: The Greek goddess of love (Roman 'Venus'), a daughter of Zeus and one of the Twelve Olympians. According to legends, she came to Greece from the Near East via the island of Cyprus. Her attributes parallel many of **Inanna**/Ishtar.

▸ **Apin**: A Sumerian astronomical name for the planet we call Mars. *See* Mars.

▸ **Apkallu**: The collective term for the first group of commanders who piloted spacecraft from Nibiru to Earth. From **Ab.gal** (= 'Great One Who Leads'), the name of the first one.

▸ Apocalypse: A term, stemming from the Greek 'To reveal', connoting prophetic revelations concerning the End—End of Time, End of the World—or the cataclysmic aspects of the End-event itself. Apocalyptic texts, that appeared both in Egypt and in Babylon more than a millennium before the biblical ones, admonished the people for religious or social transgressions, and described the coming upheavals and tribulations on a global or even cosmic scale; they also predicted the appearance of a Redeemer who will comfort and bring salvation to the masses. *See* Admonitions of Ipu-Wer, Akkadian Prophecies, Day of the Lord, End of Days, Marduk, Nabu, Prophets.

▸ Apocrypha: Ancient extra-biblical books not included in the canonical Hebrew Bible, but available in various other languages, such as the Book of Jubilees, The Book of Enoch, The Book of Noah; they purport to provide added details to biblical tales, such as the name of the leaders and the number of Nefilim (200) who took Daughters of Man as wives.

▸ Apollo: A major Greek (and later Roman) deity, god of prophecy and divination, the interpreter to mortals of the will of the gods; Delphi, ancient Greece's holiest oracle site, was the principal place of his worship. Though the firstborn son of Zeus (by the goddess Leto), he was not the Legal Heir because Zeus later had a son (Ares/Mars) by a sister-wife. He was directly involved in the Trojan War; legends had him journey to distant lands—per ZS (in *The Earth Chronicles Expeditions*) including the Americas.

▸ *Aqhat*: In Canaanite tales of gods and heroes, the son born in old age to an heirless devotee of the god El. He was presented with a magical bow by the 'Craftsman of the gods'. Coveted by the goddess Anat, she offered Aqhat lovemaking and eternal life in exchange for the bow. (The tablet with the tale's ending has not been found.)

▸ Aquarius: 'The Water Bearer', one of the twelve zodiacal constellations. The Sumerians associated this constellation with **E.a** (= 'Whose Home Is Waters') and depicted it by showing Ea seated with water streaming from him.

▸ **Arali** (= 'The place of the shining lodes by the waters'): The gold mining area of the Anunnaki in southeast Africa; Enki's headquarters in Africa.

▸ Aram, Arameans: The land peopled by speakers of a Semitic language ('Aramaic') in the upper Euphrates River region that is now mostly northeast Syria. *See* Damascus.

▸ Ararat: The highest twin mountain peaks in Western Asia (17,000 and 12,000 feet), situated in what is nowadays eastern Turkey, between Lake Van and Lake Sevan—an area known in antiquity as 'Urartu', a Hurrian kingdom in the 2nd millennium B.C. Known from the biblical tale of the Deluge as the first dry land to emerge from the Flood's receding waters, where Noah's ark could come to rest. Called 'Mount *Nitzir*' (= 'Mount of Salvation') in the Mesopotamian tale of the Deluge. According to ZS, the twin peaks were used by the Anunnaki as a visible topographic marker for laying out their pre-Diluvial as well as post-Diluvial Landing Corridors for their spacecraft.

▸ **Aratta**: A land, distant from Sumer and located beyond mountain ranges, famed for its granaries and jewels—perhaps the ancient Indus Valley metropolis Harappa. It was granted by the Great Anunnaki to the goddess Ishtar as her domain; but she kept coming back to her preferred city Uruk in Sumer, causing rivalries detailed in a Sumerian epic known as 'Enmerkar and the Lord of Aratta'. *See* Harappa.

▸ *Arba* (= H 'Four'): According to the Bible, the previous name of Hebron, "a fortified city" so named after its erstwhile ruler Arba who was "a Great Man of the *Anakim*." ZS has pointed out that 'Great Man' is a literal rendering in Hebrew of the Sumerian **Lu.gal**, which meant 'King'; and *Anakim* was the Hebrew for Anunnaki. Hebron, accordingly, was originally a stronghold of a demigod called Arba. *See* Anunnaki, Kings/ Kingship.

▸ Archaeoastronomy: The discipline that combines astronomy with archaeology and enables the dating of ancient monuments by ascertaining their astronomical orientation. First suggested by Sir Norman Lockyer in his 1894 book *The Dawn of Astronomy* (after his visit to the temples of Athena in Greece), and applied by him to the dating of Egyptian temples and of Stonehenge in Britain.

▸ Ares (Roman 'Mars'): In Greek 'mythology', the son of Zeus and Hera. He was considered the great god's legal heir (because Hera was a sister-wife of Zeus), even though Apollo, son of Zeus by the goddess Leto, was the Firstborn.

▸ Aries (**Ku.mal**): 'The Ram'. One of the twelve zodiacal constellations, associated in Mesopotamia with the god Marduk. Occupying a smaller segment of the heavens than most other zodiacal constellations, it shifts due to Precession in less years than the mathematical 2,160 years (one twelfth of the 25,920 years cycle). It was the dispute whether the Age of the Ram—the era of Marduk's pre-eminence—has arrived in the 21st century B.C. that led to the use of nuclear weapons on Earth in 2024 B.C. (Berossus, as a priest of Marduk, wrote for his Greek masters that their contemporary Age of the Ram began 1920 years before the Seleucid Era, i.e., in 2232 B.C.).

▸ *Ariokh*: The 'King of Ellasar' listed in Genesis 14 as one of the Kings of the East who invaded Canaan at the time of Abraham.

▸ Ark: A term applied in English both to Noah's submersible vessel in the biblical tale of the Deluge (H) *Tevah* (*see* Noah's Ark), and the Ark (H: *Aron*) of the Covenant, the gold-plated wooden box in which Moses placed the stone tablets inscribed with the Ten Commandments (*see* Ark of the Covenant, Deluge).

▸ Ark of the Covenant (H) *Aron Ha-Brith*: A wooden gilded box constructed according to precise instructions by God to Moses during the Exodus. Topped by two *Cherubim* fashioned and cast of solid gold whose wings touched, it served as a divine communication device. Unauthorized approach or touching led to death. The Ark, in which Moses deposited the two stone Tablets of the Law from Mount Sinai, accompanied the Israelites throughout the Exodus and played a miraculous role in the crossing of the Jordan River. It was finally placed in the Holy of Holies in the Jerusalem Temple built by king Solomon, approachable only by the High Priest. The Ark of the Covenant was gone from its hallowed place when the Babylonians sacked Jerusalem and destroyed the Temple in 587 B.C.; when and how the Ark was gone, has remained a subject of speculation and legend to this day. (An adventure-filled attempt by ZS to unravel the mystery is described by him in *The Earth Chronicles Expeditions*.)

▸ Armageddon: The term, that has come to mean a final and terrible apocalypse that will engulf the Earth and its people, comes from the New Testament's Book 'The Apocalypse of St. John the Divine' (commonly called *Revelation*). In a prophecy of a catastrophe "such as was not since men were upon the earth," the book also envisions a final terrible war when "the kings of the earth and of the whole world" shall be gathered "into a place called in the Hebrew tongue Armageddon" (16:16). The term is clearly a rendering of the Hebrew name *Har Megiddo,* the Mount of Megiddo—a place in Israel already known in biblical time as a strategic peak where many battles had been fought. In that final war, *Revelation* asserts, one of the combatant 'beasts' "shall make fire come down from heaven to Earth, in sight of men"—a statement that can be understood as predicting a nuclear explosion. ZS, in *The End of Days,* places the Armageddon oracle in the context of other prophecies of a Final War (such as that of Gog and Magog by the Prophet Ezekiel) that will precede messianic times, and views the 2007 discovery of an ancient mosaic depiction of the Sign of the Fishes at the foot of Mount Megiddo as a clue to the time of the apocalypse. *See* Ezekiel, Gog and Magog, Megiddo, Revelation.

▸ *Arpakhshad* (Arpachshad): According to the genealogical list of nations who repeopled the Earth after the Deluge (Genesis 10), one of the five sons of Shem (the eldest of the three sons of Noah) of whom Abraham was descended. Details re Arpachshad in the 'Book of Jubilees' suggest that his domain was the land later known as Elam.

▸ Aryans (also Arya): Speakers of an Indo-European language who migrated in the 2nd millennium B.C., presumably from the Caucasus area, to the Indian subcontinent, bringing with them the tales of the gods as later recorded in the Vedas. *See* Hindu Traditions, Indo-European.

▸ **Asar:** An epithet of Marduk, used in the seventh tablet of *Enuma elish* as a prefix of several of his fifty names.

▸ Ascending Passage: One of the main inner passages within the Great Pyramid in Giza, Egypt, leading to the Grand Gallery and the 'King's Chamber'.

▸ Ashanti: A tribe in west Africa renowned for its goldsmithing skills. ZS has pointed out that their males' features are akin to those of the Olmec chieftains in Mesoamerica.

▸ *Asher*: One of the twelve sons of the patriarch Jacob and the Israelite tribe named after him.

▶ *Asherah* (also *Ashtoreth* in the Bible): A Canaanite goddess widely worshipped in the Near East in the late 2nd and early 1st millennia B.C.

▶ *Ashur* (= 'The One Who Sees'): The great god of the Assyrians and the name by which they called their land (*see* Assyria) and one of its capitals. Adopting the Sumero-Akkadian pantheon, the Assyrians in their texts assigned to him the attributes of Enlil, but often referred to him as though he was Enlil's son Ninurta. He was depicted as a mature bearded deity wearing the horned helmet of the gods. When Assyria rose to supremacy in the Near East in the first half of the first millennium B.C., its military campaigns and ruthless conquests were asserted by every Assyrian king to have been carried out "on the command of my god Ashur." *See* Assyria, Nineveh, Sennacherib, Shalmaneser.

▶ Ashurbanipal (Akk. *Ashur-bani-apli* = 'A son by [the god] Ashur made'): An Assyrian king (668–630 B.C.), famed for his library in Nineveh; sometimes called 'the first archaeologist' because he had amassed inscribed clay tablets and other artifacts that were already ancient in his time. He boasted that 'the god of scribes' "initiated me into the secrets of writing," including the ability to read Sumerian, and even to understand inscriptions "from the days before the Flood"—the first discovered mention of the Deluge outside the Bible. The subjects in the accumulated tablets covered a wide range, included such masterful texts as the *Epic of Gilgamesh* (that also told the story of the Deluge), and paid particular attention to celestial information. Among the purely astronomical texts there were tablets that belonged to a series titled *The day of Bel* (= 'The Day of the Lord') and the important tablets of *Enuma elish*—the 'Epic of Creation' that told how an invading planet joined the solar system to become Nibiru, the planet from which the Anunnaki had come to Earth. ZS has concluded that both the textual collection as well as the purely astronomical tablets focused on Nibiru—starting with its original appearance, then subsequent ones, as well as the one that was anticipated; some texts, he showed, actually were intended to serve as guidelines for observing the arriving Nibiru as it attains perigee. *See* Assyria, Epic of Creation, Nineveh.

▶ Ashurnasirpal II: An Assyrian king (883–859 B.C.) who wore a cross as

part of his royal insignia and captured the Landing Place in Lebanon—
per ZS, due to the growing expectation of Nibiru's return. *See* Cross,
Landing Place.

▶ Asia Minor: The westernmost part of Asia that is shaped like an extension
of the Asian continent, protruding toward Europe. Land of the Hittites
in antiquity; nowadays Turkey. *See* Anatolia.

▶ Assembly of the gods: *See* Council of the gods.

▶ Assyria (*Ashur*): A kingdom in the upper region of the Tigris river that was
called **Subartu** in Sumerian times and became the northernmost extension of Sumer & Akkad. In language and racial origins its people—the
Assyrians—appear to have had a kinship to Sargon of Akkad, and some of
its most famous kings took the name *Sharru-kin*—Sargon—as their royal
name. (The Bible, in Genesis chapter 10, lists *Ashur* as stemming from
the line of Shem.) Religiously, the Assyrians adopted the Sumerian pantheon, with emphasis on the Enlilite deities—Enlil, Ninurta, Sin, Adad,
Shamash and Ishtar. Assyria rose to prominence in the 2nd millennium
B.C., vied with Babylonia and its god Marduk for supremacy, invaded
Egypt, and reached a dominant position in the ancient Near East in the
'Neo-Assyrian' phase in the 9th–7th centuries B.C. Its royal and religious
centers—Ashur, Nineveh, Nimrud, Calah—that have been excavated
since 1843, have brought to light vast urban centers, magnificent palaces,
great temples, immense libraries of inscribed clay tablets, and a wealth of
artifacts. Depictions and inscriptions, paying homage to Assyria's imperial
kings, enabled a reconstruction of life and events in the second and first
millennia B.C., and verified the biblical tales of the wars and conquests of
famed Assyrian kings, including the invasion of Israel by Tiglath-Pileser
III (744–727 B.C.) and the partial exile of its leaders; the attack on Israel
in 722 B.C. by his son Shalmaneser V who exiled all of its people, creating
the enigma of the 'Lost Ten Tribes'; and the attack on Judea and the failed
siege of its capital Jerusalem by Sennacherib in 702 B.C. Assyria met its
end—as predicted by the biblical prophets—in a series of military defeats
in 614–612 B.C. when it was attacked by invaders from the north. *See*
Ashur, Babylon, H̱arran, Nineveh.

▶ Asteroid Belt: A celestial zone between Mars and Jupiter replete with asteroids—small chunks of planetary remains—that keep orbiting the Sun primarily in a 'belt' between Mars and Jupiter. It is, ZS suggested in *The 12th Planet,* the celestial *Raki'a* ('Hammered Bracelet') mentioned in Genesis chapter 1, paralleling the Akkadian *Rakkis* which (according to the Mesopotamian Epic of Creation *Enuma elish*) the god-planet Nibiru/Marduk "stretched in the heavens as a hammered bracelet" after the collision with the planet Tiamat. While astronomers remain uncertain how the Asteroid Belt had come about, ZS has suggested that it is the remains of Tiamat's half that was smashed to pieces in the collision with Marduk's moons (which orbited retrogradely). The severed but unsmashed half of Tiamat, thrust to a new orbital position, became the planet Earth.

▶ Astrolabe ('Taker of stars'): A term used to describe circular clay discs, discovered in Babylonia, that were divided like a pie into twelve segments cutting through three concentric rings, resulting in a flat representation of the heavenly sphere and listing the celestial bodies in the resulting 36 astronomical segments. *See* Planispheres.

▶ Astrology: Defined as the study of the motions of the Sun, Moon and planets in the belief that their positions relative to each other and to their zodiacal 'stations' affect individual human fortunes. However, when 'astrology' began in Mesopotamia (and especially so in Babylon), it was the application of astronomical observations to affairs of state—the fate of kingdoms and their rulers, not personal horoscopes.

▶ Astronauts, ancient: *See* Apkallu, Anunnaki, Eaglemen, Nefilim.

▶ Astronomy: Scholars deciphering the tablets in the great libraries of Nineveh and Babylon, and in smaller ones in other ancient sites, were astounded both by the preponderance of astronomical texts as well as by their detail and sophistication—ranging from daily observations of celestial phenomena to tables predicting lunar eclipses fifty years ahead. Using the various stages of ziggurats (step-pyramids) for observation, special classes of priests provided daily astronomical reports to the king. While current textbooks bestow admiration on 'Babylonian astronomy', scribal notations on such texts (in Akkadian) as well as the terminology used, leave no doubt that Babylonian/Assyrian astronomy was based upon and stemmed from earlier Sumerian astronomical knowledge, records and texts—some of which were found in the ruins of Sumerian cities (such as Nippur, Eridu and Ur). The texts astounded scholars by the wealth of precise astronomical terms used, like **An.pa** for 'Zenith', **An.bil** for solstices, **An.ub** for the solstitial orientations, **An.ur** for 'Horizon'—apart from naming planet, stars and constellations and distinguishing between them. That earliest knowledge had already adopted the **Dub**, the Spherical Astronomy of 360° (which modern astronomy still follows), dividing the heavens surrounding the Earth into three "Ways"—that of Enlil in the north, of Ea/Enki in the south, and of Anu in the center. The latter hosted the twelve zodiacal constellations, whose Sumerian names and pictorial depictions (Lion, Bull, Ram, Twins, Fishes, etc.) are used to this day. Many of the tablets were grouped into series (one, known as *Enuma Anu Enlil*, consisted of thirty tablets); there were also depictions of the heavenly sphere on a flat surface, now referred to as 'astrolabes'. Central in all those texts were the references to the planet Nibiru, its orbital path, its visibility during a state visit to Earth by Anu and Antu, and its return to visibility in the first millennium B.C. *See* E.Ninnu, Gudea, Lagash, Nibiru, Temples, Ways of Heaven, Ziggurats, Zodiac. For other and later astronomical structures, see Chichén Itzá, Denderah, Gilgal Repha'im, Sacsahuaman, Sarmizegetusa, Stonehenge, Tiahuanacu, etc.

▶ Aswan: The modern name of the ancient Nile River city Syene in Upper Egypt. Situated where the navigable northern segment of the Nile is distinct from its southern cataracts-obstructed course, it marked in antiquity the border between Egypt and Nubia. Egyptian lore deemed the site to be the place where the god Ptah installed sluices to regulate the river's flow and thereby raised the land of Egypt from under the waters of the Deluge to make it habitable. It is the site of the modern Aswan Dam.

▶ Atahualpa: The pretender for the Inca throne when the Spaniards first arrived in Peru in A.D. 1530 under the leadership of Francisco Pizarro.

▶ ATEN: In the 14th century B.C., when Egypt's leading god RA became

AMON ('The Unseen'), the Egyptian Pharaoh Amenhotep/Amenophis IV proclaimed 'ATEN'—depicted as a celestial disc emitting rays—as the central object of worship, renamed himself AKHEN-ATEN ('The Servant/worshipper of Aten'), and built a brand new capital-cum-religious center named AKHET-ATEN, ('Aten of the Horizon'). Some scholars view the Aten as a 'New Sun' or 'New Ra', and explain the change as a new 'Sun Religion'; others discern elements of monotheism in the worship of the Aten. The religious revision was strongly opposed by the priests of Ra/Amen, and Akhen-Aten and his city came to a quick end in 1362 B.C. In *The End of Days* ZS explained the Aten as the planet of the gods ('Planet of millions of years')—Nibiru—in its Return format: Still unseen, but expected to return into view. He pointed out that it was then that the symbol of the Cross began to be seen on royal depictions, in Egypt as well as in Mesopotamia.

▸ Athena: The Greek goddess of war and the protectress of many demigod heroes; called Minerva by the Romans. A daughter of Zeus and one of the Twelve Olympians, her main temple was in Athens, the city named in her honor. The story of the Trojan War has her taking an active part, together with her half-brother Apollo, in the war's events.

▸ Atlantes: Colossal humanlike stone statues, more than fifteen feet high, erected atop a flat-topped Toltec pyramid at the ancient site called Tollan in Mexico. The carvings depict them with stern visages of an unfamiliar race, wearing feathered crowns decorated with star symbols, and armed with weapons that include a pistol-like ray gun.

▸ Atlantis: The legendary paradise-like island-state described in the writings of Plato, which (he wrote) was swallowed by the seas as a result of a volcanic calamity. Though searched for (and sometimes claimed to have been discovered) anywhere sunken islands or submerged structural remains are found, ZS believes that—if Atlantis or its likes had actually once existed—varied details in Greek and Mesoamerican sources point to a Mesoamerican location.

▸ *Atra-Hasis* (= 'The Exceedingly Wise'): Title given to an epic Sumerian tale, mostly known from several renditions in Akkadian, that names Atra-hasis, an Enki devotee, as the hero of the Deluge. The text begins with the division of functions between Enlil and Enki during a visit to Earth by Anu, describes a mutiny by the Anunnaki toiling in the mines that led to the fashioning by Enki and Ninharsag of a Primitive Worker, and records subsequent events that led to the Deluge. It is a text with many parallels to the Genesis tales about The Adam, Noah, the Deluge, and human ability to marry and procreate.

▸ Avebury Circle: A circular stone monument in England, not far from Stonehenge.

▸ Ayar Brothers: According to South American native legends recorded by Spanish chroniclers in Peru, four Ayar Brothers, accompanied by their sister-wives, created by the Creator God Viracocha in the heart of the Andes mountains, were instructed by him where to go, settle, and populate the lands after a Great Flood. To the Ayar couple directed to establish the sacred capital Cuzco, the god gave a golden wand with which to pinpoint the site and establish its temple's orientation. *See* Aymara, Cuzco, Tiahuanacu, Viracocha.

▸ Aymara: A native people (and their language) who inhabited the Andean highlands of southern Peru before the Incas.

▸ **Azag**: In a laudatory Sumerian poem to the god Ninurta, an epithet of the adversary he defeated in an aerial battle. *See* Anzu, Zu.

▸ Aztecs: The native tribe who peopled central Mexico when the Spaniards arrived in 1519. Their capital (now overwhelmed by Mexico City) was called Tenochtitlan and their king at the time was Moctezuma (also rendered Montezuma). Their legends described their arrival in Mexico by sea and their wanderings till they found the place earmarked for Tenochtitlan.

▸ Azt-lan: The "White Place" which, according to Aztec legends, was the ancestral home of the Aztec's first patriarchal couple and from which seven Aztec tribes migrated by sea to Mesoamerica.

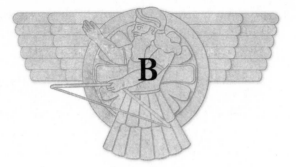

▶ *Ba'al* (= 'Lord, Master'): A major Canaanite/Phoenician god, the princi-pal son of *El*, the head of the pantheon, who attained the title *Elyon* (= 'supreme') after defeating his brothers *Yam* and *Mot*. He had the attri-butes of a 'Storm god', with thunders and lightnings as his weapons; that, and his epithet *Hadad*, suggest that he was a Canaanite adoption of **Adad** (Enlil's youngest son) who became the Hittite national god with similar 'storm weapons'. Ba'al's supremacy was manifested by his lordship over the 'Crest of Zaphon', the unique platform in the Lebanon mountains that is still called *Ba'albek*. According to Canaanite tales, when Ba'al was killed fighting Mot, he was brought back to life by the goddesses Anat and Shepesh.

▶ Ba'albek (= 'Ba'al's cleft valley'): An ancient site in the Lebanon mountains that features a vast stone-paved platform and has imposing remains of Roman temples, including the largest temple to Jupiter. These remains stand atop much earlier structures consisting of ever-rising stages of mas-sive stone blocks, including (in the western wall) the Trilithon—three colossal shaped stone blocks weighing over 1,100 tons each—the largest in the world. A similar colossal stone block, whose quarrying was not completed, still remains in the quarry in a nearby valley; local lore attri-butes to 'giants' the impossible feat of lifting the immense stone blocks, carrying them several miles up to the mountainous platform, and plac-ing them in a high row in the original ancient towering structure. ZS has identified the site as "the Landing Place" of the gods, which survived the Deluge and served as the temporary headquarters of Enlil and Enki and suggested that the rising structure served as a stone-made launch tower for rocketships—the launching of one of which Gilgamesh witnessed when he went there in his search for immortality. (*See* Agriculture, Domestication.)

▸ Babylon: From *Bab-Ili* (= 'Gateway of the gods') in Akkadian, (H) *Bab-El*. The capital city that gave its name to a kingdom (sometimes distinguished by being called Babylonia) on the Euphrates River, north of Sumer & Akkad, whose existence was first mentioned in the Bible's tale of the *Tower of Babel*. Its location and imperial extent came to light following archaeological excavations begun before World War I. The deciphering of cuneiform texts found all over the ancient Near East provided historical data about the emergence of Babylonia as an independent kingdom circa 1900 B.C., its rivalry with Assyria, and its rise to imperial status with the dynasty famed by Hammurabi (circa 1790 B.C.). Historians separate that Old Babylonian Period from the Neo-Babylonian period by an interval that lasted some five centuries, known as the Kassite Period. The Neo-Babylonian empire, that embraced the 12th to 6th centuries B.C., included in its conquests several attacks on Jerusalem and the destruction of its Temple in 587 B.C. by Nebuchadnezzar— fully corroborating the biblical tales thereof. The rise and history of Babylon were closely intertwined with the fortunes and ambitions of the god Marduk, whose main temple was the famed ziggurat (seven-stage 'pyramid') within a sprawling sacred precinct that ZS compared to the Vatican in Rome, with an array of buildings serving diverse functions and a plethora of priests hierarchically arranged, specializing in duties from cleaners and butchers and healers to administrators, astronomers, and astrologers. The latest aggrandizement of the sacred precinct, in the reign of Nebuchadnezzar II, was motivated (per ZS) by the anticipated return of the planet Nibiru and with it a repeat visit by the god Anu. The city of Babylon, as an imperial capital, a religious center and the symbol of its kingdom, came to an end in 539 B.C. by the hand of the Achaemenid-Persian king Cyrus. *See* Hammurabi, Kassites, Marduk, Ziggurats.

▸ **Bad-Tibira**: The second 'city of the gods' established by the Anunnaki in southern Mesopotamia (later Sumer); its function was that of a metal-lurgical center.

▸ Bahrein: An island in the Persian Gulf, off Arabia, that some scholars identify as **Tilmun** (= 'Land of the Missiles') of Sumerian lore. Not so, in the opinion of ZS.

▸ Bala'am (H *Bile'am*): According to the Bible, a renowned oracle priest who was retained by the king of Mo'ab during the Exodus to put a curse on the Israelites, but instead ended up pronouncing a favorable oracle in which he linked Israel's future to an appearing star.

▸ Balam: The name of a Mayan priest whose oracles were recorded in a book, sacred to the Mayans as a record of their mythical past and prophetic future, known as *Chilam Balam* (= 'The Oracles/Utterings of Balam'). ZS has wondered about the intriguing similarity, in name and function, of the Mayan Balam to the biblical Bala'am.

▸ Balikh River: An important northern tributary of the Euphrates River. The city of Harran, which has played an important role in Near Eastern events already in the time of Abraham, was situated on the Balikh River. *See* Harran, Nabunaid.

▸ Ball Courts/Games: Sacred sites in Mesoamerica, and especially Mayan sites, included game courts for playing the Tlachtli rubber-ball game. Rectangular in shape, the courts were flanked on their elongated sides (that could be 545 feet long, as in Chichén Itzá) by structures that served as viewing galleries for the spectators. In the center of each such longer side, 35 feet above the ground, the top of the wall had a protruding stone ring; the players, without using their hands, had to throw the ball through the ring. There were two teams of seven players each; the leader of the losing team also lost his head.

▸ Battle of Kadesh: A major battle between Egyptian and Hittite armies that took place in 1274 B.C. at Kadesh, a fortress on the Orontes River in what is now Syria. Recorded in detail on temple walls in Karnak,

Egypt, it involved tens of thousands of foot soldiers and archers and thousands of horse-drawn chariots, commanded by Ramses II. Though the battle itself was inconclusive, Ramses II almost lost his life there, and the battle put an end to Egyptian imperial attempts to reach and control the Upper Euphrates region. The text of a peace treaty between Egypt and Hatti that resulted from the Battle of Kadesh was found in both capitals. *See* Hittites, Karnak, Naharin.

▸ **Ba.u**: The spouse of Ninurta, nicknamed **Gula** (= 'The Big One'); known for her medical care for the people of Lagash (her 'cult center'). When the deathly nuclear cloud unleashed in the Sinai reached Sumer, Bau could not force herself to leave their beloved Lagash. The *Lamentation Over Sumer* text states that as she lingered behind, "the storm caught up with her as if she was a mortal," suggesting that she died.

▸ Bearded People: Although native Americans have had no facial hair, many monuments in Mesoamerica depict bearded men, sometimes shown in the company of typical beardless Mayan or Aztec men. ZS has pointed out that the facial features of the 'Bearded Ones' indicate they were people from the Mediterranean, and has offered explanations for this usually unexplained (and mostly ignored) puzzling aspect of Who had been to the Americas in antiquity and How.

▸ *Be'er-Sheba* (H = 'Well of Seven'): A city, existing to this day, in the *Negev* (the dry southern part of Israel) that according to the Bible served as headquarters for the Hebrew Patriarchs Abraham, Isaac and Jacob.

▸ *Bel*: An abbreviated form for *Ba'al* ("The Lord")—the principal deity. In Babylonian texts the reference was to Marduk. *See* Ba'al.

▸ *Bela*: A city near the Dead Sea, whose king is listed (Genesis 14) with the kings of Sodom and Gomorrah in a coalition of Canaanite kings who fought off an invasion from Mesopotamia at the time of Abraham.

▸ Belshazzar (*Bel-Shar-Uzur* = 'May the Lord [= Marduk] the king protect'): The last ruler in Babylon, appointed as regent by his father, king Nabuna'id; in his court, according to the Book of Daniel, a suspended hand appeared and wrote three words prophesying the coming fall of Babylon to the Persians (as indeed happened in 539 B.C.). *See* Daniel, Nabuna'id.

▸ BEN-BEN: A sacred object kept in the Holy of Holies of the main temple in the ancient Egyptian city An/Annu (later known as Heliopolis). The name could mean 'pyramidion-bird'; hieroglyphic texts depicted it as conical in shape and referred to it as the upper part of the 'Celestial Barque' in which the god Ra had arrived on Earth from "The Planet of millions of years."

▸ Benjamin: The younger of the two sons of Jacob by Rachel, full brother of Joseph. His Hebrew name, *Ben-Yamin,* reflected the name of the main tribe that lived in the Harran area, where the relatives of the Patriarchs remained after Abraham had left for Canaan. *See* H̱arran, H̱urrians, Matriarchs, Mitanni, Patriarchs.

▸ Bent Pyramid: A pyramid, attributed to the Pharaoh Sneferu (first ruler of the fourth dynasty) at Dahshur (near Maidum) in Egypt, which began to be constructed at the 52° angle as in Giza, but due to the collapse of a similar pyramid farther north was bent in mid-construction to a safer angle of 43°.

▸ Berossus (Greek from *Bel-Re'ushu* = 'The Lord [*Bel* = Marduk] is his shepherd'): A Babylonian priest-historian who, in the 3rd century B.C., was commissioned by the Greek Seleucid successors of Alexander the Great to compile for them a summary of the Sumerian/Akkadian texts dealing with the Anunnaki gods, their arrival on Earth, and the ensuing events up to the fall of Babylon and Assyria. Though the three volumes he had composed are no longer extant, portions of them were retained, having been copied and quoted by other ancient historians and savants. It is thus known that such major biblical events as Man's creation, the Deluge (with its hero here called in Greek 'Sisistrus'), the 'confusion of languages' resulting from the Tower of Babel incident, etc. were basic knowledge in Mesopotamia. A major aspect of the Berossus writings, later confirmed by discoveries of cuneiform tablets, was the use of 3,600 years as the unit of time applicable to the Anunnaki when they came to Earth—giving ZS a clue that that was the orbital period (= one 'Anunnaki year') of their planet Nibiru. His writings were the first source dating the arrival of the Anunnaki to 432,000 years (120 Sars) before the Deluge. According to Berossus fragments, he wrote that the world undergoes periodic cataclysms, which he related to the Zodiacal Ages. *See* Ages, Harran, History/Cyclical, Seleucids.

▸ **Beru**: A Sumerian unit of measurement equaling one twelfth—of time (= one 12th of our 24-hours daytime/nighttime period, translated in texts as a "double-hour"), of distance (usually translated "league"), or in astronomy (the 12th part of the celestial arc).

▸ *Beth-El* (H = 'House/Abode of [the god] *El*'): A biblical town in the vicinity of Jerusalem, situated where Abraham "built an altar to Yahweh." It also featured in the journey of the Prophet Elijah (II kings 2) via Jericho to the east bank of the Jordan River to be taken heavenwards "in a whirlwind."

▸ *Beth-Lehem* (H = 'House of Bread'): An ancient town mentioned in the Old Testament as the place where Rachel, journeying with her husband the Patriarch Jacob, died in childbirth and was buried there; her tomb, on the outskirts of present-day Bethlehem (six miles southwest of Jerusalem) is a pilgrimage site sacred to Jews and to Moslems. After the Israelite settlement, the Judean town was linked in the Bible to David—a shepherd from a Bethlehemite farming family who was anointed king by the Prophet Samuel. The New Testament, which stresses the lineage of Jesus to the House of David, identifies Bethlehem as the birthplace of Jesus (Matthew 2, Luke 2). The Church of the Nativity, built over the grotto where, according to Christian tradition, Jesus was born, is the focal point of Christian pilgrimages to Bethlehem.

▸ *Beth-Shemesh* (H = 'House/Abode of [the god] *Shamas*'): Historically, there was a southern Beth-Shemesh = Heliopolis (Annu/*On*) in Egypt, and a northern one, in the Lebanon mountains, which was later known as Baalbek. A town in Judea by that name is also mentioned in the biblical Book of Judges.

▶ Black Headed People: (a) A nickname for the Sumerians. (b) The Aztec calendar divided the past into eras called 'Suns', and called the 'Fourth Sun', when the great god Quetzalcoatl had come to Mesoamerica, "the era of the Black Headed People." ZS has calculated that the 'Fourth Sun' began circa 3500 B.C., a few centuries after the Sumerian civilization began, raising the possibility that the Mesoamerican terminology was not just a chance coincidence.

▶ Boat of Heaven: The term used in the Sumerian texts dealing with the flying-about of Inanna to denote her aerial chariot.

▶ Boghazkoi: The name of the place in north-central Turkey where the ruins of the ancient Hittite capital, Hattushas, are located.

▶ Bolivia: An Andean country, split off Peru in 1825, which retained the southern portion of Lake Titicaca and the archaeological sites of Tiahuanacu and Puma Punku.

▶ Bond Heaven-Earth: *See* **Dur.an.ki.**

▶ Book of Adam and Eve: An ancient extra-biblical book, found in several versions, that provides legendary details of the first human couple and their family after the expulsion of Adam and Eve from the Garden of Eden. References to it in the Book of Enoch suggest that an original 'Book of Adam and Eve' was held to have been among the pre-diluvial writings. Modern scholars believe, however, that the Book was composed by a Hebrew writer sometime between the first century B.C. and the first century A.D.

▶ Book of the Dead: A collection of verses inscribed in hieroglyphics on the walls of royal tombs in ancient Egypt, collectively recognized by scholars as an ancient work, divided into chapters, primarily dealing with the Pharaohs' journeys after death to an Afterlife with the gods. The texts were often accompanied by relevant illustrations. Because some portions or 'chapters' deal with the conflict between the gods Thoth and Ra, the belief in ancient Egypt was that Thoth himself was the author of the 'book'.

▶ Book of Enoch: A work, believed by scholars to have been composed in Judea in the 2nd century B.C., purporting to provide the full story of the life and celestial journeys of the biblical Enoch, the 7th pre-diluvial Patriarch, who according to the Bible (Genesis 6) did not die, but at age 365 was gone from the Earth "for the Lord had taken him." The book, versions or sources of which included works known as *The Book of the Secrets of Enoch*, *The Testimony of Enoch*, *The Words of Enoch*, and others, has survived the millennia in two principal versions: The Ethiopic Book of Enoch ('Enoch I') and the Slavonic version ('Enoch II'). The most fascinating portions of the books are the descriptions of Enoch's journeys that are filled with astronomical, calendrical, and Earth-science knowledge.

▶ Book of Jubilees: A pseudepigrapha book (a professed 'biblical book' not included in the canonical Bible), dated by scholars to second or first centuries B.C., that rewrote prehistory and history according to a calendrical count of "weeks of years" of 7 x 7, requiring the 50th year ('the Jubilee') to be one of granting freedom to people and lands. It adds many details to what is written in the canonized biblical books Genesis and the first part of Exodus; the fact that it was widely quoted in antiquity and has been found in various ancient translations of the original Hebrew and among the Dead Sea scrolls, suggests that—in antiquity—its unstated sources were deemed reliable. 'Jubilee' is a translation of the Hebrew term *Yovel* which literally means Ram.

▶ Borsippa: A city south of Babylon that was the 'cult center' of the god Nabu, the son of Marduk. During the escalating Anunnaki conflicts caused by Marduk's strife for supremacy, Borsippa was destroyed by Elamite troops on order of the opposing gods (end of 2nd millennium B.C.).

▶ Bow: In Near Eastern lore the bow was a divine weapon with magical attributes, sometimes bestowed by a god to a favored individual. A cylinder seal depiction of gods shows one, probably Enlil, armed with a bow. Inanna/Ishtar, when depicted as a goddess of war, was also shown armed with a bow. In the Bible, a divine "Bow in the Clouds" (*Keshet be-Anan*) was displayed by God after the Deluge as a sign that there will not be another Deluge; the term has thus been taken to mean a rainbow. That, ZS has shown, is not necessarily so in view of the fact that a "god in the clouds" holding a bow in his hand was depicted on Assyrian monuments.

▶ Brazil: The largest country in South America, occupying most of the continent's eastern half and its Amazon River basin. It is Portuguese speaking, unlike the Spanish-speaking rest of South America, as a result of a treaty between Spain and Portugal dividing the New World between them— a division sought by Portugal because it apparently had access to maps, from a time before the Columbus discoveries, already correctly showing the Americas. Various archaeological discoveries in Brazil of rock carvings and pottery suggest that Near Easterners had reached its shores thousands of years before the Columbus voyages.

▶ Bronze (**Za.bar** = 'Gleaming double metal'): An alloy of copper and tin that can be melted and cast, resulting in tools, utensils and sculptures of great strength. While other metals used in antiquity (gold, silver, copper and iron) are naturally found, tin is obtained by extracting it in high temperatures from a mineral called Cassiterite; the tin, malleable and soft, is useful in bronze only when added to copper in a certain proportion. In spite of these technological challenges, the 'Bronze Age' began in the Near East circa 3300 B.C. and gave way to the Iron Age circa 1100 B.C. Intriguing early use of bronze in antiquity was discovered at Puma Punku near Tiahuanacu in Bolivia, where stone blocks were held together with specially designed clamps made of bronze, in structures dated to circa 4000 B.C. That, and other evidence, has led ZS to conclude that Tiahuanacu was established by the Anunnaki as a major metallurgical center soon after the Deluge. *See* Metals/Metallurgy, Tiahuanacu, Tin.

▶ Brook of Egypt (*Nahal Mitzra'yim* in the Bible and also in Assyrian inscriptions): The shallow river (a *wadi* in Arabic) in the central plain of the Sinai peninsula that runs with water only during the rainy season, located in the peninsula's central plain. Nowadays known as *Wadi el-Arish*. It was the southern boundary of the lands promised by God to Abraham and his seed to inherit (Genesis 15). *See* Abraham, Nin.gal.

▸ Bull: A nickname of Enlil ("Bull Enlil"); his 'cult animal' as well as of his son Adad, who was depicted on Hittite and Canaanite monuments standing on a bull.

▸ Bull-men: Divine guardians, depicted in Mesopotamian monuments and on cylinder seals with a human upper part and the aft legs and tail of a bull.

▸ Bull of Heaven (**Gud.anna**): The Sumerian name of the zodiacal Constellation of the Bull (Taurus) associated with Enlil. In the Epic of Gilgamesh, the Bull of Heaven was a unique bull that was placed by Enlil in the Cedar Forest of Lebanon; it was slain by Enkidu (the companion of Gilgamesh). Incomplete portions in the Epic of Gilgamesh leave unclear whether it was a special but real bull, embellished with precious stones and metals, or a robotic creature; Egyptian illustrations that depict the slaying of the Bull of Heaven considered it a celestial event, signaling the end of Enlil's Age.

▸ Burning Bush: The bush which attracted the attention of Moses, when he shepherded a flock of sheep in the Sinai, for "it was burning with fire without being consumed." When he approached, he heard God's voice assigning to him the task of leading the Israelites out of Egypt.

▸ **Buzur**: An epithet of Enki that could mean in Sumerian both "He who knows/solves secrets" and "He of the copper mines"—per ZS, a significant clue to the identity of the 'Serpent' in the biblical Garden of Eden tale, because the Hebrew term *Nachash* also has the same multi-meanings as **Buzur**. *See* Enki, Eden, Ningishzida, Serpent.

▸ Byblos: A Phoenician city (*Gebal* in the Bible) on the Mediterranean coast in what is now Lebanon. An ancient coin discovered in its ruins depicts the nearby sacred site of Baalbek with a conical missile emplaced upon the great platform. Archaeologists found in the city's temple upright stone monoliths suggesting a 'Stonehenge-like' observatory of equinoxes and solstices.

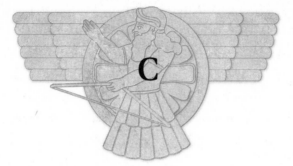

C

▸ Cain: The firstborn son of Adam and Eve. "A tiller of the soil," he killed his brother Abel who was "a keeper of herds." In punishment, God banished him to *Nod* ('Land of Migration'), where he started his own family line and settlements, but gave him a permanently distinctive protective mark. ZS cites Sumerian tales of shepherd-farmer rivalries and a tablet in the British Museum dealing with a **Ka.in** who was "doomed to roam the Earth in sorrow," and has suggested that the 'Mark of Cain' could have been a genetic marker, such as the absence of facial hair by native Americans—offering the Cain migration and lineage as an explanation for early human settlement in North America. *See* Agriculture, Domestication.

▸ *Calah*: An Assyrian city, known only from the Bible (Genesis 10) until the discovery of a tablet in which an Assyrian king described the restoration there of an olden temple. Archaeological finds identified the place as *Kalhu*, an Assyrian royal city in the 9th century B.C. The Bible listed Calah as one of the cities of the heroic hunter Nimrod; interestingly, the local name for the site is *Tel Nimrud* (= 'The Mound of Nimrod').

▸ Calendars: Calendrical timekeeping, linked to the annual Earth-Sun cycle and a monthly Moon-Earth cycle, began in Sumer, in Nippur (Sumer's religious/astronomical center); there, the term for 'month' was **Ezen**—"festival"—because each month was dedicated to celebrating one of the twelve great gods, starting with Anu. The subsequent twelve-month Babylonian calendar (including a 13th in a leap year) was based on the Sumerian one, and the Hebrew calendar used by Jews to this day is a continuation of those calendars, using the same month names, leap year arrangements, etc. Identifying the Hebrew/Jewish calendar as an uninterrupted continuation of the Calendar of Nippur, ZS has suggested that the Jewish count of years (5,768 in A.D. 2008) indicates that the Calendar of Nippur was begun in 3760 B.C. The complex luni-solar calendar, requiring sophisticated astronomical knowledge, was replaced by the later Greeks and Romans with a simplified solar-only calendar, while the Moslems have adopted a lunar-only one. The Christian or 'Common Era' (C.E.) solar calendar, whose count of 'Annu Domini' (A.D.) begins from the presumed birth of Jesus, continues the 'Julian Calendar' (so named after the Roman emperor Julius Caesar) as revised by Pope Gregory XIII in 1582.

In Mesoamerica the calendar story begins with the presentation of a golden disc by the Aztec king to the Spanish leader Hernando Cortés in A.D. 1519; while that one was promptly melted on arrival back in Spain, a stone replica of it was found and can be seen in Mexico City; it recorded the passage of time according to 'Suns' or Ages lasting an uneven number of thousands of years (see 'Ages'). In the more common meaning of the word 'calendar', the Mesoamericans had three. One, called 'Tzolkin', rotated units of 20 days 13 times to make a Sacred Year of just 260 days. Another, called 'Haab', divided the solar year into 18 units of 20, to which 5 special days were added at the end to make up a solar year of 365 days; the Haab was thus somewhat similar to the Egyptian calendar. The oldest, called 'The Long Count', was originated by the Olmecs; it recorded time by the number of days that have passed from a Day One (now calculated to equal August 13, 3113 B.C.). ZS has suggested that it was then that Thoth, renamed Quetzalcoatl by the Aztecs, came to Mesoamerica from Egypt. *See* Ages, Mayan Calendar, Nippur Calendar, Olmecs.

▶ Cambyses: The son and successor of Cyrus on the Persian throne who conquered Egypt. According to the Greek historian Herodotus, Cambyses reached Nubia in Africa in search of a Fountain of Youth.

▶ Campbell's Chamber: The uppermost of the 'Relieving Chambers' above the 'King's Chamber' in the Great Pyramid in Giza, so named by the explorer Howard Vyse in honor of Col. Colin Campbell, the British Consul in Cairo at the time (1837). (A Giza tomb known as 'Campbell's Tomb' was so named also in his honor; it is not his burial place.)

▶ Canaan, Canaanites: The biblical *Cena'an* comprised the lands that now are Israel, Jordan, Lebanon and southwestern Syria. Little was known of the Canaanites outside of the biblical information and passing references in Egyptian, Assyrian and Phoenician inscriptions, until the archaeological discovery of a major Canaanite site. Located on Syria's Mediterranean coast at a place called Ras Shamra, a trove of inscribed clay tablets found there identified the place as Ugarit and provided firsthand information on the Canaanite language, culture and religion—shown to be adaptations of the Akkadian ones. The Bible named Canaan as descended of Ham (the second son of Noah) whose lands were in Africa, not in Asia; he was thus deemed a usurper in lands belonging to Shem (Noah's Firstborn). Accordingly, Canaan (the land) was territorially available to be promised by God to Shem's descendant Abraham and his seed: "All the land of Canaan, as an everlasting possession" (Genesis 14:8).

▶ Cancer: The name of a zodiacal constellation, called **Dub** (meaning in Sumerian 'pincers', 'tongs', and depicted as a crab's claws).

▶ Capricorn: The name of a zodiacal constellation, called **Suhur.mash** (meaning in Sumerian, and depicted as, 'goat-fish').

▶ Capstones: Shaped as a pyramidion, such stones capped the pyramids, bringing all four sides to a common endpoint at the apex.

▶ Caracol (= 'The Snail' in Mayan): The astronomical observatory, so named because of its inner spiral staircase. *See* Chichén Itzá.

▶ Carchemish: A city in the Upper Euphrates region established by the Hittites to serve as a fortified gateway to Asia Minor. In 605 B.C. an invading Egyptian army led by the Pharaoh Necho was decisively defeated there by Nebuchadnezzar of Babylon—a battle and a defeat predicted by the Prophet Jeremiah (chapter 46).

▸ Carthage (*Keret-Hadashah* = 'New City'): A colony established in the 9th century B.C. on the African coast of the western Mediterranean (now in Tunisia) by the seafaring Phoenicians as a way station in their westward sailings into the Atlantic Ocean. The 'Punic Wars' in the 3rd and 2nd centuries B.C. were fought by the Carthagians against Rome for control of the sea lanes; Carthage city served as the base from which Hannibal launched attacks on Rome. *See* Phoenicians.

▸ Cassiterite: The ore from which tin (which is rarely found as a native metal in nature) is extracted ('smelted') in high temperatures in a furnace or kiln. Tin was essential for making bronze (an alloy of copper and tin); some scholars believe that the quest for Cassiterite explains some of the early settlements in the British Isles. ZS has added the Americas to the list.

▸ Cassites (or Kassites): A people, possibly from the highlands east of Mesopotamia, who excelled in metallurgy in the third and second millennia B.C. Since bronze was their preferred metal, it is possible that their name, stemming from the Greek Cassiteros, could be the source of the name Cassiterite for the tin-rich ore. *See* Kassites re their reign in Babylon.

▸ Cedars, Cedar Forest: The majestic cedar trees, extolled in the Bible for their extraordinary height (up to 150 feet), strength and beauty, were prized in antiquity as a gift of the gods, and were cut only for use in temples or consecrated royal palaces. They grew only in a special forest in the mountains of Lebanon, which is described in the 'Epic of Gilgamesh' as a hideout of the gods guarded by ferocious robotic monsters; within that "Cedar Forest" was the secret "Landing Place" of the gods—the Baalbek platform and stone launch tower, according to ZS. Cedar trees still grow in Lebanon and are its national emblem.

▸ Celestial Battle: The collision, described in *Enuma elish* (the 'Epic of Creation'), between the invading planet Nibiru/Marduk and its moons and the olden planet Tiamat and its moons, that—according to ZS, who interpreted it not as an allegorical myth but as a sophisticated cosmogony—resulted in the breakup of Tiamat, the creation of the Earth and the Asteroid Belt of her remains, and the capture of Nibiru into an elongated orbit around our Sun.

▸ Celestial Barque: The translation of the Egyptian hieroglyphic term for the vehicle in which the god Ra arrived on Earth, the forepart of which was the conical 'Ben-Ben'. In Egyptian art, the celestial star-gods were depicted traversing the heavens in boatlike barques. *See* Aerial Chariots, Spacecraft.

▸ Celestial Disk (also 'Winged Disk'): A ubiquitous celestial symbol of a disk with two outstretched wings that dominated royal and religious monuments, sculptures, cylinder seals etc. from Egypt and Nubia to Canaan, Babylon, Assyria, Hattiland and Persia for millennia. Per ZS, the symbol of the planet Nibiru.

▸ Celestial Time: A term coined by ZS to denote the zodiacal cycle of 2,160 × 12 years, which (he has suggested) the Anunnaki devised to create a workable relationship between 'Earthly Time' (one year on Earth) and 'Divine Time' (one year on Nibiru, mathematically = 3,600 Earth years). One Zodiacal Year of 2,160 Earth-years provided the 'golden ratio' of 6:10 to Nibiru's 3,600. *See* Ages, Divine Time, End of Days, Messianic Clock, Time, Zodiac, Zodiacal Ages.

▸ Chacmool: A Mesoamerican demigod whose statues always showed him lying reclined on his back.

▸ Chaldeans: A name, introduced by Greek historians, for Babylonians knowledgeable in astronomy and mathematics; hence 'Chaldea' = 'ancient Babylon' = Sumer. Scholars translate the biblical statement that Abraham came "from Ur *Khashdim*" as "Ur of the Chaldeans," referring to the city of Ur in Sumer.

▸ Chavin de Huantar: The location in the mountains of northern Peru where a culture preceding the Incas flourished circa 1500 B.C. Archaeologists have uncovered there complex earthworks, large buildings constructed of masonry stone blocks, terraces paved with marble, sunken plazas, monumental stairways, and elaborately carved and decorated monoliths depicting native deities. Though some researchers consider the 'Chavin Culture' "the matrix of Andean civilizations," who the 'Chavins' were and what was the purpose of all those structures remains an enigma. Bafflingly, also discovered there were statuettes depicting people with African, Semitic and Indo-European features. ZS has pointed out that some artifacts appear to depict a familiar Near Eastern theme: Gilgamesh wrestling two lions—all indicating that people from the 'Old World' were in the 'New World' millennia ago.

▸ Chephren (CHEF-RA; also rendered Khefra, Chefra, Chefren): The Pharaoh of the Fourth Dynasty 2650–2480 B.C.) to whom the 'Second Pyramid', adjoining the Great Pyramid in Giza, and the Sphinx are attributed by Egyptologists. For the ZS contrary findings on the subject, *see* Pyramids.

▸ Cheops: *See* Khufu.

▸ Cherubim (H *Kheruvim*): In the Bible, a class of angels who were "placed at the east of the Garden of Eden . . . to guard the way to the Tree of Life" after the expulsion of Adam and Eve (Genesis 3). According to Exodus 37, two winged Cherubim, cast of gold and facing one another, were placed atop the Ark of the Covenant. For comparative Mesopotamian and Egyptian depictions, *see* Angels, Eaglemen, Winged Beings.

▸ Chichén Itzá: A major restored Mayan site in the Yucatan peninsula of Mexico, believed to have been established circa A.D. 200 by the Mayan Itza tribe (hence the place's name, 'The Wellmouth of the Itza'); it was given its present layout and landmarks by Toltec migrants from west-central Mexico circa A.D. 1000. Spread over a large ceremonial area, the site's best known landmarks are the 'El Castillo' (a great remarkable step-pyramid), the Caracol (an astronomical observatory), a 545-foot long ballpark flanked by decorated walls, and the sacred 'Canote' (huge wellmouth pool) into which maidens, and valuable objects, were thrown as sacrifices to the gods. A large temple is formed by stone columns that are decorated with carvings of winged and bearded (!) 'Sky gods'—among them a depiction of a human hero whose beard gave him the nickname 'Uncle Sam'.

▸ Chilam Balam: 'The Oracles/Utterings of Balam'—the title of a sacred Mayan picture-book. *See* Balam/Balaam.

▸ Chimu: Tribal inhabitants in northern Peru whose culture preceded, and was overrun, by the Incas. Their capital, Chan-Chan, located where the river Moche flows into the Pacific Ocean, was a metropolis whose sacred precincts, step-pyramids, and residential compounds spread over eight square miles.

▸ Cities of the gods: According to Sumerian texts, the Anunnaki established in the E.Din a series of settlements even before Man was created by them. Destroyed in the Deluge, the cities were rebuilt after the Deluge exactly where they had been, but now were also Cities of Men. ZS has shown that the original cities were laid out in a pattern serving as a Landing Corridor. *See* Anunnaki, Eden, Erech, Eridu, Mesopotamia, Sumer.

▸ City of David: Circa 1000 B.C. king David moved the Judean capital from Hebron to Jerusalem, converting a Jebusite fortress on the promontory south of Mount Moriah to his royal city; his son Solomon and other Judean kings had there their palaces. Archaeologists, following the biblical designation, thus call the area south of the Temple Mount 'City of David'.

▸ Clay Tablets: Tablets made of clay on which scribes wrote by using a stylus to make the indentations that formed the cuneiform script. Once the clay dried (or in important cases, such as treaties, was fire-dried), a permanent written document resulted. Clay tablets, first introduced in Sumer, were of various sizes, though many were small enough to be held by the scribe in his left hand as he used the stylus in his right hand. The number of clay tablets, whole or fragmented, that have been found in the Near East runs in the tens of thousands. Many represent simple record-keeping, of temple stores, laborers' rations, or taxes collected; others recorded commercial transactions, land deeds, marriage contracts, or royal annals. In many instances the tablets recorded astronomical data, often arranged in series. And then there were the epic tales which extended over several tablets, in which case the next tablet began with the last words of the previous one, to indicate continuity. In many such cases, the scribe signed the concluding tablet with his name and title. Many temples and royal palaces had their own tablet libraries, where the tablets were arranged standing upright on shelves, with a 'catalog tablet' at the start listing the tablets on that shelf.

▶ Clovis: An archaeological site in New Mexico, USA, of early human settlement in the Americas. Dated by some researchers to 9500 B.C., it has been prominent in the debate of When and How North America was first settled.

▶ Codices: Picture-book manuscripts kept by Mesoamerica's native peoples; most were destroyed by zealous Spanish priests as heresy, but some that have been spared serve as a unique source of information on the pre-Columbian peoples, their cultures, histories, legends and religions.

▶ Coffin Texts: Hieroglyphic texts painted on wooden coffins in Egypt, mostly from the Greek and Roman periods.

▶ Comets: Small celestial objects that orbit the Sun in diverse elongated trajectories of varying periods, giving off a gaseous luminous tail as they near the Sun. Astronomers assume that comets resulted from unknown celestial collisions, but are unable to explain why many comets have a retrograde orbit—clockwise, rather than the counterclockwise direction common in our solar system. Such a retrograde orbit, ZS has pointed out, was that of the invading Nibiru/Marduk; and he suggested as an explanation of the origin of retrograde comets the statement in *Enuma elish* that, as a result of the 'Celestial battle', Tiamat's "host" of small satellites "was shattered, broken up . . . her helpers who marched at her side turned their backs about." The appearance of comets was considered a divine celestial omen in both Old World and New World cultures. *See* Bala'am, Halley's Comet.

▸ Confusion of Languages: According to the Bible (Genesis 11), prior to the Tower of Babel incident "the whole Earth had one language;" but when the incident took place, God said (to unnamed colleagues): "Come, let us go down and confuse their [Mankind's] language, that they may not understand one another's speech." A diversification of languages in the aftermath of a 'Tower of Babel' incident was reported by Berossus; several Greek historians, who repeat the tale, might have picked it up from Berossus. ZS additionally quotes references in Akkadian/Sumerian texts to a deliberate diversification of languages due to Enlil's anger with Mankind. *See* Tower of Babel.

▸ Constellations: The grouping of heavenly stars into 'constellations' and their naming go back millennia, to Sumerian times—a fact recognized by early Greek astronomers such as Eudoxus and Hipparchus. The Sumerians (and the Babylonians etc. after them) divided the heavens into three 'Ways'—the northern segment as the Way of Enlil, the southern segment as the Way of Ea/Enki, and the central segment as the Way of Anu; and numerous clay tablets listed the constellations in each such Way. The central one of Anu was devoted to the twelve zodiacal constellations, starting with Taurus (**Gu.Anna,** the Bull of Heaven), when the Sumerian civilization began (fourth millennium B.C.). Since texts dealing with much earlier times employ zodiacal terminology (the Sumerian tale of the Deluge dates it to the Age of **Ur. Gula** [= 'The Lion'] which began circa 10900 B.C.), it is certain that the concept of constellations preceded Mankind's civilizations. According to ZS, it was the Anunnaki (for whom an Earth year was a minuscule time unit), who grouped the stars and invented the zodiac as a 'Celestial Calendar' in which the mathematical length of one unit (a Zodiacal Age) was 2,160 Earth-years, giving a convenient 6:10 ratio to Nibiru's orbital period of 3,600 Earth-years. *See also* Celestial Time, Zodiac.

▸ Copan: A classic Mayan site in what is now Guatemala. Archaeological evidence suggests that it served as the seat of an astronomical academy whose savants, meeting in conclaves, determined calendrical issues.

▸ Copper (**Uru.du**): Archaeological finds indicate that copper was the first metal used by Mankind, starting in the Zagros and Taurus mountain regions of the Near East, as early as the fifth millennium B.C. Its use began with hammering soft nuggets of native copper into sheets and utensils. With the invention of the kiln furnace, mined copper ores could be smelted and refined; that made lands where copper could be mined— such as Cyprus or Crete—desired territories. The Egyptians obtained copper from mines in the southern Sinai; the famed 'King Solomon's Mines' were nearby. The discovery that copper, when alloyed with tin or zinc, acquired other useful properties, launched the Metallurgical Age. In the Bible, the word for copper—*Nehoshet*—derives from the verb that means 'to decipher'; the derived noun *Nahash* has two meanings: 'a solver/knower of secrets' and 'serpent' (as in the Garden of Eden tale); so does the parallel Sumerian terminology. Noteworthy is the report in Exodus that Moses stopped a plague afflicting the Israelites by fashioning *Nehushtan*—a copper serpent. *See* Buzur, Enki, Eden.

▸ Cori-Cancha (= 'Golden Enclosure'): The principal shrine in Cuzco, the Inca capital in Peru, dedicated to the god Viracocha. Its walls were completely encased in gold—gold that was immediately pried off the walls by the arriving Spaniards. (The bare walls still bear the marks of their golden plates.) The semi-circular section for the Holy of Holies, built of perfectly shaped ashlars, was so built that the sun's rays shone in upon the golden altar, creating a sunburst as the rays hit a huge disc of pure gold, at sunrise on the day of the winter solstice—an archaeoastronomical clue indicating that the temple's orientation was determined thousands of years before the Incas. *See* Ayar Brothers, Viracocha.

▸ Council of the gods: According to Sumerian texts, the Anunnaki's most important decisions were reached not by unilateral decrees of Anu or Enlil, but after "the great Anunnaki who decree the fates sat exchanging their counsels." Matters concerning the gods, as well as crucial decisions affecting Mankind, were debated and decided at such councils. The Anunnaki leaders (who also included Enki, Ninharsag and others) addressed the meetings, and sometimes engaged in bitter debates before reaching a decision. The Egyptian 'Chester Beatty Papyrus' also records that a Council of the Gods deliberated the conflicting claims of Horus and Seth.

▸ Covenant: (H *Brit*) Generally means a Treaty, but the term is used in the Bible to define God's promises to Abraham and his descendants as an everlasting commitment.

▸ Craftsman of the gods: Called *Kothar-Hasis* (= 'Skilled and Knowing') in Canaanite tales, he made for the god Ba'al divine weapons with which to defeat his brothers, then fortified and equipped Ba'al's redoubt of the Crest of Zaphon. He also made for a young hero a unique bow that the goddess Anat schemed to possess. Greek savants compared Kothar-Hasis to the divine craftsman Hephaestus who, according to Greek mythology, built an abode for Zeus and Hera.

▸ Creation Tales: Virtually all civilizations around the world have tales of Creation, with emphasis on how Mankind began with a First Couple. The best known is the biblical one in Genesis, which not only describes evolution on Earth, but starts with how the Earth itself, and the heavens, were created. The biblical version undoubtedly had as a source the Sumerian/Akkadian 'Epic of Creation' (*Enuma elish*). These sources attribute the Creation of The Adam to the Anunnaki/Elohim. In *The 12th Planet*, ZS provides additional Sumerian/Akkadian texts that detail how Enki (god of knowledge) and Ninharsag (goddess of medicine) used genetic engineering to upgrade Earth's hominids to *Homo sapiens*. Since the Anunnaki roamed the Earth, no wonder that Creation Tales in other parts of the world also included a First Couple fashioned by the god of science—e.g., in Mesoamerica Quetzalcoatl ('Plumed Serpent') assisted by the female Cihuacoatl ('Serpent Woman').

▸ Crest of Zaphon: The name given in Canaanite tales to Ba'al's redoubt, and in the Bible (Isaiah 14) to the Landing Site, in the Lebanon mountains, in which the term *Zaphon* can mean both 'place in the north' and 'the place of secrets'. Per ZS: The 'Landing Place' of Gilgamesh and other Sumerian texts, now called Baalbek. *See* Adad, Ba'al, Craftsman of the gods, Zaphon.

▶ Crete: A large island in the Mediterranean Sea. The locale of various 'mythological' events and of the legendary Labyrinth where the Minotaur (half man, half bull) was imprisoned, the island was where the Minoan civilization (a precursor of Greek civilization) flourished from about 1800 B.C. to 1450 B.C. Canaanite texts about *KRT* and its king could well have been related to the Greek name 'Kreta' for the island. It is mentioned in the Bible as *Caphtor*.

▶ Cro-Magnon Man: An advanced *Homo sapiens,* physically almost indistinguishable from Modern Man, who, some 40,000 years ago, inexplicably came from Western Asia and replaced the more primitive Neanderthals in Europe. Though spoken of as 'Stone-age people' and 'cavemen', they added wood, bones and clay to stones as materials for utensils, tools and weapons; wore clothing; crafted artistic artifacts (including figurines of a Mother Goddess); and decorated their caves with artful paintings that amaze to this day. In *The Wars of Gods and Men* ZS has suggested that the "accursation of Earth" which is recorded in Sumerian texts, that began some 75,000 years ago, was a new Ice Age that regressed the human race; and that about "49,000 years ago Enki and Ninharsag elevated humans of Anunnaki parentage" to be able to become rulers—a development that can explain the appearance of 'Cro-Magnon' man.

▶ Cronus: In Greek mythology, the youngest male of the twelve Titans (offspring of the first celestial couple, Gaea/Earth and Uranus/Sky). Seeking dominion, he castrated his father and imprisoned and banished the other Titans. He consorted with his sister Rhea; their three sons and three daughters made up half of the Olympian pantheon, including the great god Zeus who deposed his father Cronus.

▶ Cross: When the Spanish Conquistadors arrived in the Aztec capital Tenochtitlan (now Mexico City) in A.D. 1519, they were astounded to discover that the Cross symbol was depicted as the emblem of the chief Aztec god on his shield. This was just one instance showing that although the Cross has been assumed to be the emblem of Christianity since the crucifixion of Jesus, it has in fact been a sacred symbol found in ancient cultures. According to ZS, the 'Sign of the Cross' was the symbol, since Sumerian times, of the 'Planet of the Gods', Nibiru, whenever it came into view; thus, it came back into prominent display throughout the ancient world (as royal insignia, on monuments, in cylinder seals, etc.) as expectations of the return of Nibiru to visibility increased in the 1st millennium B.C. *See also* Aten.

▸ Cubit: An ancient unit of measuring length, presumed to have equaled 24 'fingers' in a biblical *Amah,* or 28 'fingers' in a royal Egyptian one (525 millimeters = 20.63"). Sir Isaac Newton calculated that a 'Sacred Cubit' used in the construction of the Giza pyramids and in Noah's Ark equaled 25.2".

▸ Cuneiform Script: A script introduced in Sumer in the 4th millennium B.C. and then used throughout the ancient Near East and Western Asia for more than three thousand years. Evolving from pictographs, the script expressed in wedgelike signs the syllabic sounds of the spoken words (be it Sumerian, Akkadian, Hittite, Canaanite, Persian, etc.). Scribes trained in special scribal schools had to learn more than 500 variants of the multi-wedged symbols that made up the script at the peak of its use, in Babylonia and Assyria. ZS has shown that the numerous variants were not only logically arranged, but actually followed advanced mathematical formulas.

▸ *Cush* (or *Kush*): According to Genesis, a post-Diluvial descendant of the Hamitic (= African) tribal nations, related and adjacent to *Mizra'im* (Egypt); ancient Nubia and Ethiopia.

▸ Cuzco: The Inca capital in Peru. According to native legends, the great god Viracocha began to repopulate the land after a great flood with four brother-sister couples, and gave to one brother a golden wand with which to find the place for a future center of Andean civilization— Cuzco; and that is why the temples and palaces of Cuzco, many from pre-Incan times, were covered and filled with gold. There were fourteen Inca rulers in Cuzco from A.D. 1021 to A.D. 1532. When the Spaniards reached Cuzco in A.D. 1533, it was a great metropolis divided into twelve wards matching the twelve zodiacal constellations, from which four royal roads led to the four corners of the Inca empire. Called "a nobly adorned city" by a Spanish chronicler, it was a city with squares, bridges, edifices, palaces—and the Coricancha, the 'Golden Enclosure' temple whose walls were plated with gold. After plundering the city, the Spaniards divided its edifices among themselves, in the end dismantling most of them to build Dominican churches and monasteries. Nowadays, visitors to Cuzco can still see here and there remains of the pre-Incan structures built of interlocking stone blocks.

▸ Cylinder Seals: Precursor of the modern rotary press, a 'cylinder seal' was a device originated in Sumer and then emulated throughout the ancient Near East. Small cylinders (usually an inch or so high), mostly cut from stone (in some cases, semi-precious) were engraved by an artist in reverse with an illustration, sometimes accompanied by writing. When the cylinder was rolled on wet clay, the image was impressed on the clay as a positive; when the clay dried, a permanent imprint unique to that seal was obtained. The term adds the word 'seal' to 'cylinder' because they were used to seal containers (e.g., of oil, wine) or as a seal to authenticate clay-tablet documents.

▸ Cyprus: A Mediterranean island, situated close to the present-day Syrian-Lebanese and Turkish coasts; a source of copper in antiquity. According to Greek legends, the goddess Aphrodite arrived in Greece from Cyprus.

▸ Cyrus (*Kurash*; *Koresh* in the Bible): A renowned Achaemenid-Persian king (559–530 B.C.) who—fulfilling a biblical prophecy by Jeremiah—captured Babylon in 538 B.C. His domains encompassed the ancient lands of Sumer & Akkad, Babylonia and Assyria, Mari and Mitanni, the Hittite kingdom and Greek settlements in Asia Minor, and in the east Elam and Media and beyond. One of his first acts was to issue an edict allowing the return of Jewish exiles to Judea to rebuild the Temple in Jerusalem that was destroyed by the Babylonians. The clay cylinder on which his edict is inscribed is now on display in the British Museum.

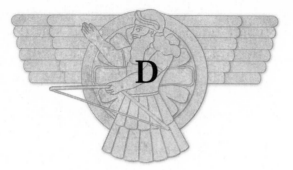

- **Dagan**: An important male deity in Mari. He complained that in old age he was not being consulted anymore by the king.

- *Dagon*: The principal deity of the Philistines. The name may mean 'He of the Fishes'—a god of the sea.

- Dahshur: The location in Egypt, south of Giza, of two famous pyramids attributed to the Pharaoh Sneferu, called the Bent Pyramid and the Red Pyramid.

- Damascus: An ancient city, now the capital of Syria, located at an intersection of major trade routes. It is first mentioned in the Bible (Genesis 14) in the tale of Abraham's pursuit of the Kings of the East who had taken his nephew captive, and was within the boundaries of the kingdom of David and Solomon. It subsequently rose to prominence as the capital of Aram, but declined after its capture by the Assyrians in 732 B.C. *See* Aram, Arameans.

- **Dam.ki.na** (= 'Lady [who] to Earth Came'): The spouse of Ea, mother of his Firstborn son Marduk, who followed Ea from Nibiru to Earth, bringing Marduk with her. She was renamed **Nin.Ki** (= 'Lady of Earth') after Ea was granted the epithet/title **En.ki** (= 'Lord of Earth').

- *Dan*: One of the twelve sons of Jacob. The Israelite tribe named after him was allotted the northernmost part of Canaan.

- *Danel* (= 'Judged by El'): The main protagonist in a Canaanite tale about an aging chieftain who could not beget a rightful heir. Righteous to the end, he kept praying for a son by his own wife. Responding to his supplications, two 'men', who turned out to be the gods El and Ba'al, appeared at his abode and enabled him to beget a rightful heir by his wife.

▸ *Daniel* (H = 'Judged by God'): The Bible's Book of Daniel identifies him as one of the sons of noblemen exiled from Judea to Babylon after Nebuchadnezzar captured Jerusalem. Taken to serve in the royal court of Belshazzar, Daniel distinguished himself as a solver of dreams and of an oracle written on the palace wall by a floating hand. Then Daniel himself began to have dreams and see visions foretelling turmoil and the rise and fall of kingdoms; the visions, involving angels, beasts and other symbolisms, are believed to have served as a model for similar visions in the New Testament's Book of Revelation. Told by angels that his dreams and visions concerned the End of Time, Daniel persisted in asking when it shall come to pass; the several enigmatic answers he received have been the subject of study and speculation ever since, including recently discovered calculations by Sir Isaac Newton. ZS, in *The End of Days*, offers his own findings. *See* Ages, Babylon, Belshazzar, End of Days, Prophets, Zodiacal Ages.

▸ Darius: An Achaemenid/Persian king (522–486 B.C.) who is mentioned in the Bible (Haggai, Zechariah, Daniel). He expanded the Persian empire westward to Thrace in southeast Europe and southward to Egypt in Africa. His royal cylinder seal, on which his name and title were inscribed in cuneiform, depicted a god hovering in the skies in a winged disk.

▸ Date Formulas: Annual Sumerian records in which each year of a king's reign was designated by its main event. These inscriptions proved invaluable not only for establishing Near Eastern chronology, but also to learning that era's major events.

▸ Date Palm: Was the Tree of Life of Garden of Eden fame a date palm? In voicing that opinion, ZS shows that in Egyptian depictions concerning the Afterlife, in Assyrian art, and in Greek drawings of Apollo's temple in Delphi, the Tree of Life is represented as a date-palm tree. Egyptian texts concerning Afterlife, the Book of Enoch, the biblical tale of the Exodus, and Canaanite tales of immortality, all associate the date palm with eternal life. Significant too is a Mesopotamian text detailing the meals of the gods in Uruk in which "108 measures of ordinary dates and dates of the land of Tilmun" (= the Sinai peninsula) were required "every day of the year, for the four daily meals." *See* Garden of Eden, Plant of Life, Tree of Life.

▸ David: The foremost Judean king whose feats, deeds and misdeeds are extensively recorded in the Bible. Son of Jesse of Bethlehem, he came to fame when, as a young shepherd, he stepped forth and slew the Philistine Goliath with a sling shot. He succeeded Israel's first king, Saul; the description in I Samuel 16 of David's anointment as the bestowing the Spirit of God upon him, established David as "God's Anointed," whose descendants alone (starting with his son Solomon) shall be the rightful heirs to kingship in Jerusalem. According to Psalm 89, David was anointed with God's Holy Oil, creating a special and everlasting bond between God and the "House of David." A warrior and a nation builder, he fought off neighboring enemies and, circa 1000 B.C., established Jerusalem as the national capital. Many Psalms, expressing unbound devotion to Yahweh, are attributed to David. The Hebrew Prophets deemed the ultimate restoration of David's throne in Jerusalem as the fulfillment of divine messianic promises; the New Testament begins the tale of Jesus with a listing of his Davidic lineage. According to ZS, the choice of David (a shepherd), his affirmation as king by the act of anointing, and the selection of Hebron as his first seat of kingship, were all symbolic links to the Kingship that "was brought down from heaven" by the Anunnaki. *See* Anunnaki, Arba, Jerusalem Temple, King/Kingship.

▸ Davison's Chamber: The first of the 'Chambers of Construction' above the 'King's Chamber' in the Great Pyramid in Giza, so named after Nathaniel Davison who discovered it in 1765.

▸ Day the Earth Stood Still: Legends concerning Teotihuacan, Mexico's 'city of the gods', link the building of its two great pyramids to a calamity that befell the Earth, when the Sun failed to rise and the night's darkness persisted. Two gods sacrificed themselves in Teothihuacan (= 'Place of the gods') in the Divine Flame to persuade the Sun and the Moon to reappear and resume their motions. The other gods commemorated the event by erecting the Pyramid of the Sun and the Pyramid of the Moon. Likewise, in South America, an Inca legend relates that at one time the Creator God became angry with the people and hid the sun from the land: "There was no dawn for twenty hours." He relented when the king hurriedly resumed the prescribed rites. A similar recollection of "a day of darkness" is included in the tales of the Uru people in the Andes. ZS, in *The Lost Realms*, recalls in that connection one of the most challenging episodes recorded in the Bible, that of the day when the Sun did not set: According to Joshua chapter 10, to help the Israelites in a battle, Yahweh made "the Sun stand still in Gibeon and the Moon in the Valley of Ayalon." The phenomenon lasted "about a whole day." Scholars have struggled for generations with this tale; unable to find a satisfactory explanation, most consider the tale to be just a myth. In response, ZS pointed out in *When Time Began* that if the Sun stood still and **did not set** on one side of the Earth (the Near East), it **did not rise** on the other side (the Americas); therefore, the opposite tales describe the effects of the same occurrence, eyewitnessed on both sides of the Earth. Citing the chronicler Montesinos, ZS has calculated South America's date of the event as 1394 B.C.—which corresponds to the time of Joshua's battle in the Valley of Ayalon. So the inexplicable event—when **the Earth** stood still—had to have actually occurred, even if science is yet to explain it. *See* Joshua, Teotihuacan.

▸ Day of the Lord: A term increasingly invoked by biblical Prophets starting in the 8th century B.C. and with rising urgency in the 6th century B.C. The Prophets described it as a time when the Celestial Lord shall appear from the south, light up Venus, come closer to Earth, and on Earth cause darkness at noon and earthquakes: Isaiah foresaw the heavens "agitated" when the celestial Lord shall reappear "from the end point of heaven" and the Earth "shaken out of its place when the Lord shall be crossing;" Amos predicted that "the Earth shall be darkened in the midst of daytime." ZS has explained that the 'Day of the Lord' was the anticipated return of the planet Nibiru to Earth's vicinity. A meticulous analysis by ZS in *The End of Days* shows how the biblical Prophets, starting in the 8th century B.C., foresaw the coming Day with mounting urgency and increased detail as the Day neared; per ZS, the event actually took place, marked by an irregular solar eclipse, in 556 B.C. (See also in *Journeys to the Mythical Past* re a date incised on the astounding 'Antikythera Mechanism'.)

▸ Dead Sea: The lakelike and lifeless body of water at the terminus of the Jordan River, now divided between Israel and the Kingdom of Jordan. Located in a deep geologic rift valley that makes it the lowest point on Earth, it is called *Yam Hamelach* (= 'The Salt Sea') in Hebrew because the high evaporation rate combined with insufficient water inflow cause an extremely high mineral-salt content that prevents any life in its waters; it is so named also in an inscription of the Assyrian king Sargon II. ZS, treating the Epic of Gilgamesh as a factual tale, has suggested that in trying to cross a "barren sea whose waters are death" Gilgamesh was actually attempting to cross the Dead Sea on the way to the spaceport in the Sinai. ZS has also suggested that the southern extension of the sea resulted from flooding caused by the nuclear upheavaling of Sodom, Gomorrah and three other "sinning cities" that had been located there. *See* Abraham, Erra, Gilgamesh, Lot, Nuclear Weapons.

▸ Dead Sea Scrolls: In the spring of 1947 a shepherd boy looking for a lost sheep in the barren cliffs overlooking the Dead Sea discovered in a cave a stack of earthenware jars in which inscribed parchment scrolls were hidden. Those scrolls and others discovered since then—collectively known as the Dead Sea Scrolls—turned out to be Hebrew manuscripts carefully hidden during the Jewish revolt against Roman rule in Judea two thousand years ago. Because most were found in caves adjoining a site called Qumran, the scrolls are presumed to have been the library of a Jewish sect known as the Essenes whose retreat Qumran was. Many of the manuscripts are copies of books of the Hebrew Bible; some are of lost extra-biblical books, confirming their existence; others pertain to the sect, its principles, customs and beliefs. While such scrolls throw light on the religious ferment at the time when Christianity began, there is no consensus regarding the Essenes, whether Qumran was indeed their hideout, or even whether the scrolls were all theirs— or perhaps brought from the Temple in Jerusalem to save them from the Roman onslaught. But all agree that the scrolls' very existence is a major attestation of the antiquity of the canonized Hebrew Bible and various apocryphal texts (that, among other things, corroborate the references to the *Nefilim*).

▸ DED (also DJED): An Egyptian hieroglyph depicting a step-pillar and meaning 'Everlastingness'.

▸ Delphi: A sacred precinct dotted with temples, located on a promontory west of Athens. It was the site of ancient Greece's most famous oracle: In the inner sanctum of the temple to Apollo, hidden in a subterranean chamber, an oracle priestess, in a trancelike state, gave enigmatic answers to kings and heroes who posed questions concerning their fates. Such an ambiguous Delphic oracle encouraged Alexander of Macedon to embark on his conquests. The topography and layout of the site and the fact that the principal sacred object there was an Omphalos, suggested to ZS that the site served as a physical base for the intrepid and continent-hopping god Apollo.

▸ Deluge: The great flood that according to the Bible engulfed the Earth and would have extinguished Mankind save for Noah and his Ark. Though the lore of virtually all cultures recalls a devastating deluge, the biblical tale was held to be just that—a tale, until a similar story was found in earlier Mesopotamian texts, (e.g., the Epic of Gilgamesh and the Atra-Hasis epic). The Sumerian and Akkadian texts provided details of the several gods' roles, their identities and motivations, and added specifics of actual locations, rulers' names (including the identity of 'Noah'— **Ziusudra** in Sumerian, *Utnapishtim* in Akkadian), and description of the Ark, a submersible vessel, per ZS. These texts enabled ZS to date the event to circa 13,000 years ago—a conclusion that links the Deluge to the scientifically established end of the last Ice Age. ZS explained the

Deluge as an engulfing tidal wave caused by the slippage of the immense ice sheet off the Antarctic continent. It was a calamity in-the-making, observed by the Anunnaki from a scientific station at the tip of Africa; and when they realized that the anticipated close passage of Nibiru at its perigee would trigger the avalanche, Enlil wanted to let Mankind be unprepared and perish; Enki, defied that by saving 'Noah'. *See* Ea/Enki, Man/Mankind, Nibiru Orbit, Noah, Ziusudra.

▸ Demigods: The written records of ancient civilizations contain as a matter of fact numerous references to 'demigods'—the offspring of parents one of whom was a god or goddess. The Sumerian King List names pre-Diluvial demigod rulers (including the names of their divine parents). In post-Diluvial times, several kings of Uruk were demigods, parented by the god Utu or (as in the case of Gilgamesh) by the goddess Ninsun. Ancient Egyptian dynastic lists provided by Manetho start with two dynasties of gods followed by a list of thirty demigods; in Pharaonic times, kings claimed to have been the offspring of gods, and included the suffix MSS (= 'Issue of' a god) in their royal titles. Alexander the Great believed palace rumors that his true father was not king Philip but the Egyptian god Ammon. Even the Hebrew Bible recognizes demigods when it tells in chapter 6 of Genesis that "the sons of the *Elohim* took Daughters of Man as wives and had children by them." In Joshua 14 the Bible lists the rulers of Hebron before the Israelite arrival as "descendants of the *Anakim*" (= Anunnaki), which makes them demigod offspring.

▸ Denderah: A site in Upper Egypt where a zodiacal map of the heavens decorated the ceiling of a temple for the goddess Hathor.

▸ Descending Passage: In the Great Pyramid in Giza, a corridor leading from the Pyramid's original entrance in the north side all the way to the Pyramid's bottom pit in its bedrock base. Similar to descending passages in other pyramids, its existence was known in antiquity; that at some point it could lead to a blocked Ascending Passage (unique to this pyramid) was discovered by chance in A.D. 820.

▸ Destiny (**Nam**): While in most modern languages, and thus in modern translations of Sumerian texts, 'Destiny' and 'Fate' are interchangeable terms, ZS has pointed out that the Sumerians distinguished between Destiny (**Nam**) that, once determined, could not be changed, and Fate (**Nam.tar**) which, though constrained by Destiny, could be modified by free will, righteous behavior, prayer, etc. A predetermined Destiny applied to people, kings, countries, the gods themselves, even to the Earth and other planets (whose 'destiny' was the orbit assigned to each one of them). But while Man's mortality was his destiny, within that inevitability was his Fate, which just behavior, following the gods' commandments etc. could result in a longer life, a healthier life, etc. In that way, the Sumerians introduced the concept of Free Will, Free Choice and Morality into Man's life and behavior.

▸ Deuteronomy (H *Devarim* = 'Sayings'): The fifth book of the so-called Five Books of Moses of the Bible, whose opening verse is "These are the words which Moses spoke to all of Israel on this side of the Jordan, in the wilderness." The book reviews the events of the Exodus and repeats the commandments by which the Israelites had to abide.

▸ **Dil.gan**: A Sumerian name for the planet Jupiter.

▸ Dilmun: *See* Tilmun.

▸ **Din.gir**: A two-syllable word that was used in Sumerian cuneiform writing as a 'determinative'—a term that defines the nature of the name that follows. Because 'din.gir' always preceded the name of a god, e.g., 'dingir Enlil', 'dingir Enki', etc., the word is taken by translators to mean 'god'—'god Enlil', the 'god Enki', etc. Ancient Akkadian-Sumerian glossaries rendered the word as *Ilu* in Akkadian (from which comes the Hebrew and Canaanite *El*, translated 'god'), and simplified the pictorial sign to that of a star. By tracing back the development of the cuneiform sign **Din.gir** from its later star symbol to its two-part pictorial origin, ZS has shown that the sign depicted a two-stage rocketship. Taken separately, **Din** meant 'Righteous' in Sumerian and **Gir** meant 'Rocket', so that what has come to mean 'god' originally meant the "Righteous one of the Rocketships." *See* God/gods.

▸ **Dir.ga** ('Dark, Crownlike'): An inner chamber in Enlil's 'Bond Heaven-Earth' facility in Nippur where "a heavenly zenith with the starry emblems" was installed.

▸ Divine Black Bird (**Im.du.gud**): The aerial vehicle of the god Ninurta in which he roamed Earth's skies. It had a wing span of about 75 feet and its depictions showed it with two arching dual wings. It was kept in a special enclosure built on an artificial platform in the sacred precinct of Lagash (Ninurta's 'cult center').

▸ Divine Formulas: One way that translators use to convey the elusive meaning of the Sumerian term 'Me' that described small portable objects that contained and provided secret knowledge or 'formulas' for each and every aspect of a high civilization, from space travel to temple rituals. The **Me** was not just something on which data was encoded (we would now say 'a computer chip' or 'memory disc'), but also provided the ability, the authority and the power to exercise such knowledge. A text titled 'A Hymn to Eridu' recorded a complaint by Enlil that Enki, the custodian of the **Me**, withheld from him the **Me** needed to establish Nippur as his command center. A subsequent description of Enlil's Mission Control Center in Nippur lists **Me** alongside "Tablets of Destinies" as essential equipment. Another text tells how Inanna, visiting Enki to obtain the **Me** needed to make her city Uruk a center of kingship and priesthood, stole and escaped holding one hundred of them in her hand. Scholars have also translated the term as 'Divine powers', 'Divine commandments', 'Mythic virtues'. *See* Dur.an.ki, Enlil, Zu.

▸ Divine Ranks: The principal deities of the Sumerian-Akkadian pantheon had a numerical rank. Culling the information from a variety of texts, ZS has determined that these ranks followed the Sumerian sexagesimal ('Base 60') system, assigning to Anu (chief of the twelve Great Gods) the rank of 60, 50 to Enlil, 40 to Ea/Enki, 30 to Nannar/Sin, 20 to Utu/Shamash, 10 to Ishkur/Adad. Their female counterparts bore the 'half ranks' of 55 to Antu, 45 to Ninlil, 35 to Ninki, 25 to Ningal, 15 to Inanna/Ishtar (who pushed Ninharsag down to 5). In the struggle for succession, Ninurta claimed Enlil's rank of 50—only to see Marduk obtain the rank and its "Fifty Names" after the nuclear blast of 2024 B.C. In sculptures and other depictions, the deity's standing was indicated by the number of pairs of horns on their helmets.

▸ Divine Scribe: One of the titles of the Egyptian god Thoth, who wrote down the decisions of the Council of the Gods. It was stated that he "wrote with his own fingers" the composition known as the Egyptian Book of the Dead.

▸ Divine Time: A term coined by ZS in *When Time Began* for the Anunnaki's one year on Nibiru (one orbit = 3,600 Earth years), as distinguished from 'Earthly Time' (one year = one Earth orbit). *See* Sar.

▸ DNA: The chains of molecules of four nucleic acids (known by their initials A-C-G-T) within every living cell that combine to form 'genes' which determine whether the life form shall be a lowly bacterium, a flower or fish, a bird, animal or human. The key to unlocking the genetic secrets was the discovery that the genetic chains are paired to form a Double Helix. ZS has pointed out, in *The Cosmic Code*, that in antiquity such a spiraling double helix was depicted as Entwined Serpents—it was the Egyptian hieroglyphic symbol for 'Ptah' (= Enki, Mankind's creator by genetic engineering and the 'Serpent' in the biblical tale of Adam and Eve). Entwined Serpents—a symbol of medicine to this day—was also the Sumerian symbol of Enki's son and helper **Nin.gish.zid.da** ('Lord/Artificer of the Tree of Life'). The human genome is arranged in 22 'chromosomes' (plus two to determine sex); DNA works when three of its four 'letters' combine into 22 different sets of 'trios' of amino acid that act as 'verbs' from which protein 'words' are formed. ZS has found it remarkable that the Hebrew language also uses 22 letters to make up 'trios' that serve as 'root verbs'—emulating the way DNA works.

▸ Dome of the Rock: An octagonal structure on the Temple Mount in Jerusalem built as a protective housing over the sacred 'Foundation Rock'—a large and unusually formed rock outcropping on which the Ark of the Covenant in the Holy of Holies of Solomon's Temple had stood (and where, according to tradition, Abraham was ready to sacrifice his son Isaac). The structure was built by the Moslems after they captured Jerusalem in the 7th century A.D.; the Moslems believe that it was from that sacred rock that Mohammed was taken aloft to visit heaven. The structure's gilded dome, that gave the building its name, was brought over by the Caliph Abd al-Malik from Baalbek in Lebanon, where it roofed over a Byzantine church. *See* Ark of the Covenant.

▸ Domestication: The process of adapting wild plants (such as barley, wheat) or wild animals (such as sheep, goats) to human needs and raising them in controlled circumstances (as agricultural crops in fields, in herds, etc.). By and large, the process began in the Near East circa 10000–9000 B.C., in the area that is now Lebanon/Syria. While scientists and sociologists theorize how Mankind switched from 'hunting-gathering' to agriculture and husbandry, Sumerian texts attributed the feat to a deliberate decision by the gods in the aftermath of Earth's devastation by the Deluge circa 11000 B.C. Texts, such as the Tale of **Lahar** ('woolly creatures' = sheep) and **Anshan** ('grain cereals'), state that both emanated from a "Creation Chamber," a "House of Fashioning" set up by Enlil and Enki right after the Deluge on "the Pure Mound," in the "Mountain of aromatic cedars" (per ZS, the Landing Place of the Anunnaki = Baalbek in Lebanon). Then the gods taught **Nam.lu.gallu** (= 'Civilized Mankind') the "tilling of the land" and "the keeping of sheep"—first and foremost so that the gods themselves would be satiated. Other Sumerian texts attributed the teaching of agriculture to Enlil and his son Ninurta; of animal husbandry, to Enki.

▸ Duat: The Egyptian hieroglyphic name, meaning 'Abode for ascending to the stars', for the Pharaohs' first destination in their Afterlife Journey. The Pyramid Texts and the Book of the Dead described it as a place with underground passages and chambers leading to where the 'Gates to Heaven' would open and the king would be taken heavenwards in a 'Divine Ascender', to join the gods on the 'Planet of Millions of Years'. Treating the Journey's details in those texts as factual geographic and topographic indicators, ZS has concluded that the Duat was located in the central plain of the Sinai peninsula—the site of the Anunnaki's post-Diluvial spaceport.

▸ **Dumu.zi** (= 'Son who is Life'): The youngest of the six sons of Enki who was betrothed to Inanna/Ishtar (Enlil's granddaughter). His elder brother Marduk opposed the marriage, and brought about Dumuzi's death. Many Sumerian texts describe that godly 'Romeo and Juliet' tragic love, and how the distraught Inanna went in search of her beloved's body in an effort to resurrect him. Additionally studying relevant Egyptian texts, ZS has suggested that it was Inanna who began the custom of mummification, hoping to preserve Dumuzi until he comes back to life. The 10th Mesopotamian month (called *Tammuz* in Akkadian and in Hebrew) was named for Dumuzi, and he was bewailed in that month even in biblical times.

▸ **Dur.an.ki** (= 'Bond Heaven-Earth'): The innermost secret chamber or Holy of Holies in Enlil's pre-Diluvial Mission Control Center in Nippur, from which the space operations of the Anunnaki were controlled with the aid of 'Tablets of Destinies'—devices encoded with sky maps, planetary orbits, and other space data. ZS has suggested that after the Deluge, Jerusalem fulfilled this function. Because Nippur was also deemed to be the Navel of the Earth, the **Dur.an.ki** could be compared to a virtual Umbilical Cord between the Anunnaki on Earth and their mother planet, Nibiru. *See* Nippur, Omphalos.

▸ *Dvir*: According to the Book of Exodus God spoke to Moses from the space between the spread pairs of wings of the golden *Cherubim*, located atop the Ark of the Covenant. After the Temple was built in Jerusalem, the Ark of the Covenant was placed in the Holy of Holies which only the High Priest was allowed to enter and (in a strictly prescribed manner) approach the *Dvir* "and hear the voice [of the Lord] speak unto him from off the overlay which is upon the Ark of the Covenant." The term, which the King James Bible translated "oracle," is nowadays usually translated "shrine," "inner shrine"; but ZS has pointed out that in Hebrew, *Dvir* literally means 'Speaker'—a voice communication device!

▶ Dzibilchaltun: A Mayan site on the Gulf of Mexico coast of the Yucatan peninsula whose remains—plazas, pyramids and temples—cover an astounding area of some twenty square miles. Archaeological evidence supports local lore that that is where Mayan and pre-Mayan civilization began when people led by 'Can' (meaning 'Serpent') arrived by boats. The site's leading attraction is the astronomically aligned Temple of the Seven Dolls, so called because seven figurines were found there, standing in a circle. ZS reported in *The Earth Chronicles Expeditions* that the figurines (now in the site's small museum) resemble astronauts wearing backpacks.

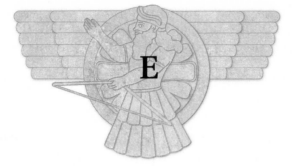

▶ **E.a** (= 'Whose abode is water'): The epithet-name of the leader of the first group of 50 Anunnaki who arrived on Earth, splashing down in the Persian Gulf. Chosen for his scientific knowledge, his mission was to obtain gold from the Gulf's waters; depicted with flowing streams of water, he was the prototype 'Aquarius'. He was the Firstborn son of Anu, Nibiru's ruler, but was not the Legal Heir, for he was mothered by one of Anu's concubines; the succession privilege belonged to his half-brother Enlil, whose mother was not only Anu's official spouse but also Anu's half-sister. Many of the conflicts on Earth stemmed from the rivalry between the two half-brothers; as an accommodation, Anu granted Ea the title **En.Ki** (= 'Lord [of] Earth'); but his numerical rank, 40, remained below Enlil's 50. When the initial plans failed, he was put in charge of the gold mining operations in southeast Africa. There he discovered the existence of hominids genetically akin to the Anunnaki—leading to his most important feat: The genetic engineering to fashion The Adam. As the creator of Mankind, he frustrated the plan to have it perish in the Deluge, by instructing his faithful follower to build the famed Ark. His 'cult center' in Sumer was Eridu; his domain, which he divided between his six sons, was Africa. The Egyptians called him PTAH ('The Developer'). Described in the texts as a 'ladies' man', his many infidelities included affairs with female Earthlings. His autobiography, found on partly damaged clay tablets, has been used by ZS to compose *The Lost Book of Enki*.

▶ Eaglemen: An epithet for Anunnaki astronauts, often depicted as gods with human bodies, eagle or bird heads, and one or two pairs of wings.

They were usually linked with Enlilites; Utu/Shamash, Enlil's grandson, was at times their commander. Enlilite priests were sometimes distinguished from Enkiite ones by being dressed as Eaglemen. *See* Cherubim, Utu, Winged Beings.

▸ **E.Anna** (= 'House/Abode of Anu'): The main ziggurat-temple in Uruk.

▸ Earth (**Ki**, *Gi* = 'The Cleaved One'—from which 'Gaea' in Greek, and Latin 'Geo' as in Geography): According to the Epic of Creation as interpreted by ZS, Earth was the remaining half of the planet Tiamat that broke up in the 'Celestial Battle' with Nibiru/Marduk, shunted by the force of the collision to its present orbit, and pulling along with it Tiamat's principal satellite to become our Moon. It was nicknamed "the Seventh" because, counting from the outside in as one enters our solar system from way out, Earth is the seventh planet. Its cuneiform sign represented a globe crisscrossed by longitude lines. *See* Celestial Battle.

▸ Earthling: The literal meaning of the biblical (H) "The *Adam*," which stems from *Adamah*—'Earth' in Hebrew. *See* Adam.

▸ **E.babbar** ('House of the Bright One'): The name of the temple of Utu/Shamash, the so-called "sun god," in his cult center Sippar.

▸ *Eber*: According to the Bible's Table of Nations (Genesis 10) it was through this descendant that Shem, the oldest son of Noah, became the "father of all the children of Eber" of whom Abram/Abraham the *Ibri* (= 'The Hebrew') stemmed. ZS, in *The Wars of Gods and Men*, has linked these designations to the Sumerian **Ni.Ibru** (= 'The Comely Place [of] Crossing")—which was the name of Nippur in Sumerian, concluding that Abraham's designation as *Ibri* meant that he was born in Nippur.

▸ Ebla (*Ibla* in ancient annals): A city-state (its site, Tell Mardikh, is in northern Syria) that flourished for a thousand years since circa 2400 B.C. Archaeologists have discovered there tablets in which the capture of this formidable center is directly attributed to the god Nergal.

▸ Eclipses: As the Earth orbits the Sun and the Moon orbits the Earth, the Earth's shadow sometimes hides the Moon, causing a Lunar Eclipse.

Occurring regularly, Lunar Eclipses could be predicted, and a tablet now in the British Museum contained formulas for predicting Lunar Eclipses fifty years ahead. Sometimes, the Moon's shadow hides the Sun, causing a Solar Eclipse. Occurring more rarely, Solar Eclipses were deemed in antiquity omens of great significance. Biblical and Mesopotamian prophecies regarding the Day of the Lord—the return of Nibiru to Earth's vicinity per ZS—described the event in terms of a solar eclipse; an extraordinary total solar eclipse, according to ZS in *The End of Days*, occurred in 556 B.C. *See* Day of the Lord, Harran, Nibiru.

▶ Ecuador: A country in western South America, so named because it lies astride the Equator. According to local traditions, it was at its Cape Santa Helena which protrudes into the Pacific Ocean that the first settlers to the equatorial regions had arrived by boats, guided by divine instructions emanating from a green stone; archaeological finds there are dated to circa 2500 B.C. It was also there, according to legends, that the "route of Viracocha" led away over the ocean as he left the Americas. When the Incas of Peru extended their empire, Ecuador was their northernmost outpost. The Museo del Banco Central in Quito, the capital, displays some amazing golden artifacts from pre-Colombian times.

▶ *Eden*: Coming from the Sumerian **E.din**—'Home/Abode of the Righteous Ones'—it was the area, later Sumer, where the Anunnaki established their settlements in pre-Diluvial times. *See* Eden.

▶ Edfu: A site in Upper Egypt, where hieroglyphic inscriptions on the walls of the great temple assert that the god Horus, fighting his father's murderer the god Seth, established there a foundry and enlisted humans in his fight, arming them with weapons "forged of divine metal." The temple inscription also states that Horus kept there his great Winged Disc; "when the doors of the foundry open, the Disc riseth up." *See* Aerial Chariots, Iron.

▶ *Edom*: A kingdom in biblical times, located to the southeast of Judea.

▶ Egypt (**Magan**), (H) *Mitzrayim*: The ancient Egyptians called their land HM-Ta (= 'Dark Land'), the land of the Hamitic people—in accord with the biblical statement (Genesis 10) that it was the land of the descendants of Noah's second son Ham. Sumerian tales of the Anunnaki assert that "when Earth was divided," Africa was allotted to Enki; according to Egyptian lore, the fertile Nile Valley was ruled by the god PTAH (= Enki) and his descendants. After it was inundated by the Deluge, Ptah erected dams and "raised Egypt from under the waters" to make it habitable; then, circa 3100 B.C., Egyptian civilization with Pharaonic dynasties began. *See* Ham.

▸ Egyptian Religion: The ancient Egyptians' word for 'gods' was NTR, meaning 'Guardians'; they were Gods of Heaven who, in times immemorial, arrived on Earth from the 'Planet of Millions of Years' (represented by the celestial Winged Disk). At first only gods reigned in Egypt; according to the priest-historian Manetho the god Ptah, followed by his son Ra and the gods Shu, Geb, Osiris, Seth and Horus, reigned for a total of 12,300 years, followed by a divine dynasty led by Thoth for another 1,570 years. Those gods married half-sisters, fought and even killed each other. Thirty demigods then preceded the Pharaonic dynasties that began circa 3100 B.C.—a reason for Pharaohs to claim they too were demigods, entitled to an eternal Afterlife. Memphis in central Egypt was the first royal and religious capital; circa 2200 B.C. upheavals shifted the power center to Thebes in Upper (= southern) Egypt. In time Ra (= Marduk per ZS) became 'Amen' (the 'Hidden/Unseen' god). *See* Aten, Ben-Ben.

▸ **E.hul.hul** ('House/Temple of Double Joy'): The main temple of the god Nannar/Sin in Harran, second in importance only to his ziggurat-temple in Ur. *See* Adda-Guppi, Harran, Nabu'naid, Nannar, Ur.

▸ *Ekhal* (from **E.gal**, 'Great Abode'): The great hall, the main middle part in Solomon's Temple in Jerusalem, following the tripartite architecture of Near Eastern temples (Hallway, Great Hall, Holy of Holies).

▸ **E.kur** ('House which is like a mountain'): The name of Enlil's pre-Diluvial ziggurat-temple in Nippur, as well as of the post-Diluvial "house with a pointed peak" whose mistress was Ninharsag—which ZS has identified as the Great Pyramid in Giza. Sumerian and Akkadian texts dealing with 'Ekur wars of the gods' (that scholars title "Myths of Kur") have been shown by ZS to chronicle what he has termed 'The Pyramid Wars' (that have actually taken place).

▸ *El*: Literally meaning 'Lofty', the term derived from the Akkadian *Ilu* where it designated 'deity'. In the Hebrew Bible too it was the generic word for 'deity', but in Canaanite texts *El* was the personal name of the head of the pantheon—once an active god of Heaven and Earth, but in time aloof and ready to retire together with his spouse *Asherah*—quite possibly the Moon god Sin and his spouse Nikkal. According to Canaanite texts discovered at a site called Ras Shamra (ancient Ugarit), the couple had three sons, the gods *Yam* ('Ocean/Sea'), *Ba'al* ('Lord') and *Mot* ('Smiter, Annihilator') who were busy fighting each other. The (H) Bible uses *Elim* as the plural of *El* in the generic sense, and *Elohim* when the Anunnaki are involved. *See* Canaanites, God/gods.

▸ Elam: An ancient kingdom in the mountainlands southeast of Sumer; it is first mentioned in the Bible as the land of Shem's offspring *Elam*, and its capital Susa was the biblical *Shushan* in Persian times. An extension of the Sumerian civilization, it was allotted by Enlil to his son Ninurta (whom the Elamites called In-shushinak = 'Lord of Shushin'). A warrior people, the Elamites were proficient makers of metal weapons and provided troops for various military campaigns, such as the 'War of the Kings' described in Genesis 14.

▸ *el-Arish*: The Arabic name of a town and a *wadi* (a river bed that flows with water only in the rainy season) in the Sinai peninsula. The *wadi* (that was called The Brook of Egypt in the Bible) fills with water flowing from the mountainous southern part of the peninsula, irrigates the central caravan and pilgrim town of *Nakhal*, and outflows to the Mediterranean Sea at the town of el-Arish. ZS has pointed out that *el-Arish* comes from **Urash** (= 'The Ploughman'), a Sumerian epithet for Ninurta, and *Nakhal* comes from *Nikkal* (in Akkadian, **Nin.gal** in Sumerian), Ninurta's spouse. *See* Sinai Peninsula, Ways.

▸ El Castillo (= 'The Castle'): The name given by the Spaniards to the imposing pyramid that dominates the skyline in Chichén Itzá. Believed to be
Toltec rather than Mayan in origin, it rises in nine stages to a height of
about 185 feet. Its astronomical features include 91 steps on each of its
four sides, that with the topmost platform add up to 365 (= days of a solar
year) and the phenomenon on Equinox days, when the sun's rays striking
the staircase leading up simulate a wriggling serpent—the symbol of the
god Kukulkan in whose honor the pyramid was built. *See* Chichén Itzá.

▸ El Dorado: Short for 'El hombré dorado', "The Gilded Man"—a legendary
ruler of a kingdom on an island of pure gold who was covered with gold
dust for his daily swim. The legend lured the Spanish Conquistadors and
many other adventurers to keep searching in central and south America
for the golden city, "el Dorado."

▸ Elijah (H) *Eli-Yahu*, 'My God is Yahweh': A Prophet renowned in biblical
times for varied miracles, and for not dying on Earth for he was taken
aloft heavenwards "in a chariot of fire, in a whirlwind." Subsequent biblical Prophets held that he will return to herald messianic times—a belief
proclaimed annually during the Jewish Passover meal. *See* Jericho, Last
Supper, Tell Ghassul.

▸ *Elisha*: The principal disciple of the Prophet Elijah who witnessed his master's heavenly ascent and, having grabbed hold of his mantle, acquired
the ability to perform miracles.

▸ Elixirs: Virtually universally, tales of the gods include references to an
elixir eaten or drunk by the gods to sustain their 'immortality'. When
the Earthling Adapa was taken to Nibiru to be presented to Anu, Enki
made sure that he would not partake of the "Food of Life" and the
"Waters of Life" lest he attain the "Life of a god." In the biblical tale of
Adam and Eve in the Garden of Eden, 'Yahweh-Elohim' expels them lest
they "Take also of the Tree of Life and eat and live forever." Egyptian
texts dealing with the Pharaohs' Afterlife refer to the gods' 'eternal sus-
tenance' and in particular to "the everlasting beverage"—paralleling the
'Soma' elixir of Hindo-Aryan tales.

▸ *Elohim* (H): Though usually translated 'God', this biblical word is a plural of *El* not only grammatically but also in context, as when the *Elohim* said "let **us** fashion the Adam in **our** image and after **our** likeness" (Genesis 1). Genesis 6 refers to the "sons of the *Elohim*" who took Daughters of Man as wives. ZS has pointed out that the parallel Sumerian sources of this and other relevant passages in the Bible attribute the events to the Anunnaki. *See* Anunnaki, Nefilim.

▸ End of Days (H *Aḥarit Hayamim*): A biblical term, first used in Jacob's oracle about the distant future, but mainly used by the Prophets to describe a future Messianic Time, when evil shall be gone from the Earth, justice and peace will reign—but not without a preceding terrible cataclysm, an apocalypse; then there will be a New Beginning, and all nations shall flock to Jerusalem to worship Yahweh. According to the Prophet Jeremiah, Yahweh had planned that ending from the very beginning; the Prophet Isaiah considered the "bowing down" and "cowering" of Marduk and Nabu as essential steps in resuming the "Kingdom of God"; and the Prophet Hosea asserted that the "Kingdom of God" will return at the 'End of Days' "through the House of David," in Jerusalem, on the Temple Mount. The biblical Prophets also asserted that what was to come had been planned by God all along—"From the Beginning the Ending I foretell, from ancient times the things that are not yet done [I told]" God was saying to Isaiah. ZS has stressed that the prophesied 'End of Days' and the 'Day of the Lord', usually treated by scholars as the same set of events, are completely separate and distinct anticipated occurrences: The Day of the Lord was the anticipated return of Nibiru, which took place within the biblical time frame; the timing of the messianic End of Days continued to intrigue beyond the Hebrew Bible's final book, the Book of Daniel. In *The End of Days*, ZS, reviewing the various olden and current predictions, has concluded that the "time, times and a half time" told to Daniel by an angel refers to Zodiacal Time. *See* Apocalypse, Armageddon, Celestial Time, Daniel, Megiddo, Pisces, Revelation, Zodiacal Ages.

▸ End of Time, End Time: *See* End of Days.

▸ **En̲heduanna**: The daughter of king Sargon of Akkad who served as a high priestess in Ur. She composed a series of hymns to all the main temples in Sumer, in which each one was described; the tablets have been found by archaeologists, and are in the British Museum. The University Museum in Philadelphia has on display a round clay plaque that depicts Enheduanna performing a libation ceremony.

▸ **E.ninnu** (= 'House/Temple of Fifty'): An elaborate temple built in the sacred precinct of Lagash as new headquarters for the god **Ninurta** and his spouse **Bau**, to mark the granting to him of the Rank of Fifty—affirming Ninurta's status as Enlil's Successor (per ZS, in the crucial year 2160 B.C. when Marduk became the "Unseen" god Amon in Egypt). The builder, the king Gudea, recorded on clay cylinders (now in the Louvre in Paris) how he received in a dream divine instructions, architectural plans, and objects that ended up physically by his side, all to guide him precisely in the building project. The new temple included a facility for Ninurta's aircraft **Im.du.gud** (= 'Divine Black Bird') and unique features that, according to ZS, formed an inner planetarium (**Shu.gu.lam**) aligned to the zodiacal constellations, and an outer structure aligned to sunrise that acted as a 'Stonehenge on the Euphrates'. *See* Gudea, Lagash, Ninurta.

▸ **En.ki** (= 'Lord [of] Earth'): *See* E.a.

▸ **Enki.du**: (= 'By Enki created'): According to the Epic of Gilgamesh and other Sumerian texts, a kind of 'stone-age man' who acquired human qualities after intercourse with a harlot. Fashioned to subdue Gilgamesh by wrestling with him in Uruk, he became his guardian and companion on the quests for immortality. In the end, he was punished for destroying Enlil's Bull of Heaven while protecting Gilgamesh. *See* Cedar Forest, Landing Place, Uruk.

▸ **En.lil** (= 'Lord of the Command'): The son of Anu by his spouse and half-sister Antu, and thus the Legal Heir to Nibiru's throne; his numerical rank was 50. A commander and disciplinarian, he was sent to organize Earth Mission after Ea's first efforts to obtain gold for Nibiru's survival failed. His rivalry with Ea/Enki regarding the Succession was aggravated by their both being in love with their half-sister Ninharsag. Enlil—who had a son by her out of wedlock—ended up espousing the nurse Sud (renamed **Nin.lil**). He deemed intermarriage between young Anunnaki (the biblical *Nefilim*) and the "Daughters of Man" inappropriate to Earth Mission, and opposed the saving of Mankind from the Deluge. But once he accepted Mankind's survival (due to Enki) as an accomplished fact, he granted Mankind agriculture and kingship, and was revered and loved by the Sumerians, who called him "Father Enlil." His city Nippur served as Sumer's religious center. His 'Foremost Son', **Ninurta** (mothered by Ninharsag) was born on Nibiru; his sons **Nannar**/*Sin* and **Ishkur**/*Adad* were born on Earth.

▸ **En.me.dur.an.ki** (= 'Master of the **Me** of the Bond-Heaven-Earth'): According to Sumerian lore, an Earthling who was transported by the gods Utu/Shamash and Ishkur/Adad to the 'Celestial Abode', where he was initiated into heavenly secrets, and was then returned to Earth to serve in a priestly capacity—a possible prototype of the biblical Enoch. A text in which his name was spelled **En.me.dur.anna** ('Master of the **Me** of Heaven-Bond') describes him as a demigod, the son of Utu/Shamash by an Earthling mother. The Sumerian term '**Me**' is usually translated in these texts as 'Divine Formulas' (*see* Divine Formulas).

▸ Enoch (H *Hanokh*): First listed in the Bible as the son of Cain (Genesis 4), but mostly recalled as another Enoch who was the seventh pre-Diluvial Patriarch in the line of Adam through Seth, who did not die on Earth, but instead "walked with the *Elohim* and was gone, for the *Elohim* had taken him away." The biblical passage (Genesis 5) is substantially enlarged upon in the Book of Enoch, in which his first celestial trip and then his final heavenly journey are described. ZS has compared the tale of Enoch to that of the Sumerian **Enmeduranki**.

▸ *Enosh*: The third son of Adam and Eve, of whom the line from Adam to Noah continued.

▸ **En.sag/En.shag** (= 'Lofty Lord'): Marduk's son by his Earthling wife, better known by his epithet-title **Nabu** (= 'The Spokesman'). A Sumerian text states that Enki, Ensag's grandfather, reached an agreement with Ninharsag (in whose custody the neutral Fourth Region, the Sinai, was placed) to make En.Shag "Lord of **Tilmun**" (= "Land of Missiles"), the part of the Sinai where the Spaceport was. In *The End of Days* ZS has wondered whether that Enki-Ninharsag deal might have triggered the War of the Kings described in Genesis 14. *See* Abraham, Nabu, Spaceport, Tilmun, War of the Kings.

▸ Entwined Serpents: The symbol of healing and medicine to this day, it was the hieroglyph for PTAH, the Egyptian name for Enki, and the symbol of his son and aide Ningishzidda (Thoth in Egypt).

▸ *Enuma elish* (= 'When in the High Above'): The title of the Akkadian/Babylonian version of the 'Epic of Creation'. It tells, on seven clay tablets, the story of the creation "high above" of celestial gods, the appearance from "the great deep" of the god Marduk and his battle with the olden goddess Tiamat and her "swirling host," leading to the formation of "the hammered bracelet" and Earth; it then describes the settling of the Anunnaki on Earth and their feats under the leadership of Marduk. Scholars treat the Epic as a myth or an allegorical tale of good versus evil struggle; ZS has suggested that it is a Babylonian rewrite of a sophisticated—and scientifically plausible—Sumerian cosmogony of how our Solar System was formed and how it was changed by the invading planet Nibiru. *See* Asteroid Belt, Celestial Battle, Earth, Nibiru.

▸ Epic of Creation: *See* Enuma elish.

▸ Epic of Gilgamesh: *See* Gilgamesh; *also* Ale-woman, Baalbek, Dead Sea, Deluge, Enkidu, Eternal Youth.

▸ Equinox: An astronomical term connected with the Sun's apparent annual migration from north to south and back, giving rise to the summer and winter seasons. In this apparent migration, the Sun passes twice over the Earth's Equator—once in March (the 'Spring Equinox' for dwellers of Earth's northern hemisphere) and then in September (the 'Autumnal Equinox'), when daytime and nighttime are exactly equal. In ancient Mesopotamia, the New Year began on the day of the Spring Equinox.

Many ancient Near Eastern temples (such as the ones in Jerusalem and Baalbek) were "equinoctial," as is St. Peter's basilica in the Vatican; and various Mayan and Incan temples included orientations to the Equinoxes.

▸ Erech: The (H) biblical name (*Erekh*) for the Sumerian city Uruk. Not one of the original seven 'cities of the gods' of the Anunnaki, it was established as a place for Anu and Antu to stay during a visit to Earth (circa 4000 B.C. per ZS), and its temple was named **E.Anna**—'Home/Abode of Anu'. Anu then gave it as a present to his great-granddaughter Inanna. Through determination, trickery and her feminine charms, Inanna/Ishtar made Uruk an important city, with a line of heroic kings that included Gilgamesh.

▸ **Eresh.ki.gal** (= 'Scented Mistress of the Great Land'): A granddaughter of Enlil and sister of Inanna. She was married to Enki's son Nergal; together, they reigned over the "Lower World" (the southern tip of Africa) where a scientific facility (per ZS: to observe conditions in Antarctica) was located. A text known as 'Inanna's Descent to the Lower World' describes Ereshkigal's domain and certain major events there.

▸ **E.ri.du** (= 'House in the Faraway Built'): The 'home away from home' of the Anunnaki—the first settlement established at the edge of the southern marshlands when Enki first landed on Earth. Destroyed as were all the Cities of the Gods by the Deluge, it was rebuilt circa 3800 B.C. (precisely at its original location) as the first Sumerian city. Though Enki's domain was in Africa, Eridu remained his permanent city and 'cult center' in Mesopotamia. Hymns extolled his temple/home there, revealing that it was there that he kept the enigmatic 'Divine Formulas' **Me**. Per ZS, the word for 'Earth' in many languages—'Erda' in Old High German, 'Erde' in German, 'Jord' in Danish, 'Jordh' in Icelandic, 'Airtha' in Gothic, 'Erthe' in Middle English, 'Erd' in Kurdish, 'Eredz' in Aramaic, and 'Eretz' in Hebrew—all stem from that first **'Eridu'**.

▸ **Erra** (= 'The Annihilator'): An epithet for **Nergal**, coming from the 'Erra Epic' text that describes the events leading to the use of "awesome weapons" (= nuclear weapons, per ZS) to obliterate the spaceport of the Anunnaki in the Sinai and the "sinning cities" in the plain of the Dead Sea, in 2024 B.C. *See* Nergal.

▸ **E.sag.il** ('House Whose Head is Lofty'): The name of Marduk's ziggurat-temple in Babylon. Completed circa 1960 B.C. after he had attained supremacy as an affirmation of that supremacy, it was designed in accordance with celestial orientations pointing to *Iku*, the lead star of the Constellation of the Ram; its seven stages were designed to enable continuous astronomical observations. The Esagil was also Marduk's official residence, attended by a hierarchy of priests. Babylonian, Assyrian and Persian kings came there to receive the god's blessing for their claim to Babylon's throne, the last one on record being Cyrus. After the death of Marduk (in 323 B.C. per ZS in *The End of Days*), the ziggurat served as the god's tomb. *See* Babylon, Marduk, Ziggurats.

▸ Esarhaddon (also written Asarhaddon): An Assyrian king (680–669 B.C.). The biblical account of the violent circumstances of his succession to the throne in faraway Nineveh, long doubted, were in time corroborated by discovered Assyrian texts. He invaded Egypt and his annals mention the Brook of Egypt in the Sinai and the Qenites residing there, confirming the biblical references to both. His annals report that before embarking on the invasion of Egypt, he went to Harran and paid homage there to an aging god Sin. A stela of Esarhaddon, now in the British Museum, depicts all the emblems of the twelve members of our solar system.

▸ Esau: Son of Isaac and Rebecca, twin brother of Jacob.

▸ Essenes: The presumed name of the ascetic group that dwelt in Qumran on the shores of the Dead Sea, where the Dead Sea Scrolls were found.

▸ **Etana**: A ruler in the Sumerian city Kish. The Sumerian King Lists simply observed after his name: "The one who to Heaven ascended." But tablets were found with a long text, The Epic of Etana, that tells how this righteous king, deprived of a son to succeed him, was provided by the god Utu/Shamash with an 'Eagle' to take him to the Divine Abode, there to obtain the "Plant of Birth." The text describes how, as he was carried by the Eagle ever higher, the Earth appeared smaller and smaller until it disappeared from view; at which point the increasingly scared Etana asked to be brought down back to Earth.

▸ Eternal Life: A variant on Eternal Youth; *see* Immortality.

▸ Eternal Youth: According to the Epic of Gilgamesh, in his search for immortality he met the still living hero of the Deluge who was granted the longevity of the gods; and he revealed to Gilgamesh "a secret of the gods"—the whereabouts of a "Plant of Life" whose berries endow Eternal Youth. (Gilgamesh managed to obtain the plant, only to have it snatched from him by a serpent.) Millennia later, the Spaniards led by Ponce de Leon explored Florida for a rumored Fountain of Eternal Youth there. *See also* Elixirs, Food of Life, Fountain of Youth, Water of Life.

▸ Ethiopia: A land in east Africa, south of the Sudan. Local lore deems it to have been the kingdom of the Queen of Sheba who visited king Solomon in Jerusalem, and considers Ethiopian kings as descended of Solomon.

▸ Euphrates River: A major river that, together with the Tigris River, irrigates and delineates Mesopotamia ('The Land Between The Rivers'). Starting in the north in the mountains in Anatolia, and enhanced there by several tributaries, it flows all the way to the Persian Gulf in the south. Many major cities and cultural centers from Sumer on dotted the river's course; being navigable once it left the highlands, it was also an essential transportation and trade route. Called *Puratu* in Akkadian, it is the biblical river *Prath* that was one of the four 'Rivers of Paradise'. According to the Bible, the Euphrates River delineated the eastern boundary of the lands covenanted by God to Abraham and his descendants.

▸ Eve: The name of Adam's female counterpart and wife. The Bible calls her (H) *Hava* (= 'She of Life'), and had her fashioned out of Adam's rib (thus, 'She of the Rib')—two aspects that may stem from the Sumerian word **Ti** that means both 'Life' and 'Rib'. For ZS on the Sumerian/genetic aspects of the biblical tale of Eve and the Serpent in the Garden of Eden, *see* Copper, Ea/Enki.

▸ Evil Wind: The term used in the Sumerian lamentation texts to describe the deathly wind that blew toward Sumer and caused terrible and gruesome death to people and animals alike, poisoning the air and the waters—but leaving the buildings intact. The Lamentation Texts clearly state that the "baleful storm," that brought to an end the great Sumerian civilization, was caused by "an evil blast"—"an evil blast was its forerunner; in a flash of lightning it was created." ZS has suggested that the Evil Wind was a nuclear cloud blown eastward from the Sinai peninsula and the nearby Dead Sea plain when nuclear weapons were used there by the warring Anunnaki. *See* Lamentation Texts, Nuclear Weapons.

▸ Exodus: The miracle-filled Israelite departure from bondage in Egypt and wanderings in the Sinai wilderness, as told in the Bible's second book. Titled *Shemoth* ('Names') in Hebrew, after its opening verse ("Now these are the names of the children of Israel"), it is called 'Exodus' in English. Because most scholars identify the oppressive Pharaoh of the events as Ramses II, the Exodus is usually dated to the mid 13th century B.C. The Bible itself, however, states that the Exodus took place 480 years before Solomon began to build the Temple in Jerusalem (I Kings 6); this and other synchronizations have led ZS to conclude that the Exodus began in 1433 B.C. Such dating places the Exodus in the context of geopolitical and religious events of the time: The palace intrigues involving the 18th dynasty in Egypt, the Egyptian military thrusts against Mitanni and Hatti, and the contests for control of the Space-related sites of the Anunnaki. *See* Battle of Kadesh, Harran, Hatshepsut, Hittites, Mission Control Center, Mitanni, Moses, Mount Sinai, Naharin, Promised Land, Sinai Peninsula, Spaceport, Thothmes.

▸ Ezekiel: A major biblical Prophet, he was one of the Judean priests and noblemen exiled from Jerusalem after the city's first capture by the Babylonian king Nebuchadnezzar in 598 B.C.; they dwelt near the Khabur River, in the vicinity of Harran—the Patriarchs' ancestral district. The Book of Ezekiel begins with a "vision of *Elohim*"—his sighting of a divine 'sky chamber' whose occupant instructed him to convey to the people the Words of God. In his extensive prophecies, Ezekiel described a virtual tour of a rebuilt future Temple and a resurrection of the dead from their dried out bones, and prophesied about the End of Days and a Final War that will precede messianic times. Noteworthy is the reference in chapter 28 to the "Place of the Elohim" with its "fiery stones" in Lebanon—the place, per ZS, now called Baalbek. In *The End of Days*, ZS has placed Ezekiel's visions, their locale and their timing in the context of historic events at the end of Babylon and Assyria, the departure of the Anunnaki in the 6th century B.C., and of prophecies regarding their return. *See* Adda-Guppi, Aerial Chariots, Baalbek, Harran, Jerusalem, Nabunaid, Sin, Temples.

▶ Falcon god: An epithet and the hieroglyph for the Egyptian god Horus, who was usually depicted with a falcon's head.

▶ Fastness of Zaphon: A Canaanite descriptive name for Ba'al's redoubt in the Lebanon mountains (the site now known as Ba'albek). *See* Crest of Zaphon.

▶ Fate (**Nam.tar**): *See* Destiny.

▶ Fifty: A number that signified the hierarchical rank of Enlil (next to Anu's sixty). In the struggle for succession on Earth, the Rank of Fifty was extended by Enlil to his Legal Heir Ninurta by naming a new temple for Ninurta **E.Ninnu**, "House/temple of Fifty." When Marduk finally assumed supremacy on Earth, it was formalized by granting him "The Fifty Names" at an Assembly of the 'Fifty Great Gods'. Those fifty names were added to the original six-tablet Sumerian 'Epic of Creation' as a seventh tablet in its Babylonian version. The last, fiftieth name in the list, was **Nibiru**—making Marduk both the supreme god on Earth and the supreme planet in the heavens. In *The End of Days*, ZS explains the motives for and significance of the introduction of the count of 'Jubilees' (50-year periods) during the Exodus. *See* Book of Jubilees, Divine Ranks, Marduk.

▶ Fifty-two: The magical or secret number of Thoth. *See* Calendars, Quetzalcoatl, Thoth.

▶ Fish-men: Priests wearing garb whose upper part resembled a fish—the uniform of certain Enkiite priests. *See also* Eaglemen.

▶ Flood ('Great Flood', 'Flood of Noah'): *See* Deluge.

▶ Forty: The hierarchical rank of Enki; the duration of the Israelite wandering (forty years) in the Sinai during the Exodus.

▶ Food of Life: Sumerian texts refer to 'Food of Life' and 'Water of Life' as nourishments of the Anunnaki, available on their home planet and brought over from Nibiru to sustain their longevity while on Earth. When the Earthling Adapa was taken to visit Nibiru, Enki made sure he would not get the 'Food of Life' and the 'Water of Life', lest he attain the gods' longevity. *See* Elixirs, Plant of Life.

▶ Foundation Stone (H *Even Shatit*): The name of the unusual stone outcropping on the Temple Mount in Jerusalem on which Solomon's Temple's Holy of Holies was located to house the Ark of the Covenant; and on which—according to Jewish tradition—Isaac was about to be offered as a sacrifice to God by Abraham. Moslems revere the Rock because, according to their tradition, Mohammed was lofted there for a nighttime visit to Heaven. (ZS describes his adventurous foray to the mysterious cave below the Rock in *The Earth Chronicles Expeditions.*) *See* Dome of the Rock.

▶ Fountain of Youth: Legendary waters the drinker of which shall be rejuvenated and become young again. The exploration of Florida by Ponce de Leon, ZS wrote in *The Stairway to Heaven,* was one example of Man's unending search for such a miraculous antidote to aging and death. *See* Eternal Youth, Waters of Life.

▶ Four Corners of the Earth: A Biblical term, sometimes rendered in the Bible as the "Four Wings" of the Earth, conveying the notion of everywhere on Earth, the whole Earth. It may have stemmed from the way Babylonian maps indicated the four orientations.

▶ Four Regions: Sumerian texts frequently refer to 'The Four **Ub** (= Regions)'; ZS has traced their formation to a peace treaty that brought to an end the 'Pyramid Wars'. The First Region, that of the Tigris-Euphrates Rivers, gave rise (circa 3800 B.C.) to the Sumerian civilization and its offshoots, under the aegis of the Enlilites. The Second Region was that of the Nile River civilizations in Africa, under the Enki'ites (begun circa 3100 B.C.). The Third Region, that of the Indus River Valley civilization (circa 2900 B.C.) was set aside for the betrothed Inanna (Enlil's granddaughter) and Dumuzi (Enki's son). The Fourth Region was "sacred"—the gods' alone, in the Sinai peninsula: A prohibited zone where the Spaceport of the Anunnaki was located.

- *Gabriel*: An archangel who, according to the Book of Enoch, took Enoch to the Divine Presence in the Seventh Heaven. Moslems believe that the prophet Mohammed was taken by Gabriel from Mecca to Jerusalem, and from there heavenwards to the presence of God.

- Gaea: In Greek mythology, a primeval goddess whose name meant 'Earth', who emanated from Chaos and gave birth to Uranus (= 'Starry Heaven').

- **Gaga**: The name, in the Epic of Creation, of the Counselor of the celestial Anshar, sent out on a mission toward other celestial bodies. Per ZS, a satellite/moon of the planet we call Saturn, that was shunted off course (to a different orbit) by the approaching invading planet Nibiru/Marduk to become the planet we call Pluto.

- Garden of Eden: *See* Eden.

- Gate of the Sun: The name given to one of the three principal monuments in Tiahuanacu, Bolivia. It is a colossal stand-alone gateway whose large doorway, decorated arch, jambs, lintels, niches and false windows are all cut and shaped from a single huge stone block weighing over one hundred tons. *See* Tiahuanacu.

- Gates of Heaven: According to Genesis 28, Jacob—on his way from Canaan to Harran—had a dream-vision in which he saw angels ascending and descending a Ladder to Heaven; and he realized that the place was *Sha'ar Hashama'yim* (= 'Gate of Heaven'). According to the Egyptian

'Book of the Dead' and Pyramid Texts, the deceased Pharaoh's journey to the Afterlife takes him to the 'Planet of Millions of Years', where the 'Gates of Heaven' would be opened for him to join the Eternals.

▸ Gateway of the gods: The meaning of *Bab-Ili*, the name 'Babylon' in Akkadian.

▸ Gaza (*Azzah*): A city on the Mediterranean coast; according to Genesis 10, the southernmost Canaanite city. It was occupied by Philistine 'People of the Sea' in the 12th century B.C. and formed one of their five strongholds west of Judea. It is listed in the annals of the Assyrian king Sennacherib.

▸ GEB (= 'He who heaps up'): An early Egyptian deity. Representing the deified Earth, he fathered together with NUT (= 'Sky') the male gods Osiris and Seth and their sisters Isis and Nephtys—four major great gods of the Egyptian pantheon.

▸ *Gebal*: The (H) biblical name for the Phoenician city known as Byblos.

▸ Gemini: The zodiacal constellation of 'The Twins' whose Sumerian name was **Mash.tab.ba** (= 'Twins')—so named, per ZS, in honor of the twin grandchildren of Enlil, Utu/Shamash and Inanna/Ishtar.

▸ Genesis: The name, in English, of the Bible's first book, in Hebrew *Bereshit* after its opening words—*Bereshit bara Elohim et Hashama'yim v'et Ha'aretz* (translated "In the beginning God created the heaven and the earth"). Starting with the creation of the heavens and the Earth, it describes Evolution, explains the role of the Elohim in Man's coming into being, records Mankind's pre-diluvial history, and traces post-diluvial events to the chosen line of Abraham. Puzzled why the first word in the Bible's first verse in the Bible's first book starts with the second letter of the alphabet (*Beth* = 'B') and not with the first one (*Aleph* = 'A'), ZS has shown how the meaning will change if the start had indeed been an 'A': *Ab-reshit bara Elohim, et Hashama'yim, v'et Ha'aretz* = "The Father-of-Beginning created the Elohim, the Heavens, and the Earth." ZS, in *Genesis Revisited*, has also shown that the opening biblical narrative matches the section of *Enuma elish* that describes the celestial collision between Nibiru/Marduk and Tiamat.

▸ Genetic Engineering: The Sumerian Creation Texts describe in great detail the process by which Enki and Ninharsag fashioned Man. ZS shows that the texts describe a process of genetic engineering—upgrading the hominid that (in Enki's words) "already exists" by adding genes of the Anunnaki to bring about a more advanced *Homo sapiens*; then by a second feat of genetic engineering, the 'Serpent' (i.e., Enki) gave the infertile hybrid the ability to procreate.

▸ Giants: The lore of many peoples includes tales of giants, especially so when it comes to explaining who was able to haul and emplace the colossal stone blocks at such sites as Baalbek in Lebanon, the promontory above Cuzco in Peru, or the edifices in Tiahuanacu in Bolivia. In Mexico, the Aztec stone calendar depicts four Ages, the first of which was that of the "White Haired Giants;" a giant statue of the Goddess of Water was discovered in Mexico City, and at Tula there stand the statues of the giant 'Atlantes'. In Mexico's central zone bordering the Gulf of Mexico, giant stone heads of African-looking men were found at Olmec sites. In South America, varied legends tell of 'giants' who arrived by sea and settled on the Pacific coast; there, Mochica paintings depict giants, with black or blackened faces, being served by smaller enslaved natives; and the great Temple of Pachacamac south of Lima had a golden statue of a giant. In the ancient Near East, Hittite kings were depicted being embraced by a god double the kings' size; and the Bible speaks of the giantlike Og, king of Bashan, and of Goliath the Philistine whose height of "six cubits and a span" equaled more than 9 feet. ZS tells how he was drawn to the subject of his writings when, as a schoolboy, he questioned the reading in Genesis 6 of the word *Nefilim* as 'giants' because they were *Anakim*—a term commonly taken to mean 'giants' but which ZS has shown to be the rendering in Hebrew of the Sumerian **Anunnaki**. Were then Anunnaki 'gods' tall and giant-like? Depictions on cylinder seals that show a great god approached by a king suggest that the god was indeed bigger and more than one third taller than the king. *See* Gilgal Repha'im, Repha'im.

▸ **Gibil** (From **Gish.bil**, 'He Who Has/Uses Fire'): A son of Enki who was taught by his father the arts of mining and metallurgy. A prototype of Ephaestus, the Greek god of fire and metallurgy (= the Roman god Vulcan). In the texts dealing with the conflict that led to the use of nuclear weapons, Gibil is described as the god in whose African domain the seven "Awesome Weapons" had been hidden. *See* Nuclear Weapons.

▸ *Gilgal* (H = 'Circle of Heaped Stones'): The name given to the place, "east of Jericho," where Joshua put up twelve stones to commemorate the miraculous crossing of the Jordan River by the Israelites as they entered the promised Land at the end of the Exodus. It was also the place where, centuries later, the Prophet Elijah was told by God to cross back the Jordan, to be taken heavenwards in a fiery Whirlwind.

▸ *Gilgal Repha'im*: A Stonehenge-like structure on the Golan Heights, east of the Sea of Galilee. It consists of four concentric circles of crude stone walls, rising eight feet, with a complex entryway built of more massive stone boulders and oriented to the winter solstice, suggesting a 3rd millennium B.C. date. An artificial mound in the circles' center contains a paved vaulted chamber, eleven feet long, that may have served as a burial place. Some objects discovered in the burial chamber are dated to mid-2nd millennium B.C., but the tale in Genesis 31 about a circular stone monument erected by Jacob could support an earlier date. Because the Bible (books of Numbers and Joshua) reported that a giantlike king named Og had once reigned in that area, and he was (like Goliath) a descendant of a godlike race called *Repha'im*, Israeli archaeologists gave the site its current name *Gilgal Repha'im* (= 'The Stone Circles of the Repha'im'). *See* Giants, Gilgal, Repha'im.

▸ Gilgamesh (From **Gish.bil.ga.mesh** = 'Firebrand Offspring'): A Sumerian king of Uruk (biblical *Erech*) circa 2900 B.C. Known primarily from the 'Epic of Gilgamesh', he is also listed in the chronicles called the 'Sumerian King Lists' and is the subject of other texts; thus there is no doubt about his being a historical figure. The son of the city's High Priest and the goddess Ninsun, he was not just a demi-god but "two-thirds divine." This, he believed, entitled him to avoid man's mortality, and the Epic relates his search for immortality. That the tale of Gilgamesh and its moral ("Man was given knowledge, the life of a god he was not given") was known throughout the ancient world is evident not only from the various renderings that have been discovered, but also from widespread depictions (including in South America!) of an episode in the tale—the wrestling of Gilgamesh with two lions. ZS has pinpointed the two destinations of Gilgamesh's quest—the "Landing Place" of Baalbek in the "Cedar Forest" and the Spaceport in the Sinai. *See* Epic of Gilgamesh *and related entries.*

▸ **Girsu**: The sacred precinct of Lagash, where Gudea built a new temple; hence the other name, **Nin.girsu** (= 'Lord of Girsu') for the god Ninurta. Included in the Girsu was a specially constructed enclosure for the god's aircraft. *See* Eninnu, Lagash, Ninurta.

▸ Giza: The site, near Cairo in Egypt, where three major pyramids and the Sphinx are located. Apart from all other features unique to these three pyramids, they are the only ones in Egypt without the customary inscriptions and colorful depictions. *See* Great Pyramid, Khufu, Pyramids, Radedef.

▸ God Lists: Clay tablet texts that listed gods by their family groups, providing their genealogies and giving their varied epithet-names, often in both Sumerian and their Akkadian equivalents.

▸ God, gods: The tales and records of all ancient peoples speak of anthropomorphic super-beings who were the object of veneration and worship by Mankind. The terms by which they were called in the various languages are commonly rendered in modern languages by the word 'gods' (with a small 'g'!); but the ancient terms were actually descriptive epithets: **Din.gir** in Sumerian meant 'The righteous ones of the rocketships'; NETERU in Egyptian meant 'Guardians'; *Ilu* in Akkadian (from which the biblical Hebrew singular *El* and plural *Elohim*) meant 'Lofty Ones'; the Greek *Theos* (from which the Roman *Deus*) meant 'Divine'. Tales of the gods, usually treated by scholars as myths, universally attributed their origin to the heavens, described several generations leading to ones born on Earth, detailed struggles, fighting and wars among them, and ascribed to them the creation of Mankind, mostly through the fashioning of a First Couple; the biblical tale of Adam and Eve is no exception. ZS has treated such 'myths' as records and recollections of actual events, and has suggested that the similarities are due to the fact that worldwide these gods were the same original group of the Sumerian **Anunnaki** (= 'Those who from heaven to Earth came'): The Hittite *Teshub* was the Akkadian *Adad*, and so was (per ZS) the Andean *Viracocha*; the Mesoamerican *Quetzalcoatl* was (per ZS) the Egyptian *Thoth* (and the Sumerian **Ningishzidda**); the Greek *Cronus* paralleled the Sumerian **Anu**, the Olympian *Zeus* and *Poseidon* reflected the Mesopotamian *Ea* and *Enlil*, as did the Canaanite *Ba'al* and *Yam*, and so were the legendary Hindu gods *Vishnu*, *Indra* and *Vritra*. The aerial battles of Zeus versus Typhon or Horus versus Seth paralleled those of Ninurta versus Zu, and so on and on. Capable of roaming the skies and possessing extraordinary weapons, they were all so humanlike—except for one crucial difference from Mankind: their presumed immortality. But in fact all the tales, including Sumerian, Akkadian, Canaanite, Egyptian, Aztec etc., recorded instances of the death of gods (such as Zu and Dumuzi in Sumerian lore, Osiris in Egyptian, Ba'al in Canaanite, the Aztec goddess Coyolxauhqui). The 'immortality' (per ZS) was simply extreme longevity, stemming from the fact that for the Anunnaki (and their life cycle) one year on Nibiru—meaning one orbit around the Sun—equaled some 3,600 Earth-years. The existence of those gods with a small 'g' not only does not conflict with the belief in a sole universal God with a capital 'G', but confirms the view (held by the Anunnaki themselves) of a cosmic 'Creator of All'—the biblical *Yahweh*, whom the Bible calls "*El Elohim*"—'God of the gods'. and who told the *Elohim* gods per Psalm 82: "You are Elohim, all of you sons of the Most High; but you shall die as men do." *See* An (Anu), Anunnaki, Enki, Enlil, Marduk, Yahweh.

▸ Gog and Magog: In the prophecies of Ezekiel (chapters 38 and 39), a major combatant (together with, or of the land of, *Magog*) in a World War that shall culminate a period of troubles and tribulations that shall precede and usher a messianic time. The list of nations that will get involved in that Final War begins—"chillingly," per ZS—with Persia (today's Iran). Those apocalyptic events, according to the Prophets, shall come at and signify the End of Days. *See* Armageddon, Apocalypse, End of Days, Ezekiel, Revelation.

▸ Gold (**Gush.kin, Ku.gi** = 'bright out of the earth'; also **Zu.ab** = 'bright from the primeval deep', from which probably (H) *Zahab* = gold): A precious shiny bright metal found on Earth in natural form, both as veins in rocks deep inside the earth, as pure nuggets lying about in river-beds, or as grains mixed in seawater. It is the most malleable and ductile of all known metals; it can be stretched, made into thinnest wires, sheets, foil, grains or dust (and nowadays even reduced to its atoms); it can be melted, cast, shaped, hammered and alloyed; it is non-corrosive, and a perfect electrical conductor. The first metal known to Mankind, it was considered from the earliest times the property of the gods; it was used by them when communicating with mankind (a golden wand given by Viracocha in Peru, golden Cherubim upon the Ark of the Covenant to hear Yahweh). In both the Old World and the New World, Holy of Holies and divine abodes were entirely covered with gold to form golden enclosures, outfitted with golden emblems, golden ritual objects, and golden utensils. According to Sumerian texts the Anunnaki mined gold in southeast Africa (**Arali** = 'Place of the shiny lodes'), from the mines of the **Ab.zu** (= 'Primeval Deep'). The texts attributed the gods' decision to fashion Man to a need for Primitive Workers in order to take over the Anunnaki's toil in the mines after a mutiny of the Anunnaki. Utilizing extant texts to reconstruct a cohesive narrative, ZS saw the Anunnaki's need of gold with which to protect the dwindling atmosphere of Nibiru as their reason for coming to Earth. At first Ea arrived with fifty Anunnaki hoping to obtain gold from the waters of the Persian Gulf; when that failed, a full fledged Earth Mission under Enlil's command was put into operation, requiring mining of gold in southeast Africa. When the Anunnaki there mutinied, Man was fashioned. When all that was wiped out by the Deluge, a new source of ready-to-collect gold nuggets was exposed by the same Deluge in South America, leading to the settlements and operations centered in Tiahuanacu. This explains the incredibly vast quantities of gold and gold artifacts obtained by the Spanish Conquistadores in the Andean lands of South America, whose natives were completely ignorant of mining. *See* Abzu, Coricancha, El Dorado, Golden Enclosure, Golden Wand.

▸ Golden Enclosure: While the term usually refers to the 'Coricancha' (= 'Golden Enclosure' in the Quechua language), the Inca temple in Cuzco whose walls were plated with gold, other golden enclosures are known from antiquity. There was a golden enclosure in the main shrine of the Chimu people in northern Peru. In Puma Punku in Bolivia, four chambers, each hewn out of a colossal rock, were completely covered inside with plates of gold. ZS has suggested that it was done there when Anu and Antu visited the place circa 4000 B.C. because Mesopotamian texts describing that divine couple's stay in Uruk state that their quarters were in an edifice whose walls, ceiling and cornices were covered with gold— a true golden enclosure. The Holy of Holies in Solomon's Temple in Jerusalem was similarly entirely plated within with gold.

▸ Golden Wand: Andean legends assert that Mankind's spread and settlement there began when the creator god Viracocha gave a chosen man or couple a golden wand with which to find a place to settle. Mummies found in 'cities of the dead' along the Peruvian Pacific coast were wrapped in ornamented textiles that depicted the god holding in one hand a lightning rod and in the other a golden wand. *See* Ayar Brothers, Gold.

▸ Goliath (H *Golyat*): A fearsome giantlike Philistine warrior, wearing awesome armor and heavily armed, who was slain by the young Judean shepherd David with a slingshot. The Bible (I Samuel 17) gives his height as "six cubits and a span," which equals nine and a half feet. According to II Samuel 21, which describes later fighting with kinfolk of Goliath, suggests that they were descended of the *Rephaim* demigods. *See* Giants, Rephaim.

▸ Gomorrah (H *Amorrah*): One of the five cities in the plain south of the Dead Sea whose kings banded together to withstand an attack of an alliance of four 'kings of the east' (Genesis 14). It is named in the Bible (Genesis 19) together with Sodom as having been upheavaled from the skies on divine orders at the time of Abraham. ZS has linked the biblical tale of the 'War of the Kings' to Akkadian records known as the Khedorlaomer Texts, and the upheavaling of Sodom and Gomorrah to the use of nuclear weapons in 2024 B.C. as described in the Sumerian Erra Epos and Lamentation Texts. *See* Bela, Dead Sea, Sodom.

▸ Great Flood: *See* Deluge.

▸ Great Pyramid of Giza: Forming a distinct group with two companions and the Great Sphinx, the Great Pyramid is the world's largest single stone building of all time. Perfectly shaped with four sides each measuring 756 feet at its base, it rises to a height of 480 feet; it is built of an estimated 2,300,000 to 2,500,000 grayish limestone blocks averaging 2.5 tons (apart from inner features using rarer limestone or more massive granite). Its sides were originally covered by a casing of white limestone blocks of about 15 tons each, angled to have the pyramid rise at the steep angle of 52°. The Pyramid's total mass is calculated to have been 93 million cubic feet, weighing some 7,000,000 tons. Inside, the pyramid contains an amazing array of perfectly aligned chambers, passages, shafts, niches, and a grand gallery, whose purposes or functions remain a mystery. All that rests on a precisely formed and positioned stone platform, on the 30th parallel north. And all that immense architectural and technological marvel is attributed to a single Pharaoh—Cheops (KHUFU)—who reigned more than 4,500 years ago. Though all attempts in modern times to show how such construction by Cheops was possible have failed, Egyptologists continue to maintain so—the sole evidence being the discovery of that Pharaoh's hieroglyphic name inscribed in a sealed chamber of the Pyramid. ZS has maintained that the Giza pyramids were built by the Anunnaki as part of the Landing Corridor that served the post-Diluvial Spaceport in the Sinai (on the 30th parallel!), providing in his books (primarily *The Stairway to Heaven* and *Journeys to the Mythical Past*) textual and pictorial evidence that the Giza pyramids and Sphinx had existed for millennia before

Cheops—evidence that links and explains varied inner features to the Anunnaki's Pyramid Wars and Marduk's imprisonment in this pyramid. As to the inscribed 'Khufu' name, ZS analyzed its discovery in 1837 and concluded that it was a deliberate archaeological forgery. Except for the Vyse Markings, this pyramid (as the other two and the Sphinx at Giza) are totally devoid of any inscription or depiction, quite unlike all other Egyptian pyramids. *See* Ascending Passage, Davison's Chamber, Giza, Inventory Stela, Landing Corridor, Marduk, Ninurta, Pyramids, Pyramid Texts, Queen's Chamber.

▸ Great Sea: The Sumerian/Akkadian term denoting the Mediterranean Sea. *See also* Upper Sea.

▸ Great Year: An astronomical term used to denote the number of years required to complete the cycle of the twelve zodiacal constellations. The retardation in the shift from one Zodiacal House to another, known as Precession of the Equinoxes, amounts to one degree in 72 years, so to retard the full 360° takes a total of 25,920 years (72 × 360) = one 'Great Year'.

▸ Greece, Greek Civilization: Greece as a country—Hellas in Greek—extends in southern Europe into the Mediterranean Sea, encompassing the large island of Crete, the renowned island of Rhodes, and many other islands in the eastern Mediterranean; Greek settlements (including the famed Troy) extended into Asia Minor. As a result, Greece formed a cultural bridge between Europe and the Near Eastern civilizations, borrowing their scientific knowledge, alphabet, religions, and pantheon. The Greeks described their gods as anthropomorphic, akin to men and women physically and in character, but immortal; led by a pantheon of twelve Olympians headed by Zeus, who attained his supremacy after many conflicts and wars. According to Greek legends, Zeus arrived in Greece via the island of Crete, having swum there after abducting Europa, the daughter of a Phoenician king. Treated by scholars as myths, the tales echo Canaanite tales of *Krt*, emulate Hittite tales of the gods, and (as shown by ZS) can be traced to Sumerian tales of the Anunnaki and their pantheon of twelve.

▸ **Gud.anna:** *See* Bull of Heaven, Taurus.

▸ **Gudea:** A Sumerian king of Lagash circa 2200 B.C., who left behind a large number of statues of himself (many now on display in the Louvre in Paris), as well as long inscriptions detailing how, in a kind of a 'Twilight Zone' dream, several gods gave him detailed instructions (including a tablet with architectural plans), celestial orientations, and an actual brick model, for the building of a new temple for the god Ninurta; how he went about building it; and how it was inaugurated when the god and his spouse moved in. *See* Lagash, Ninurta.

▸ **Gula:** Ninurta's spouse. *See* Bau, Isin.

▸ Gutium: An ancient kingdom in the mountains northeast of Mesopotamia. Though worshippers of Enlil, its people were feared as uncouth marauders. Derogatorily called *Umman-Manda* (possibly 'Hordes of far/strong brothers') in a text known as 'The Legend of Naram-Sin', they are recorded to have invaded Sumer & Akkad in the 22nd century B.C. Gutian troops again occupied northern Sumer after its devastation by the nuclear Evil Wind in 2024 B.C.

- Haab: A solar-year calendar, one of Mesoamerica's three calendars. It consisted of 18 'months' of 20 days each, plus an additional 5 special days to complete a total of 365 days. *See* Calendars.

- *Habakuk*: A biblical Prophet (circa 600 B.C.) whose prophecies regarding the coming "Day of the Lord" are distinguished from previous Prophets not only by announcing that the "Appointed Time" is at hand, but also by their detailed description of the Celestial Lord's course ("The Lord from the south shall come"), radiance ("His rays shine forth . . . his splendor shall fill the Earth"), and the celestial disturbances accompanying the Lord's appearance ("The stars of heaven and their constellations shall not give light, the Sun shall be darkened at its rising, the Moon shall not shine its light"). Per ZS, these are all references to the expected Return of Nibiru. *See* Day of the Lord.

- Habiru: In the 18th and 17th centuries B.C., Assyrian and Babylonian annals made references to bands of marauders, calling them *Hapiru*. In the 15th century B.C. a message from an Egyptian commander in Canaan to his superiors in Egypt complained of attacks by APIRU. Some scholars have suggested that those were references to *Hebrew* tribes who entered Egypt. However, apart from the similar sound of the names, there appears to be no basis for these theories. *See also* Hyksos.

- Hades: In classical Greek tales, the third generation of gods, born of Cronos and Rhea, included three daughters and the three sons Hades,

Poseidon, and Zeus. After defeating the Titans, the three drew lots; Zeus won the heavens and the Upper World, Poseidon the oceans, and Hades the Lower World. In time the domain of Hades became synonymous with a 'Netherworld' realm of the dead. ZS has pointed out that a similar division (between Anu, Enlil and Enki), resulting from the drawing of lots, is described in the Mesopotamian *Atra-Hasis* Epic.

▸ Hagar: The handmaiden of Sarah who bore Abraham's son Ishmael. *See* Ishmael.

▸ *Haggai*: A biblical Prophet during the reign of the Persian king Darius who urged the rebuilding of the temple in Jerusalem ahead of the coming upheavals, in the heavens and on Earth, on the 'Day of the Lord'.

▸ Halley's Comet: A short-term comet that orbits the Sun and is seen from Earth every 76/77 years. It is named after the British Astronomer Edward Halley who at the end of the 17th century A.D. determined the comet's orbital period and correctly predicted its next visibility. Astronomers and historians have since ascertained that the comet was known (and observed) in antiquity, when it was deemed a harbinger of events in heaven and on Earth. It was extensively studied during its most recent near-Earth passage, in 1986. ZS has compared Halley's comet and its inclined orbit to a "mini Nibiru" and attached significance to the fact that its elliptical orbit crosses the Ecliptic near Uranus. *See* Comets, Hasmoneans, Nibiru, Uranus.

▸ *Ham*: The second of the three sons of Noah. The connotation of the name in Hebrew ('Hot', 'Brown') matched both the biblical designation of Egypt and Nubia in Africa as the Lands of Ham, as well as Egypt's ancient hieroglyphic name, HM-Ta. *See* Egypt.

▸ Hammered Bracelet: *See* Asteroid Belt.

▸ Hammurabi: A Babylonian king (1792–1750 B.C.) known for his Code of Laws that was inscribed on a stone column (now on view in the Louvre Museum, Paris). A devout follower of the god Marduk, Hammurabi is credited with making Babylon (the city) a great sprawling capital, with a sky-scraping ziggurat-temple for Marduk at the center of a large sacred precinct. Of his military campaigns to make Babylonia a great empire, archaeological evidence and writings from the time highlight his duplicitous attack on Mari, an important Sumerian city-state on the Euphrates River. *See* Babylon, Esagil, Marduk, Mari.

▸ Harappa: A major center of the 2nd millennium B.C. Indus Valley Civilization where brick-walled remains of extensive granaries and images of a bejeweled goddess have been found. ZS has raised the possibility that she might have been Inanna/Ishtar, who was assigned the distant and differently-speaking kingdom of **Aratta** (which archaeologists have not yet identified, but could be Harappa). *See* Indus Valley Civilization.

▸ *Harran* (= 'The Caravanry'): An ancient city in the Upper Euphrates region, astride the Balikh River (now in eastern Turkey), which is still inhabited (though as a ramshackle remnant of its erstwhile greatness). Situated at the intersection of trade routes, it became a major home-away-from-home for the famed 'Merchants of Ur' who bought there sheepskins and wool and sold there woven fabrics and garments. In time, the temple in Harran to Ur's god Nannar/Sin became second in importance to the one in Ur. The Bible relates that Abraham's father Terah moved from Ur to Harran with his family; and after Abraham moved on to Canaan, the wives of his son Isaac and grandson Jacob were chosen from the Terahites who stayed on in Harran. Harran also played major roles in the affairs of the gods and the histories of Babylonia and Assyria: Marduk stayed there in a crucial period of his struggle for supremacy. (For the significance of these interwoven events, and the crucial year 2048 B.C., see *The End of Days* by ZS.) As events neared the End, the Assyrian royal family made its last stand in Harran before Assyria's demise; and the last king of Babylon was granted there the throne due to his mother who was High Priestess in Harran. At the closing chapter of the Anunnaki tale, Nannar/Sin left Earth from Harran (but relented and returned); Harran was thus a witness and a stage for 4,000 years of history. (For a description of a visit to Harran, see *The Earth Chronicles Expeditions*.)

‣ Hasmoneans (H *Hashmona'yim,* also known as the *Maccabees*): A devout Jewish family in Judea that led, in the 2nd century B.C., an uprising against the Seleucid (Greek-Syrian) rulers of the country who tried to forcefully Hellenize the Jews and set up worship of Zeus in the Jerusalem Temple. The local skirmishes grew to a countrywide revolt, and in a series of fierce battles the Hashmoneans succeeded to free the land, cleanse the Temple of the idols, and restart the Holy Flame in 160 B.C.; the miracle of a bit of sacred oil lasting eight days has since been celebrated by Jews as the holiday of Hanukkah. The Hashmoneans re-established Judea as an independent Jewish state, and ruled it as its kings until the Romans occupied the land a century later. ZS has linked the Hasmonean uprising and the imperative of restarting the Temple's Holy Flame by 160 B.C. to the Calendar of Nippur and to the End of Days prophecies in the Book of Daniel. *See* Daniel, Jerusalem Temple, Maccabees, Nippur Calendar, Seleucid Dynasty.

‣ HATHOR (Hat-Hor, 'Abode of Horus'): A great early Egyptian goddess whose domain was the Sinai peninsula—especially its southern mountainous part, where turquoise mines were located (and thus her epithet, 'Lady of the Mines'). She was depicted in Egyptian art with cow's horns flanking a planet as her headdress, and as she grew older she was nicknamed 'The Cow'. ZS has suggested that she was the goddess whom the Sumerians called **Ninmah**, who as a peacemaker between the warring Anunnaki clans was assigned the neutral Fourth Region—the Sinai peninsula. There, her son **Ninurta** built her a mountain abode, and she was granted the epithet **Ninharsag** (= 'Lady of the Mountain Peak'). As she aged, the Sumerians depicted her with a cowlike head.

‣ HATSHEPSUT (= 'Noblest Lady'): A female Pharaoh of the 18th dynasty, the daughter and sole legitimate heir of Thothmose I. Forced to marry her half-brother Thothmes II but childless, she reigned after his death, from 1479 to 1458 B.C., part of the time as Queen of Egypt and part of the time as co-regent with her rival, a royal son by a harem girl, who in time became Thothmose III. Her mortuary temple on the west side of the Nile opposite Luxor is one of the most impressive temples of ancient

Egypt. ZS believes that it was she who was the Bible's "Pharaoh's daughter" who—childless herself—adopted a castoff Hebrew baby—Moses (*Moshe* in Hebrew). The 18th dynasty assumed theophoric names that included the suffix 'MOSE' (hieroglyphic 'MSS') which implied divine descent, such as AhMOSE and ThothMOSE. Giving the adopted child a name that included MOSE was thus in line with that dynasty's custom. The standard dating of the Exodus to the 13th century B.C. places the story of Moses in the context of Ramses II and Egypt's 19th dynasty; but ZS has shown that the biblical dating of Solomon's Temple in relation to the Exodus (I Kings 6:1 and I Chronicles 5:36) places Moses in the 15th century B.C., exactly at the time of Hatshepsut.

▶ *Hatti*: The Akkadian name for the Hittite kingdom. *See* Hittites.

▶ Hattusshas: The capital of the ancient Hittite kingdom. Located near present-day Boghazkoy in central Turkey, the site has been extensively excavated. *See* Hittites.

▶ Hebat: A Hurrian-Hittite goddess, wife of the god Teshub.

▶ Hebrew: The term *Ibri* (a 'Hebrew man') is first used in the Bible by Abraham to introduce himself to the reigning Pharaoh in Egypt; it stems from the verb-root that means 'To Cross', and has been generally interpreted to mean that Abraham said that he had come from 'across the river' (Euphrates), i.e. that he came from Mesopotamia. ZS has taken this further by linking the term specifically to Nippur (Sumer's religious center) which in Sumerian was called **Ni.Ibru**, suggesting that Abraham identified himself as a Nippurite, a 'Man from Nippur'. *See* Abram/Abraham.

▶ Hebrew Language: A Semitic language, stemming from Akkadian, spoken by the biblical 'Children of Israel' (now the Jewish people) and in which the Hebrew Bible ('Old Testament') was written. It uses the 22 letter alphabet that originated in the Sinai during the Exodus. *See* Alphabet, DNA, Hebrew.

▶ Hebron (H *Hevron*): Located in Judea south of Jerusalem, it was an important city already in the time of Abraham (end of 3rd millennium B.C.), when it was called *Kiryat Arba* (= "The Stronghold of Four"). Abraham purchased the Cave of Machpelah in Hebron to serve as the burial place for his wife Sarah, then for himself; in time the Patriarchs Isaac and Jacob and their wives were also buried there. When David became king, Hebron served as his capital until the royal seat was established in Jerusalem circa 1000 B.C.

▸ Heel Stone: The name given to the stone pillar posted beyond the stone circles of Stonehenge; it directed the monument's sightline to sunrise on summer Solstice Day.

▸ Heliopolis (= 'City of Helios', the sun god): (a) The Greek name for the Egyptian city whose original ancient name was AN (*On* in the Bible): *See* An, Annu. (b) The Greek name for Baalbek in Lebanon.

▸ Hephaestus: The Greek name for the Divine Craftsman and the god of metallurgy (called Vulcan by the Romans). He built the abode of Zeus and Hera (who is presumed to have been his mother), and crafted many magical objects for gods and heroes. Scholars have found parallels between the Greek tales about him and *Kothar-Hasis*, the Divine Craftsman of Canaanite lore; both were associated with the Island of Crete.

▸ Hera: Per classical Greek tales, the sister-wife of Zeus, mother of the god Ares.

▸ Herakles (Hercules): A son of Zeus by a mortal woman, he was a heroic demigod and the subject of many tales, the best known of which is that of his Twelve Labors. On his death, he was invited to join the 'Immortals' on Mount Olympus.

▸ Hermes: The Divine Messenger in Greek tales of the gods (called Mercury by the Romans), a son of Zeus by the nymph Maia. He was considered a patron of shepherds, athletes and merchants, and his prerogatives included distant travel, weights and measures, oratory, literature, cunning and shrewdness. He brought dreams to mortals, and guided the souls of the dead. Hermes was depicted with a winged cap, winged sandals and a winged staff adorned with intertwined serpents—the symbol, ZS has pointed out, of the god **Ningishzidda** (= the Egyptian god THOTH). Indeed, in time the Greeks identified 'Hermes Trismegistus' (= 'Thrice Great') with Thoth as the god of knowledge and science.

▸ Herod: A king of Judea under ruthless Roman rule (also known as Herod I or Herod the Great), who was granted the throne in Jerusalem in 36 B.C. as a result of Roman imperial intrigues. Descended of Edomites who had converted to Judaism a century earlier, when Judea was independent under Hashmonean rule, he attempted to balance his dubious religious qualifications and national identity by marrying a Hashmonean princess and by extensive construction works, including monumental works at the Temple Mount in Jerusalem and construction of the Massadah Fortress. Herod is mentioned in the New Testament, in a tale of a massacre described by Matthew. He reigned until his death in 4 B.C. *See* Hashmoneans.

▸ Herodotus: A 5th century B.C. Greek historian whose writings provided invaluable information on the Greek-Persian Wars. His 'Histories' include first-hand reports on his travels to Egypt, Asia Minor, and other Mediterranean and Black Sea lands. His story-telling style provides unique eye-witness information on Egypt and Babylonia of his time, but also includes much unverified hearsay, the validity of which has come into question.

▸ Hesiod (Hesiodos): A Greek poet of the 8th century B.C. whose work 'Theogony', has served as a prime source for knowledge of Greek mythology.

▸ Hezekiah (H *Hizki-Yahu* = 'Yahweh Is My Strength'): A Judean king (715–687 B.C.) who, according to the Bible (II Kings 20 and II Chronicles 32), dug a subterranean water tunnel from the Gihon Spring outside the city to a reservoir within the city walls in anticipation of an Assyrian attack on Jerusalem. The ensuing siege is described both in the Bible and in the annals of the Assyrian king Sennacherib. The tunnel, bearing an inscription by its diggers, was discovered in 1880 and is described in *The Earth Chronicles Expeditions* by ZS. *See* Tunnel of Hezekiah.

▸ Hieroglyphs, Hieroglyphic Writing: The writing system of ancient Egypt associated with temples of the priesthood ('hiero-') that used glyphs ('picture symbols'), in which such icons represented the drawn objects, a concept, or a verbal sound.

▸ Hindu Traditions: Knowledge of the historical, prehistorical and religious traditions of the ancient peoples of the Indian subcontinent comes from texts in the Sanskrit language (such as the Vedas, Puranas and other 'ancient writings') together with epic tales (such as the Mahabharata and the Ramayana); though written down circa 200 B.C., they are revered as being "not of human origin," held to have been originally composed by the gods themselves; but, scholars believe, brought to the Indian subcontinent by 2nd millennium migrants from the Caucasus. The complex tales of the Hindu gods and demigods parallel in many aspects the Greek ones, with three principal victors of divine conflicts—Indra, Agni, and Surya (as the three Greek Zeus, Poseidon and Hades). Many similarities to Hittite and Hurrian tales (scholars call them all 'mythologies') naturally suggest a common source, such as the Sumerian three: Anu, Enki and Enlil. *See* Indo-European, Indra.

▸ Hipparchus: A Greek astronomer from Asia Minor who, in the 2nd century B.C., discussed "the displacement of the solstitial and equinoctial signs"—the retardation that causes the zodiacal shift from Age to Age. This has led scholars to credit Hipparchus with discovering the phenomenon now called Precession and the resulting system of zodiacal constellations. ZS has shown, however, that such knowledge had been possessed by the Sumerians millennia before Hipparchus. Although Hipparchus himself acknowledged that he drew on earlier knowledge of "Babylonian astronomers of Erech, Borsippa and Babylon," current textbooks continue to name Hipparchus as the discoverer of Precession.

▸ Hispaniola: The name given by Columbus to the island, now shared by Haiti and the Dominican Republic, that he discovered in 1492.

▸ History, cyclical: The concept of history as a series of Ages, common to all ancient civilizations—found already in the writings of Berossus—is one aspect of the notion that 'history repeats itself'; both are in league with the biblical view of history as a Beginning and an End in which one leads to and follows the other. "I am He, I am the First and also the Last I am," God told the Prophet Isaiah; "I am Alpha and Omega, the Beginning and the Ending, sayeth the Lord," according to Revelation; and since God is everlasting, not only is the Ending a new Beginning—it was all also foretold, pre-planned: "From the Beginning the Ending I foretell, from ancient times the things that are not yet done [I tell]" God revealed to Isaiah. ZS holds that such a *cyclical* view of history rules out 'End of Time' considerations according to *linear* calendars (such as the A.D. one, or the Mayan one), and that speculation regarding the timing of the 'End of Days' can take place only in terms of a *cyclical calendar*, such as that of the Zodiacal Ages. *See* Ages, Apocalypse, Berossus, End of Days, Zodiacal Ages.

▸ Hittites: An Indo-European speaking people in Asia Minor who were known at first only from their mention in the Bible as *Hittim*: Abraham bought the burial cave of Machpelah in Hebron from "Ephron the Hittite," and "Uriah the Hittite" was a captain in King David's army. Archaeological discoveries in central Turkey (where the Hittite capital Hattu-shas was located) and royal records uncovered in Egypt, Assyria, and Babylon confirmed the existence of a once mighty Kingdom of Hatti that, at the end of the 2nd millennium B.C., vied with those other empires for control of the ancient Near East. Though Hittite tales of the wars of gods and demigods resemble the Hindu-Aryan tales in the Vedas, it is certain that they adopted the Sumerian pantheon, venerating Enlil's son **Ishkur**/*Adad* as their national god *Teshub* (= 'The Windblower'— 'The Storm God' in most current translations). The Hittites might have been the first to introduce horse-drawn chariots into battle, and in 1595 B.C. they successfully invaded Babylon and took Marduk prisoner. Two centuries later they brought to a halt Egyptian expansion at the Battle of Kadesh; the text of the peace treaty was found in both kingdoms' capitals. ZS has suggested that Teshub/Adad, sent to supervise the gold and tin metallurgical center in the Andes, brought over with him trained Hittite miners and metallurgists. *See* Anatolia, Asia Minor, Hebat, Indo-Europeans, Tiahuanacu, Yazilikaya.

▸ Holy of Holies: The biblical architectural details of the Temple built by Solomon in Jerusalem describe its division into an anteroom (*Ulam*), a main large rituals hall (*Hekhal*), and the innermost and most sacred chamber, the Holy of Holies, where the Ark of the Covenant with the *Dvir* ('Speaker') was emplaced—paralleling the tripartite division of the portable Tent of Appointment during the Exodus. Archaeologists have found such a tripartite division in other Near Eastern temples, with architectural names harking back to Akkadian (*Ulammu*) and Sumerian (**E.gal**). Remarkably, Inca and pre-Inca temples in South America also included a sacred Holy of Holies that—like the one constructed by Solomon—were encased in gold. But there, as in Egyptian temples, the Holy of Holies was so built that on Solstice Day the sun's rays would shine in and light up a god's effigy; the Jerusalem Temple was built on an East-West (equinoctial) alignment. The Holy of Holies in the Jerusalem Temple was completely inlaid with gold, making it similar in this respect to the Golden Enclosures associated with Anu's visits to Earth. *See* Coricancha, Dvir, Golden Enclosure, Temples.

▸ Homer: A Greek historian-storyteller of the 8th century B.C. whose epic poems, the 'Iliad' and the 'Odyssey' have been a major source for the tale of the Trojan War and the role in it of Odysseus, King of Ithaca. The existence of a 'Homer' (although Herodotus wrote of him), the authorship of those epics by a sole author, and most of all the very existence of a city called Troy, have all come into question by modern scholars—until the discovery of Troy by Heinrich Schliemann in the 19th century in western Turkey, exactly where it was supposed to have been according to Homer.

▸ Homo erectus (Latin: 'Upright Man'): A transitional species in the hominid evolution who, about two million years ago, began to walk upright.

▸ Homo sapiens (Latin: 'Wise Man', 'Knowing Man'): Modern man, who appeared in southeast Africa some 250,000 years ago, with no anthropological evidence to explain his almost overnight appearance when previous hominid evolutionary advances took millions of years; the enigma is known as the problem of the 'Missing Link'. While Bible adherents explain the Missing Link by attributing to God the act of creating us, ZS has identified the biblical *Elohim* as the Sumerian Anunnaki, and amassed Sumerian texts that show why and how the Anunnaki upgraded *Homo erectus* to *Homo sapiens* through genetic engineering some 250,000 years ago. *See* Adam, Anunnaki, Enki, Entwined Serpents, Genetic Engineering, Ninharsag.

▸ *Horeb*: Another biblical name for Mount Sinai, meaning the 'Mount in the Dryness'.

▸ Horned Headdress: The Sumerians, and others after them, depicted gods by showing them wearing horned helmetlike headdresses.

▸ Horus (HOR; *Horon* in the Bible): A great Egyptian god, the son of Osiris and Isis, who was born when Isis impregnated herself with the semen of the slain and dismembered Osiris. When he grew up, he challenged his father's murderer, the god Seth, for control of Egypt, and defeated him in an aerial battle in the skies of the Sinai peninsula. Horus was depicted with a falcon's head and was often called the Falcon God.

▸ HUI (or HUY): A high Egyptian official who served in Nubia and in the Sinai as viceroy of the Pharaoh Tutankhamen (circa 1350 B.C.). His tomb in Thebes was decorated with colorful scenes from the lands he governed. ZS has reproduced in his books a particular scene from the Sinai peninsula that shows a large multi-stage rocketship in an underground silo, with its conical command module above ground (where palm trees and giraffes are depicted). ZS has also shown that the shape of the rocketship with its command module matches the Sumerian pictograph for **Din.Gir**—the Sumerian term for 'The Righteous Ones [of the] Rocketships.'

▸ Hurrians: Called *Horim* (= 'Free People') in the Bible, the Hurrians—perhaps of Indo-European origin—settled in the 3rd millennium B.C. in the Upper Euphrates region, and extended their influence from a heartland centered on the Khabur River—an area named *Naharin* in ancient documents and *Aram Naharayim* (= 'The West of the Two Rivers') in the Bible. Important archaeological finds in ancient sites called Nuzi, Carchemish and Alalakh indicate that the Hurrians served as a cultural and religious bridge between Sumer & Akkad in the south and the Hittites in the north, retaining names and words akin to Sanskrit. By the mid-2nd millennium B.C., spreading southward, they established a kingdom called Mitanni; though powerful culturally and economically, it could not withstand for long the assaults of its militarily mighty neighbors. *See* Exodus, Mitanni, Naharin, New Kingdom (Egypt).

▶ **Huwawa**: According to the Epic of Gilgamesh, an artificial, robotic monstrous guardian of the entrance to the abode of the gods in the Cedar Forest: "The fiery warrior . . . his roar is like a flood, his mouth is fire, his breath is death." This description, and a cylinder seal depiction of a robotic Huwawa waving a sword, reminded ZS of the biblical description of the guardian to the Garden of Eden's entrance as a *Cherub* "with a sword of fire that revolveth" (Genesis 3:24). Gilgamesh and his comrade Enkidu managed to overcome the monster by first blinding it with dust. *See* Cedar Forest, Gilgamesh, Landing Place.

▶ Hyksos: The Greek rendering of the Egyptian name for Asiatic migrants who, in mid-17th century B.C., seized control of Egypt. Known as 'Shepherd Kings', they formed Egypt's 15th and 16th reigning dynasties with the city of Avaris as their capital. They were eventually forcefully expelled circa 1560 B.C. Some scholars, seeking in Egyptian records evidence for the Israelite sojourn in Egypt and the Exodus, have raised the possibility that those "Asiatic shepherd kings" were the Israelites. The dates, however, do not synchronize.

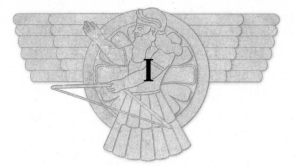

I

▸ **Ibbi-Sin**: The last king of Ur, Sumer's last capital, who reigned for six years until the Year of Doom (2024 B.C.), when the great Sumerian civilization came to a tragic end. *See* Nuclear Weapons, Sumer, Ur.

▸ *Ibri*: A Hebrew; per ZS, a native of Nippur (**Ni.Ibru** in Sumerian). *See* Abraham.

▸ Ica: A town in southern Peru, not far from the Nazca Lines, where pottery purported to depict prehistoric scenes and animals is on display in a private museum.

▸ Ice Ages: Geological and other evidences indicate that Earth had undergone periodic Ice Ages, with warming periods in-between. The last recorded ice age ended abruptly about 13,000 years ago—at the time of the Deluge (Great Flood or Noah's Flood) per ZS, caused by the slippage of Antarctica's ice sheet into the surrounding ocean.

▸ **Igi.gi** (= 'Those Who Observe and See'): A class of Nibiruans, numbering three hundred, whose duties differed from those of the 600 Anunnaki on Earth. Ancient texts recorded the Igigi's dissatisfaction with being stationed "in the heavens" lacking female companionship, a situation that led to their forceful seizing of Earthling women as wives. Per ZS, the Igigi operated the shuttlecraft between Earth and the space base on Mars, where they were stationed, and the tale had to be the origin of the enigmatic verses in Genesis 6 about the *Nefilim* (= 'Those Who Have Come Down') who "took the Daughters of Man as wives whichever way they chose." *See* Nefilim.

▶ **Im.du.gud** (= 'That which like a storm runs'): The 'Divine Black Bird' (aerial vehicle) of the god Ninurta.

▶ Immortality, Immortals: The ancient Greeks referred to the gods as 'The Immortals,' thereby distinguishing them from mortal Man. The distinction, and Man's unending search for the elusive Immortality, go back to Sumerian times, when texts such as the Epic of Gilgamesh dealt with his search for immortality and asserted that he had met the hero of the Deluge, who by the grace of Enlil avoided aging and death for thousands of years. The Bible tells of Enoch, who did not die on Earth for he was taken to be with the *Elohim*, and of the Prophet Elijah who was likewise transported. ZS, citing examples of ancient tales of gods' aging and even death, has explained their wonted 'immortality' as in reality extreme longevity on Earth because of their life cycle in terms of their planet Nibiru, where one 'year' (i.e., one orbit around the Sun) equals about 3,600 Earth years. The notion that being transported to the gods' planet will grant long life underlied the simulated Afterlife Journey of Egyptian Pharaohs to join the gods on the 'Planet of Millions of Years'. *See* Afterlife, Eternal life, Nibiru, Sar.

▶ **In.anna** (= 'An's Lady'): Better known by her Akkadian name *Ishtar*, she was born on Earth, together with her twin brother Utu/*Shamash*, to their parents Nannar/*Sin*—the middle son of Enlil—and his spouse Ningal. When her great-grandparents Anu and Antu, rulers of Nibiru, completed a state visit to Earth, Anu gave the place erected for their stay as a gift to his great-granddaughter, whom he nicknamed **Anunitum** (= 'Anu's Beloved'). The beautiful and ambitious Inanna managed to turn the place into a great city called Uruk (the biblical Erech). Her love affair and betrothal to Enki's youngest son Dumuzi ended abruptly by Dumuzi's drowning, for which his older brother Marduk was blamed—a tragedy that triggered long and bloody Anunnaki wars on Earth, leading to Inanna/Ishtar's reputation as a never-married goddess of both love and war—a prototype of the Roman Venus and likewise associated with the planet of that name (as well as with the Constellation of the Maiden, 'Virgo'). Though offered distant Aratta as her domain, she preferred Uruk and roamed Earth's skies in her "Boat of Heaven," enticing gods, kings and heroes, including the famed Gilgamesh and Sargon. In the pantheon of twelve her original rank was 5, but in time she replaced the aging Ninmah in the rank of 15. *See* Aratta, Gilgamesh, Lower World, Mari, Sargon, Uruk.

▶ Inca, Incas: The predominant inhabitants of what is now Peru, in South America, when the Spaniards arrived in 1532. 'Inca' was the word, in their Quechua language (distinct from the 'Aymara' of the central-south Andes) for 'Lord/Sovereign', and it became the name for the people themselves. From their mountainous capital Cuzco, where the first Inca reigned circa A.D. 1020, they extended their control to the coastal areas; and by the time of the Spanish conquest the 12th Incan king oversaw an empire connected by highways that extended from today's Ecuador in the north to Chile in the South. As a result of recent archaeological and cultural studies the separate identities and cultures of other Andean peoples who had preceded the Incas in the conquered lands have been identified; but scholars continue to attribute to the Incas many of Peru's ancient highland sites and "lost cities" (such as Machu-Picchu) that are distinguished by astounding stone structures. ZS, in *The Lost Realms*, gives credence to the writings of early Spanish chroniclers who recounted the existence of a pre-Incan 'Ancient Empire', going back to 2400 B.C., that had intriguing material and cultural similarities to Old World cultures.

▶ Inca Rocca: The first Incan king of the twelve who reigned in Cuzco from A.D. 1021 to 1532 Incan lore asserted that, after a long interruption in kingship because the gods had been angry, 'Inca Rocca' was a youth taken away by the Sun God, who returned wearing golden garments and announced that kingship would be restored in Cuzco once he resumed the custom of marrying a half-sister. Other versions of the tale call the restorer of kingship Manco Capac.

▶ Indo-European: A classification based on linguistic similarities between Sanskrit, the language of the sacred Hindu writings, and that of many European languages (including the Slavonic, Germanic, Italic, Greek,

Armenian, etc., groups)—a result, it is believed, of migrations of people from a core area in the Caucasus northward and southward, but mostly to the east and west. Ancient Hurrian and Hittite were predecessor Indo-European languages and cultures that served as a bridge to the Mesopotamian cultures of the Middle East. It is noteworthy that this classification of nations by their common linguistic origin matches the biblical Table of Nations (Genesis 10) and the list for the offspring of Noah's son Japhet.

▶ Indra: A major member of the Hindu pantheon. He slew his father, and fought his own brothers (using missiles in aerial battles) for the leadership of the gods; but though supreme in the end, he had to share control with his brothers Agni and Surya. The tales parallel those about the Greek gods. *See* Aditi, Hindu Traditions, Jupiter, Zeus.

▶ Indus Valley Civilization: A major civilization that developed in the 3rd millennium B.C. in the Indian subcontinent, along the Indus River, and lasted till mid-2nd millennium B.C. Archaeological remains of two main urban centers, Harrapa and Mohenjo-Daru, suggest an agriculture-based hierarchical society that started suddenly and ended abruptly. ZS believes that this was the Third Region of civilization the Anunnaki granted to Mankind, circa 2800 B.C. under the aegis of Inanna. The very few artifacts discovered depict gods with horned headdresses and worship of a naked and bejeweled goddess; but with no written texts discovered, a possible kinship to Sumer can only be surmised from Sumerian texts. *See* Aratta, Harappa, Inanna.

▶ Inventory Stela: A large limestone stela discovered in the 1850s by the famed Egyptologist Auguste Mariette and donated by him to the Egyptian Museum in Cairo (which he had established). In its clear hieroglyphic inscription the Pharaoh Khufu (Cheops) takes credit for building a shrine to the goddess Isis, "Mistress of the Pyramid," "beside the House of the Sphinx." ZS provided a rare photo of the stela and reproduced the inscription in *The Wars of Gods and Men* (1980), asserting that this was another proof that the Great Pyramid (attributed to Khufu) and the Sphinx (attributed to a successor, Khefra), had already existed in Khufu's time. In *Journeys to the Mythical Past* (2007) ZS reported that the stela is no longer on display in the Museum.

▶ Iran: *See* Persia.

▶ Iron (**An.ta**), Iron Age: The change from bronze as the strongest metal for tools and weapons to iron required major technological advances, ranging from mining, smelting, refining, and melting to casting. Archaeological evidence indicates that the change took place in the ancient Near East circa 1200 B.C. Textual evidence, however, suggests earlier familiarity with iron: Egyptian tales of the contending of Horus and Seth—long before Pharaonic times—describe the granting by Horus to his human followers of "weapons that were forged" (i.e., made of iron). The Bible (Genesis 4) records that Tobal-Kain, a descendant of the accursed Cain, was "an artificer of gold and copper and iron," presumably even before the Deluge. In Deuteronomy, the Promised Land is described—at the time of the Exodus, 15th century B.C.—as "a land whose stones are iron and of whose mountains thou canst hew copper."

▶ Isaac (H *Itzhak*): The second Patriarch of the Hebrew people, Abraham's son by his wife Sarah, born to both in old age as predicted by one of three divine beings who paid the couple a visit. Though Abraham already had a son by Sarah's handmaiden Hagar, it was Isaac who was the legal heir and patriarchal successor. ZS has postulated that this paralleled the succession rules of the Anunnaki, in accordance with which a son born by a sister-wife was the Legal Heir even if not the Firstborn; and the Bible identified Sarah as a half-sister of Abraham ("Indeed she is my sister, the daughter of my father but not of my mother"). The Hebrew patriarchal line then continued through Isaac's son Jacob.

▶ Isaiah (H *Yesha-yahu* = 'Yahweh [is] Salvation'): A major biblical Prophet, who preached and conveyed the Words of God in Jerusalem at the end of the 8th century B.C. Fully aware of history and current events, of national affairs (such as the relations with the sister-kingdom of Israel) and of international events (such as the rise of Assyria and Babylon and their confrontations with Egypt), his admonitions were as much moral and religious as geopolitical prophecies; they reached a peak with his prediction that Yahweh would destroy the army of the Assyrian king Sennacherib that besieged Jerusalem (702 B.C.). Switching from the past and present to the future, Isaiah first spoke of the coming Day of the Lord—when "the stars of Heaven and its constellations shall not give their light, the Sun shall be darkened and the Moon shall not shine its light"—a day of upheavals and judgments upon all nations; then he foresaw at the 'End of Days' an era of peace and justice, when Jerusalem shall be a "Light unto the Nations," and multitudes from all over shall throng to "the Mount of the Temple of Yahweh." *See* Day of the Lord, End of Days, Hezekiah, Jerusalem.

▶ **Ish.kur** (= 'He of the Mountains'): *See* Adad.

▶ *Ishmael* (= *'El* will hear'): Abraham's son by Hagar, the handmaiden of his wife Sarah, conceived at Sarah's own suggestion so that Abraham, already in his nineties, should not die without a male heir. When Sarah herself had later a son (Isaac) as a result of divine intervention, the older Ishmael mocked Isaac, and Sarah insisted that Hagar and Ishmael leave Abraham's household. Under the patriarchal succession rules, Isaac, having been born to Abraham by a wife who was a half-sister, was the Legal heir even though not the Firstborn; but Ishmael too was blessed by God to have numerous offspring, including "twelve chieftains."

▶ Ishtar: *See* Inanna.

▶ *Ishum* (= 'The Scorcher'): The name by which Ninurta is called in the Babylonian version of the epic text dealing with the use of nuclear weapons in 2024 B.C.

▶ **Isin**: An early city in southern Sumer whose principal deity was **Gula** (Ninurta's spouse, also known as **Bau**). The city played an important role in Mesopotamian history when it became the capital of Sumer & Akkad after the nuclear "Evil Wind" killed off all life in its wake seven years earlier. The 'Dynasty of Isin' began in 2017 B.C. and endured for two centuries.

▸ Isis (AST = 'She of the Throne'): A major Egyptian goddess who was depicted with the hieroglyph for 'Throne' on her head. She was the sister-wife of the god Osiris; and after he had been murdered by his brother Seth, she retrieved her husband's dismembered body and managed to give birth to Horus (his father's avenger when he grew up).

▸ *Israel* (H = 'He wrestled with *El*'): A new name granted Jacob, Abraham's grandson, after he came face to face and wrestled with an *El* (Genesis 32). *El* is commonly translated 'angel', but literally is the singular of *Elohim* = per ZS, one of the Anunnaki. The biblical term 'Children of Israel' refers to the Israelites of the Exodus from Egypt. *See* Jacob.

▸ Israel (Kingdom): After the death of king Solomon (928 B.C.) succession conflicts among his heirs led to the seceding of the northern tribes from the Judean kingdom and the establishment of a separate kingship, 'Israel'. The Kingdom of Israel was subjugated by the Assyrian king Tiglat-Pileser III (744–727 B.C.) and came to an end when his successor Shalmaneser V, in 722 B.C., made the land an Assyrian province and exiled its people—dispersing them in other parts of the Assyrian empire (and thus giving rise to the enigma and legends of the 'Ten Lost Tribes' of Israel). *See* Judea.

▸ Itza: The name of a Mesoamerican tribe whose people were first to venerate gods at the site the Mayas later called Chichén Itzá (= 'The wellmouth of the Itzas').

▶ Jacob (H *Ya'akov* = 'Who follows by the heel'): The third Hebrew Patriarch, the son of Isaac, so named because he was born holding on to the heel of his twin brother Esau. He went from Canaan to Harran, his grandparents' (Abraham and Sarah) and his mother's (Rebecca) ancestral home, to choose a wife, and married there his cousins Leah and Rachel. He had twelve sons, the forefathers of the Twelve Tribes of Israel. On one of his divine encounters, he wrestled with an angelic person, who renamed Jacob *Isra-El*, "for thou hast wrestled with *El*." For the other divine encounter, *see* Jacob's Dream. Before he died, Jacob blessed his twelve sons in an oracle about the End of Days, in which scholars find hints of the twelve zodiacal constellations. ZS has pointed out that before the twelfth son (Benjamin) was born in Canaan, the Bible lists Jacob's Harran offspring as eleven sons and one daughter—paralleling the Sumerian count of eleven 'male' and one 'female' (Ishtar = Venus) members of the Solar System. *See* Harran, Israel.

▶ Jacob's Dream: According to Genesis 28, as Jacob (on his way from Beer-Sheba in Canaan to Harran) lay to sleep one night in a field, he was awakened by a dream-vision of "a ladder set up on the earth and its top reaching heavenwards" on which "angels of the *Elohim* were going up and down;" and God appeared and spoke to him. Realizing what he had witnessed, Jacob said: "How awesome is this place! Indeed, this is none but an abode of the *Elohim*, and this is the Gateway to Heaven;" and he named the place *Beth-El*, God's Abode. ZS has suggested that Jacob had witnessed what some call nowadays a UFO.

▶ Jade: A bright green semiprecious stone associated with the gods in Mesoamerica and the Far East. Though available in Mesoamerica only from mines in Guatemala, hundreds of jade objects were found at Olmec, Aztec and Maya sites. *See also* Turquoise.

▶ Jaguar: The great feline of the New World, it was revered both in Mesoamerica and in South America as a symbol of strength. The great Mesoamerican god Quetzalcoatl was sometimes depicted with a jaguar mask, and a hidden staircase inside the main pyramid at Chichén Itzá leads up to a statue of a jaguar. The name of the oracle priest Balam, author of the Mayan sacred 'Book of Balam', meant 'Jaguar'. Mayan priests wore jaguar skins; and ZS has drawn attention to the fact that in ancient Egypt, parallel priests wore leopard skins.

▶ Japhet (H *Yefet* = 'The good looking'): The third son of Noah, whose nation-lands, according to the Bible, paralleled the Indo-European ones.

▶ Jehu: A king in ancient Israel who is depicted bowing to the Assyrian king Shalmaneser III (858–824 B.C.) on the latter's memorial stone column (now on display in the British Museum).

▶ Jeremiah (H *Yirme-Yahu* = 'Yahweh will lift me'): A major biblical Prophet in Jerusalem during the politically and militarily turbulent times (626–586 B.C.), when Assyria, Babylonia and Egypt contended for domination in the Near East. Guided by his faith, high moral principles of justice, and impressively versed in international affairs, Jeremiah called on the people to put their faith in Yahweh as he foresaw coming events—including the destruction of the Temple in Jerusalem by the Babylonians (and the subsequent fall of Babylon!)—as part of a divine plan to mete out punishment where due, and salvation when it was earned, "at the End of Days."

▶ Jericho (H *Yeriḫo* = '[City] of the Moon [god]'): A city just north of the Dead Sea, on the way from Jerusalem to the east side of the Jordan River, that has been continuously settled from very ancient times—archaeological evidence suggests as far back as 7500 B.C. The Epic of Gilgamesh describes his arrival at a city near "the low lying sea" (the Dead Sea lies at the lowest point on Earth) whose temple was dedicated to Sin, the Moon God—a reference to Jericho, per ZS. The Bible describes at length the Israelites' siege of the walled city of Jericho after they had crossed the Jordan River, and the trumpeting and other means taken to topple its walls. Jericho also featured in the journey of the Prophet Elijah, to go across the Jordan River in order to be taken aloft by a fiery whirlwind. *See* Elijah, Joshua, Siduri, Tell Ghassul.

▸ Jerusalem: (H *Yeru-shala'yim*, probably from *Ur-Shalem* = 'City of the Complete One'): Already a sacred city at the time of Abraham (he was greeted there by the priest of "The God Most High" during the War of the Kings), it was where—presumably on Mount Moriah, the city's site of a great artificial platform—Abraham was ready to sacrifice Isaac on God's command. Though situated neither at a trade or military crossroads nor on the banks of a river, always short of water, not surrounded by farmland or grazing meadows, and with no natural resources of any kind, Jerusalem has remained settled and coveted by conquerors throughout the millennia. David made it his capital, and Solomon built on the platform the Temple to Yahweh; Jesus' coming there launched Christianity, and Moslems believe that Mohammed went there for an ascent to Heaven. Why Jerusalem, why there? In his writings, ZS has shown that after the Deluge had destroyed the Anunnaki's Mission Control Center (Nippur) in Mesopotamia, they relocated the Spaceport to the Sinai peninsula and chose Jerusalem, for its geographic location, to serve as the post-Diluvial Mission Control Center at an equidistant point in the new Landing Corridor. ZS suggests in *The End of Days* that past attacks on Jerusalem by the Egyptians, Assyrians and Babylonians, as recorded in the Bible, were fights for controlling this 'Bond-Heaven Earth'—a role that has been central to the messianic prophecies about a future "New Jerusalem" to come after 'Armageddon', and thus also central to current events. *See* David, Judea, Shalem, Solomon, Temple.

▶ Jerusalem Temples: The 'First Temple' was built in Jerusalem by king Solomon upon an ancient stone platform on Mount Moriah, in accordance with a *Tavnit* (= a 'Scale Model') that Yahweh showed king David and detailed architectural instructions recounted in I Kings 5–7. It was a tripartite structure with its innermost section serving as a Holy of Holies, with the Ark of the Covenant placed upon the Sacred Rock where (according to tradition) Abraham was ready to sacrifice Isaac. Oriented east-west, the Temple was an eternal equinoctial temple. Called in Hebrew *Beth Ha-Mikdash* (= 'The Dedicated/Sacred House'), it was intended, according to the Bible, to serve a dual purpose: As the place for Yahweh's *Shem* (translated 'Presence') on Earth, and the place where He could hear the people's prayers, when the High Priest entered the Holy of Holies and approached the Ark of the Covenant. With all the similarities to other temples, the Jerusalem temple was unique in that it contained absolutely no statue or effigy; the only object within it was the Ark of the Covenant. That temple, completed after seven years in 953 B.C., was destroyed by the Babylonian king Nebuchadnezzar in 587/586 B.C. After the Achaemean/Persian king Cyrus captured Babylon in 539 B.C., he allowed Judean exiles to return and rebuild the Temple in Jerusalem. Known as the 'Second Temple', its rebuilding was completed exactly on the 70th anniversary of its destruction, as had been predicted by the Prophet Jeremiah. In the 2nd century B.C., the Greek-Seleucid rulers of the Asian parts of Alexander the Great's empire became intent on Hellenizing Judea and converting the Temple to the worship of Zeus—actions that triggered the Jewish revolt of 164 B.C. and the rededication of the Temple in 160 B.C. The Second Temple was aggrandized by king Herod (1st century B.C.), only to be destroyed again, by the Romans, in A.D. 70. The victory Arch of Titus in Rome depicts Roman soldiers carrying off some of the Temple's sacred objects. The 'Temple Mount', where both Temples stood, was the focal point of the messianic pronouncements of the biblical Prophets and of the messianic expectations after 160 B.C. *See* Ark of the Covenant, Cyrus, David, Dome of the Rock,

Dvir, End of Days, Hasmoneans, Herod, Holy of Holies, Jerusalem, Seleucids, Solomon, Temple Mount.

▶ Jesus (H *Yehu-shu'ah* = 'Yahweh Saves'): The son of Joseph and Mary born in Bethlehem, conceived, according to Christian beliefs, immaculately, as a Son of God. He grew up in the Galilee; but following a family tradition to spend the Passover holiday in Jerusalem, came to Jerusalem in the spring of A.D. 30 (or 33) with his twelve disciples, preaching to his fellow Jews and challenging the city's Roman masters (Pontius Pilate was the governing Procurator). The events described in the Gospels culminated during the 'Last Supper'—actually, the Jewish *Seder,* the symbol-filled ritual evening meal that ushers in the Passover holiday—when Jesus was arrested, then tried and executed on the cross by the Romans. The mysterious disappearance of his body from the temporary burial cave gave rise to the belief in his resurrection and divinity, and eventually to Christianity. ZS, in *The End of Days,* puts those events in the context of the messianic expectations of that time, in which the resumption of the Davidic kingship by an 'Anointed One' (*Mashi'ah* in Hebrew, from which **Chrystos** in Greek and Messiah/Christ in English) was required as a prelude to the return of the Kingdom of Heaven, and suggests that the traditional *Seder* wine chalice, mentioned in the New Testament, is an important clue in understanding the prophetic background of those events.

▶ Jews: Descendants of the Israelites who had inhabited Canaan after the Exodus, but primarily of the kingdom of Judea with Jerusalem as its capital, who abide by the religious commandments and social code contained in the Bible's 'Five Books of Moses'. They were exiled and dispersed after the Romans destroyed the Second Temple in A.D. 70. *See* Hebrews, Israel, Jerusalem, Judah, Judea.

▶ Job (H *I'yov*): The principal persona in the biblical book by that name, which deals with the issue of why do the righteous suffer—in spite of being benevolent, just, pious. Though filled with wisdom, astounding scientific knowledge, and familiarity with Sumerian texts (per ZS, including about the Celestial Battle and Nibiru's orbit), the book's authorship and date, whether there really was a 'Job', and if so where—remain unknown.

▸ Joel (H *Yo-el* = 'Yahweh is God'): One of the biblical Prophets who, at the start of the 6th century B.C., announced that "the Day of the Lord is at hand," and described it as a day when "the Sun and Moon shall be darkened, the stars shall withdraw their radiance"—per ZS, references to the return of Nibiru. *See* Day of the Lord.

▸ Jordan (H *Yarden* = 'Which flows down'): The river which winds its way down from northern Israel at Mount Hermon, at an elevation of some 2,000 feet, until it reaches the Dead Sea in the south at over 1,000 feet below sea level. Though it is neither a mighty river nor really running deep, it has served from time immemorial as a natural divide between the desertlike lands to its east and the more fertile lands to its west. Crossing the Jordan River was a major step recorded in biblical and other lore; one memorable crossing took place at the end of the Exodus. The River's waters have also played a religious role, as in baptisms described in the New Testament.

▸ Joseph (H *Yosef* = 'God has added'): The eleventh of the twelve sons of Jacob, born after a long time to Rachel, Jacob's favored wife (who died giving birth to Jacob's twelfth son, Benjamin). Spoiled by his father, Joseph aroused the jealousy of his older brothers and irritated them with tales of dreams in which his superiority was the theme. According to the book of Genesis, the brothers got rid of him by selling him into slavery in Egypt. But there his dream-solving abilities led the Pharaoh to name him Viceroy with unlimited authority to save Egypt from a coming seven-year famine. Ultimately, his father and brothers came to Egypt to sojourn there during the famine, but stayed on; their descendants finally left at the time of the Exodus. The Bible records that Moses took the coffin of the mummified Joseph for burial in the Land of Israel.

▸ Joshua (H *Yehu-shu'ah* = 'Yahweh Saves'): The leader of the Israelites after the death of Moses, who led the conquest and settlement of the

Promised Land. The Bible's 'Book of Joshua' records inter alia the miraculous crossing of the Jordan River, the toppling of Jericho's walls, and the Day the Earth Stood Still.

▶ Journey to the Afterlife: According to the Egyptian 'Book of the Dead' and 'Pyramid Texts' the KA ('Double', 'Spirit' or 'Alter Ego') of the embalmed and mummified Pharaoh—after his heart was weighed and found worthy—embarked on a Journey to the Afterlife, for an everlasting existence with the gods on their planet. Simulating the journey to heaven of the resurrected god Osiris, the Pharaoh would leave his tomb—considered only a temporary rest place—through a false door, and then through subterranean passageways travel to a launching site where the Pharaoh's alter ego, seated between astronaut-gods in a rocketship, would ascend heavenwards to the gods' planet. ZS, in *The Stairway to Heaven* and *The Cosmic Code*, has shown that the texts described landmarks leading from Egypt to the Sinai Peninsula, where the post-Diluvial spaceport of the Anunnaki was. The evidence includes a depiction of a multi-stage rocketship in an underground silo. *See* Afterlife.

▶ Jubilee: The name for the Year of Freedom, required by biblical commandments, after the count of 7 × 7 years—i.e., the 50th year. *See* Book of Jubilees.

▶ Judah (H *Yehudah* = 'Who knows Yahweh'): Jacob's fourth son by his wife Leah who stood out among his brothers, as a spokesman and leader. In his Oracle of Blessing before his death, Jacob compared Judah to a fearless lion—a connotation with zodiacal implications, by some scholarly opinions. The tribe of Judah inherited the southern part of the Promised Land; its territory in time absorbed that of Benjamin (including Jerusalem), giving its name to the Kingdom of Judea. The term 'Jew', *Yehudi* in Hebrew, stems from Judah's name.

▶ Judea (Judaea): After the death of Solomon, the name of the southern kingdom, inhabited by the tribes of Judah and Benjamin, that split with the kingdom of Israel in the north at the time of the First Temple, and of subsequent Jewish independent states there during the Second Temple in Greek and Roman times. Thereafter, the geographical name for that part of the Holy Land. *See* Israel, Jerusalem, Judah.

▸ Jupiter: The Roman name for Zeus, derived from the Sanskrit 'Deus Pitar'—'Father of the gods'. The remains of the largest temple to Jupiter in the Roman empire are in Baalbek in Lebanon. The planet given the name 'Jupiter' was called **Ki.shar** by the Sumerians.

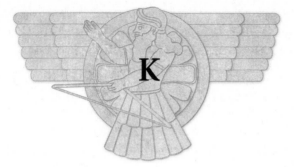

▸ KA: An Egyptian hieroglyphic term, applied to a Pharaoh in his Afterlife journey, that is variably translated as 'Alter Ego', 'Double', 'Personality' or 'a mortal's personification of a god'. *See* Journey to the Afterlife.

▸ *Kabbalah* (= 'That which was received'): A form of Jewish mysticism that searches for divine guidance through understanding secret biblical codes. Developed during the Middle Ages, it is based on the same two pillars of divine revelation of scientific knowledge as in the Bible's Book of Job—*Hokhmah* (= Wisdom) and *Binah* (= Understanding).

▸ Kadesh: *See* Battle of Kadesh.

▸ *Kadesh-Barne'a*: An ancient habitat marking the border between southern Canaan and the Sinai peninsula. Called simply *Kadesh* (= 'The Sanctified [Place]') in Canaanite texts, it is named *Kadesh [of] Barne'a* in the Bible, to distinguish it from Kadesh in the north. The Israelites spent there most of the forty years of the Exodus.

▸ *Kakkabu* (= 'Celestial body'): The Akkadian determinative term before the name of a star or planet (but initially also a constellation). The Bible similarly used the term *Kochav*; but modern Hebrew distinguishes between *Kokhav* as 'star' and *Khokhav Lekhet* ('moving star') for 'planet'. *See* Astronomy, Planets.

▸ Kalasasaya: One of the three prominent features of the ancient site of Tiahuanacu in Bolivia, near the shores of Lake Titicaca. Delineated by a series of standing stone pillars (which is what the name means in the local tongue), it is a rectangular enclosure of about 400 × 450 feet that included a sunken court. The east-west orientation, and the number of pillars and their positions, suggest an astronomical function relating to both equinoxes and solstices. The angle (or 'obliquity') for the solstices conforms to a construction date of either circa 10000 B.C. or 4000 B.C.—the latter conforming, per ZS, to Anu's state visit to Earth. *See* Solstices, Tiahuanacu.

▶ Karnak: The site of major temples in the area of Thebes, ancient Egypt's capital during the New Kingdom.

▶ Kassites: A tribe either from northeast or northwest of Babylon that, in vague circumstances, rose to power in Babylon when the dynasty to which Hammurabi belonged lost power after military defeats and the taking of Marduk hostage by the Hittites. Speaking an unfamiliar language, Kassite kings bearing names such as Karaindash and Kadashman ruled over Babylon (which they called Karduniash) from at least 1560 B.C. to 1160 B.C. Their sparse written records credit them with returning Marduk to Babylon from captivity; but whether that was how they seized power, and who they were, remains an historical enigma. *See* Cassites.

▶ *Kavod*: A Hebrew term, usually transliterated 'Kabod', that the Bible employs when describing the appearing of Yahweh, as when the Israelites could see God's *Kavod* landing upon Mount Sinai in a "cloud of devouring fire" (Exodus 10, 19, 24), or when the Prophet Ezekiel described the divine chariot operated by Cherubim. The term, that can mean Honor or Magnificence, is most often translated in English versions of the Bible 'Glory', 'Glory of the Lord'. It stems from the Hebrew verb that means 'heavy, massive,' and ZS has suggested that in the context of the Exodus and Ezekiel sightings it referred to a heavy physical object, such as a spacecraft. *See also* Aerial Chariots, Spacecraft.

▶ *Keret*: Among the trove of inscribed clay tablets discovered in Ras Shamra in Syria—the site of the Canaanite city Ugarit—was the tale of *Keret*, a name that could be both of a walled capital city, or of its king. While it deals with Man's striving for immortality, it bears similarities both to the biblical tale of Abraham (who needed divine help to have an heir by his wife) and of Job (a prosperous man who loses all, though he is righteous). It has been assumed that the tale's *KRT* refers to the island of Crete.

▸ Khabur River: A major tributary of the Euphrates River where Mesopotamia and Anatolia meet. Called River Khebar in the Bible, it was where the Prophet Ezekiel (one of the Judean nobility exiled to that area by the Babylonians), saw the Divine Chariot.

▸ *Khedorla'omer*, Khedorla'omer Texts: Genesis chapter 14, that describes the international 'War of the Kings' at the time of Abraham, lists "Khedorla'omer, king of Elam" among the 'Kings of the East' who invaded Canaan. The veracity of the biblical tale depended on scholarly identifications of the named kings and kingdoms. That changed in 1897, when the Assyriologist Theophilus Pinches reported at the Victoria Institute in London that a group of clay tablets in the British Museum, which has since been known as 'The Khedorla'omer Texts', described such a war and named the Elamite king **Kudur-Lagamar** as a participant. Pinches identified Kudur-Lagamar, who was known from Elamite and Sumerian tablets, as the Hebrew Bible's '*Khedorla'omer*'. (ZS has also pointed to passages in the Khedorla'omer Texts that might refer to Abraham as "the son of the priest whom the gods in their true counsel have anointed"). *See* Abraham, Gomorrah, Sodom, War of the Kings.

▸ KHNUM (also KHNEMU): An Egyptian name for the 'Divine Craftsman', the god who fashioned Man—another name for PTAH (= **Enki** per ZS).

▸ Khorsabad: The modern name of the site of the capital city of the Assyrian king Sargon II (721–705 B.C.) that was named by him *Dur Sharru-kin* (= 'Fort of the Righteous King'), where magnificent palaces, wall reliefs, great sculptures and a hoard of inscribed tablets were found.

▸ KHUFU: The Egyptian hieroglyphic name of the Pharaoh we call Cheops. *See* Giza, Khufu, Pyramids.

▶ **Ki**: The Sumerian term for Earth (as a 'firm land' rather than a gaseous planet), from which Akkadian *Gi*, Greek ***Gaea***, then 'Geo', derive.

▶ King, Kingship: The institution of kings and kingship was begun in Sumer. Texts known as the 'Sumerian King Lists' assert that "Kingship was brought down from Heaven," not merely suggesting that Kingship was a gift of the gods to Mankind, but also that it instituted on Earth a form of government practiced by the Anunnaki themselves on their home planet. The symbols of Kingship—a tiara or crown, a scepter, and a shepherd's staff—were stated in the texts to have been brought down to Earth by Anu. The Sumerian term for 'king' was **Lu.gal** (= 'Great Man') who at first was a demigod and later on an 'Anointed One' chosen by the gods, intermediary between the gods and Mankind whose role was to be a shepherd of the people, and Sumerian kings strived to attain, through justice and benevolent rule, the title **En.si** (= 'Righteous Shepherd'). In the Bible, anointing (with oil) as signifying choice and appointment to kingship was performed by the prophet Samuel in respect to David. *See also* Arba.

▶ King Lists: While the most familiar record of the succession of kings (in this case, of Judea and Israel) are the Bible's books I and II Kings, the custom of listing kings in a chronological order with information about their reigns was started in Sumer; the texts known as the 'Sumerian King Lists' in fact begin with ten pre-Diluvial rulers (eight of them divine, two demigods) and resumed the kingship after the Deluge. The Babylonians and Assyrians etc. continued the tradition of king lists. In Egypt, the priest Manetho (3rd century B.C.) listed the rulers by dynasties, also starting with a divine one, followed by demigods, and then by Pharaohs. Various records that have been discovered by archaeologists corroborate the Pharaonic dynasties listed by Manetho. *See* Anunnaki, Civilizations, Deluge, E.din.

▶ King's Chamber: An inner bare-walled chamber inside the Great Pyramid in Giza, located at the top of the Grand Gallery, beyond an elaborate Ante-chamber. A lidless stone coffer standing in the chamber has given rise to the notion that it was a Pharaoh's coffin, leading to the chamber's name. No evidence whatsoever was ever found to support this assumption of the Chamber's (and coffer's) functions. ZS, in *The Wars of Gods and Men*, quotes Sumerian texts to suggest that the chamber served, during what he has termed 'The Pyramid Wars', as the place where the god Marduk was imprisoned.

▸ King's Highway: A vital ancient north-south route in the Near East, running along the central mountain range on the east side of the Jordan River, linked by several east-west river crossing points to a counterpart 'Way of the Sea' along the Mediterranean coast on the west side of the Jordan.

▸ **Kin.gu** (= 'Great Emissary'): In the tale (in the 'Epic of Creation') of the Celestial Battle between Marduk and Tiamat, Kingu was the oldest and largest of Tiamat's "host" of satellites/moons. After Tiamat was vanquished, one part of her was smashed to bits and pieces and one part was thrust to another orbit—per ZS, to become the planet Earth (**Ki** in Sumerian). Kingu, according to the text, became **Shesh.Ki** (= 'Brother/Companion of Earth')—Earth's Moon, per ZS.

▸ **Kish**: The first Sumerian city to serve as a seat of kingship, under the aegis of Ninurta—and thus the first Royal City of Men after the Deluge.

▸ **Ki.shar** (= 'Foremost of firm lands'): Per ZS, the planet we call Saturn. It played an important role in the celestial events described in the Epic of Creation.

▸ Knossos: The capital of the ancient Minoan kingdom on the island of Crete, where the legendary Minotaur (half man, half bull) was kept in a labyrinth.

▸ Koran (= 'That which is read/recited'): The holy book of Moslems, who believe that it was revealed to the prophet Muhammed by the angel Gabriel.

▸ *Kothar-Hasis*: *See* Craftsman of the gods.

▸ **Ku.babbar**: Silver.

▸ Kukulkan (also Kukulcan): The Mayan name for Quetzalcoatl, the 'Winged Serpent' god.

▸ **Ku.mal** (= 'Field dweller'): The Sumerian name for the zodiacal constellation of Aries (= The Ram).

▸ Kumarbi (also Kumarbis): In Hittite tales of the gods, an adversary of the god Teshub.

L

▶ *Laban*: The brother, back in H̲arran, of Jacob's mother Rebecca. He was the wily father of Leah and Rachel whom Jacob ended up marrying when he went from Canaan to Harran to find a wife from among his mother's relatives. *See* Harran, Matriarchs, Naharin, Patriarchs.

▶ Labyrinth: The maze built in Crete to keep the Minotaur half-man/half-bull creature. *See* Keret.

▶ *Lachish*: A fortified city in Judea whose capture by the Assyrian king Sennacherib (701 B.C.) is recorded in the Bible (2 Kings and Isaiah)—and corroborated by the Assyrian king, who depicted the capture on his monuments.

▶ **Lagash**: A Sumerian city that served as the 'cult center' of the god Ninurta, where—already in the 24th century B.C.—its king Urukagina promulgated a Code of Laws based on social justice. One of its famed kings, Gudea (22nd century B.C.), described in detailed texts inscribed on two large clay cylinders (that can now be seen in the Louvre in Paris) how he built a new temple for the god Ninurta and his spouse Bau in the **Girsu**, the city's sacred precinct. The instructions for the temple's building were given to the king in a kind of 'Twilight Zone' dream, parts of which turned out to be real. *See* E.ninnu, Girsu, Gudea, Ninurta.

▶ *Lamech*: The name of two early biblical Patriarchs: One of the line of Cain, born in the enigmatic distant 'Land of *Nod*' to which Cain was exiled after he had slain Abel; and the other of the line of Seth (the third son of Adam and Eve)—a son of Metushelah and, more importantly, the father of Noah (the hero of the Deluge tale). According to the Bible, Lamech lived 777 years.

▶ Lamentation Texts: A collection of texts, written after the demise of the Sumerian civilization, that lament the desolation and absence of human, animal and plant life in Sumer's cities, temples and countryside after the "Evil Wind" had swept over the land—per ZS, as a result of the use of nuclear weapons in 2024 B.C. *See* Evil Wind, Nuclear Weapons, Sumer.

▶ Landing Corridor: Per ZS, the Anunnaki located their spaceports—the pre-Diluvial and the post-Diluvial ones—as part of patterns of natural and artificial landmarks forming a triangular Landing Corridor, anchored on the twin peaks of Ararat as an apex. At the epicenter, equidistant from other landmarks, was Mission Control Center—Nippur the first time, Jerusalem after the Deluge. The two great pyramids of Giza, ZS showed in diagrams, were part of the post-Diluvial landmark and landing system. *See* Jerusalem, Nippur, Spaceport.

▶ Landing Place: The term used in the Epic of Gilgamesh to describe his first destination in his Search For Immortality: "A secret place of the Anunnaki" in the Cedar Forest, a place guarded by a ferocious artificial or robotic creature—Baalbek in Lebanon, per ZS. Gilgamesh described seeing there a fiery rocket launched heavenwards. *See* Baalbek, Cedar Forest, Gilgamesh, Huwawa.

▶ Larak (**La.ra.ak** = 'Seeing the bright halo'): The third 'City of the gods' established by the Anunnaki in the **E.din.** ZS has shown that it was located so that it served as a component of the pre-Diluvial Landing Corridor.

▶ Larsa (**La.ar.sa** = 'Seeing the red light'): A seventh 'City of the gods' in the **E.din** that, per ZS, served as a component of the pre-Diluvial Landing Corridor.

▶ Last Supper: The term applied to the last evening meal of Jesus with his twelve disciples, when Jesus came to Jerusalem to celebrate the Passover holiday. It undoubtedly was the traditional Jewish *Seder*, the evening meal ushering the weeklong holiday whose rituals of unleavened bread and wine include a ceremonial wine cup for the prophet Elijah. ZS, in *The End of Days*, points to messianic clues both in the Gospels' narrative and the famous painting by Leonardo da Vinci, and suggests that the 'Holy Chalice' of Christian traditions (that evolved to the legendary Holy Grail) was the wine cup set aside for Elijah. *See* Elijah, Jerusalem, Jesus, Passover.

▶ La Venta: A major Olmec site near the Gulf of Mexico coast, where some of the first Olmec colossal sculpted stone heads were found.

▶ Law Codes: Though the Law Code of Hammurabi, the 18th century B.C. Babylonian king, comes mostly to people's minds, the fact is that the practice of enacting a series of laws to form a 'law code' goes back to ancient Sumer—the oldest of which (thus far discovered) was by king Urukagina six centuries earlier. While the Hammurabi and other Babylonian decrees were primarily lists of crimes and their punishments, the Sumerian ones were laws of social justice, protecting the poor, the daily laborers, widows. The Ten Commandments that Moses received on Mount Sinai (15th century B.C.) are a unique law code that lists with brevity and clarity the essential religious, social and moral do's and don'ts.

▶ Lebanon: So named after its *Lebanon* (= 'The Place of Whiteness') mountain ranges, which are snow covered in winter in the otherwise semi-tropical Near East. Famed from antiquity for its unique Cedar Forest—the location, according to the Epic of Gilgamesh, of the gods' Landing Place and its awesome guardians. Present-day Lebanon is the post World War I political entity that, in ancient times, was home to the Phoenicians. *See* Baalbek.

▶ *Levi*: One of Jacob's twelve sons. Aaron and Moses belonged to the tribe of Levi. The Jewish tradition of Levites serving as priests and Temple attendants began with Aaron during the Exodus.

▶ Libra (= 'The scales'; and so in Hebrew, *Mozna'yim*): The zodiacal constellation that the Sumerians called **Ziba.anna** (= 'Heavenly Fate/ Decision'); it was connected, by some opinions, to the Autumnal Equinox when day/ night are balanced. In ancient Egypt it was believed that a Pharaoh could not journey to the Afterlife unless the god Thoth weighed the king's heart in balancing scales, and found it "not wanting."

▶ Lion: The zodiacal constellation the Sumerians called **Ur.gal** (= 'Lion'), and so depicted it. The lion was considered the 'cult animal' of Inanna/ Ishtar, and she was frequently depicted standing upon a lion. The Epic of Gilgamesh relates that when he was wandering lost in a desert, he encountered two lions and slew them both with his bare hands. The feat assumed legendary status and depictions of Gilgamesh wrestling the lions have been found throughout the ancient world—and, ZS has pointed out, even in pre-Columbian South America.

▶ Long Count Calendar: A Mesoamerican calendar, introduced by the Olmecs and used by the Mayans, that recorded dates by counting the number of days that had passed from a "Day One" in 3113 B.C. (Per ZS, when the god Thoth arrived in Mesoamerica with a group of his African followers). Various numbers of days were grouped and represented by a hieroglyph; the one called Baktun (= 144,000 days) features in so-called 'Mayan Prophecies' regarding the year A.D. 2012. *See* Calendars, Mayas, Olmecs, Quetzalcoatl.

▶ Lost Tribes of Israel: The disappeared descendants of the ten tribes that broke off from Judea after the death of king Solomon and formed the Kingdom of Israel, who were exiled en masse by the Assyrians in 724/720 B.C. and vanished in the fog of history. Because of many similarities in tales and customs by the native Americans, the first European explorers of the New World believed that they had found the 'Ten Lost Tribes'. *See* Israel (Kingdom).

▶ *Lot*: Abraham's orphaned nephew whom he took along with him when he left Harran for Canaan. During the War of the Kings, the eastern attackers took Lot captive when they overran Sodom, and Abraham chased them all the way to Damascus to have Lot released. The Bible tells that Lot and his family were warned by two *Malachim* (literally 'emissaries' but translated 'Angels') to leave Sodom before it was upheavaled; Lot's wife, who stopped and looked back, was turned to a "pillar of salt." ZS has suggested that the 'upheavaling' was part of the nuclear attack on the nearby Spaceport and the "five sinning cities," and that the Sumerian text that served as a source of the biblical tale used a term that is better translated as 'vaporized' to describe Lot's wife's fate. *See* Erra, War of the Kings.

▸ Lower Sea: The Sumerian/Akkadian name for what is now called the Persian Gulf.

▸ Lower World: In Mesopotamian texts, the designation of the southern tip of Africa that was the domain of Ereshkigal (a sister of Inanna) and her spouse Nergal (a son of Enki). An array of scientific instruments located there predicted the Deluge. A text titled 'Inanna's Descent to the Lower World' describes the place and tells how Inanna, going there uninvited, was put to death (and how she was brought back to life). *See* Dumuzi, Ereshkigal, Inanna, Nergal.

▸ **Lu.gal** (= 'Great Man'): The Sumerian term translated 'king'.

▸ **Lugal.banda**: A king of Uruk (Inanna's center in Sumer) who, according to the Sumerian King Lists and other texts, was a demigod—the son of Inanna by Uruk's previous king, Enmerkar. Several epic texts described Lugalbanda's adventures in distant lands, including his attempt to be taken aloft as a god.

▸ *Lu.lu* (= 'The mixed one'): An Akkadian term, found in Creation Texts, that designates the intelligent being who was fashioned by Enki and Ninti/Ninharsag by mixing Anunnaki genes with those of *Homo erectus,* creating a hybrid.

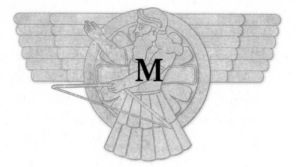

M

▸ *Maccabees*: Jewish zealots, also known as <u>H</u>ashmone'ans, who led the success-ful uprising against the Seleucid-Greeks (who ruled Judea after the death of Alexander) and re-established the independence of Judea. The cleans-ing of the Temple in Jerusalem of heathen idols and its rededication (in 160 B.C.) has since been celebrated by Jews as the Festival of Hanukkah. The circumstances that led to the uprising and the Maccabean feats are detailed in the two-part Book of Maccabees, which is included in the Vulgate translation of the Hebrew Bible and in some Christian bibles, but not in the Hebrew Bible (or in Christian Protestant versions). The <u>H</u>ashmonean dynasty reigned in Judea until the Roman occupation in the first century B.C. *See* Hasmoneans, Herod, Jerusalem, Jerusalem Temple, Nippur Calendar.

▸ Machu Picchu: In 1911 the American archaeologist Hiram Bingham found an abandoned city in the Incan realm in Peru, and described it in his books *Machu Picchu, a Citadel of the Incas* and *The Lost City of the Incas*—an epithet that has become inseparable from the place. Situated on a mountain peak amongst skyscraping Andean mountains, it is an enchanting place of mystery, featuring walls of large interlocking stone blocks, a row of three windows, a stone sun dial, a semi-circular win-dowed structure built with perfect ashlars, a sacred rock within a cave. ZS, in *The Lost Realms*, believes that the place was what local legends tell—the capital, and an astronomical observatory, of an 'Old Empire' that preceded the Incas.

▶ **Magan**: The Sumerian name for Egypt.

▶ *Magog*: *See* Gog and Magog.

▶ Mahabharata: A long sacred Hindu epic text, written in Sanskrit, that tells tales of Heaven and Earth, of gods and heroes in ancient India. Believed to have been written between the 5th century B.C. and the 4th century A.D., the tales frequently relate how the gods traveled "in cloud-borne chariots," and "made themselves metal fortresses in the skies."

▶ Maidum: The location in Egypt, south of Giza, of the 'Collapsed Pyramid'—a failed attempt to build a smooth-sided pyramid at the steep 52° angle. Did its builders, who preceded the presumed builders of the 52° Giza pyramids, pioneer the idea of such pyramids (as most Egyptologists think) or try (as some, including ZS, believe) to emulate the Giza ones that had already existed? The puzzle of this pyramid has thus a bearing on the issue of When and By Whom were the unique Giza pyramids built.

▶ *Mal'akhim*: A biblical Hebrew term literally meaning 'Emissaries', but usually translated 'angels'. *See* Angels.

▶ Man, Mankind: Discoveries in East Africa of hominid skeletal remains document the slow progression of the human species over millions of years from ancestral apelike primates; but this evolutionary evidence has failed to explain the sudden transformation—overnight, in evolutionary timetables—from a bipedal 'Homo erectus' to 'Homo sapiens' ('Thinking Man')—us—that occurred inexplicably some 300,000 years ago. ZS has suggested that this problem of the "Missing Link" is resolved by the Sumerian texts that describe a deliberate feat by the Anunnaki (specifically, Enki and Ninharsag) of genetic engineering, of adding some of their genes to those of a *Homo erectus*. It is a feat, he claims, that also explains the biblical assertion in Genesis that *The Adam* was fashioned deliberately by the *Elohim* "in **their** image and after **their** likeness." The Garden of Eden episode with the 'Serpent', ZS wrote, deals with a second genetic engineering feat by Enki, of granting to the hybrid the ability to procreate. Sumerian and Akkadian texts disclose Enlil's unhappiness with all that, and his anger when some of the Anunnaki began to conjugate with female Earthlings—leading to his wish to see Mankind perish in the Deluge. *See* Adam, Buzur, Creation Tales, Deluge, Eden, Enki, Eve, Nefilim, Ningishzidda, Ninharsag.

▸ Manco Capac: The name given by the Incas both to a legendary founder of Cuzco, and to the actual first 'Capac' (= king), also known as Inca Rocca, who began Inca rule in A.D. 1021. *See* Cuzco, Incas.

▸ Manetho (Greek from MEN-THOTH = 'Gift of Thoth'): A 3rd century B.C. Egyptian priest who was retained by the Ptolemaic-Greek rulers of Egypt (after the death of Alexander) to write for them the history of Egypt and its kings. His writings arranged the rulers by dynasties— beginning with a time when gods alone ruled, then demigods, then Pharaohs. The first divine dynasty of seven gods was begun by PTAH (= Enki, per ZS) who was succeeded by his son RA (= Marduk per ZS). The total length of time of the pre-Pharaonic reigns was 17,870 years, i.e. started some 10,000 years before the Deluge. Manetho also provided the estimated "duration of the world" as 2,160,000 years (a number, ZS has pointed out, that represented 1,000 zodiacal ages of 2,160 years each). *See* Ages, Demigods, History/Cyclical, Zodiac.

▸ **Mar.duk** (= 'Son of the Pure Mound'): Best known as the national god of Babylon, where earlier canonical texts, such as the Epic of Creation, were revised to grant him also celestial supremacy as the Creator Planet, changing its name from Nibiru to 'Marduk'. He was the Foremost son of Ea/Enki, born on Nibiru and brought over to Earth by his mother Damkina. Found guilty of the death of his younger brother Dumuzi, Marduk was buried alive inside the Great Pyramid but was spared and was exiled—but then alienated the other Anunnaki leaders, and espe- cially Enlil, when he broke a taboo by taking an Earthling female as a wife (who bore him a son, Nabu). Witnessing his father's constant yet futile contesting with Enlil for the succession rights, he took up the struggle for supremacy of which, he believed, his father was unjustly deprived. Limited at first to the Enki'ite domain of Egypt (where, per ZS, he was worshipped as RA), his repeated attempts to establish himself also in the Enlilite domains led to such incidents as that of the 'Tower of Babel', brutal warfare, and the climactic use of nuclear weapons on Earth. Vying with Enlil's son Ninurta for the Succession, he did attain in the end the "Rank of Fifty"—but only after the great Sumerian civilization succumbed to the nuclear wind. It was then that Babylon was made an imperial city, with an imposing sacred precinct dominated by a seven-stage ziggurat, the **Esagil**; it served as the god's abode, headquarters, and finally as his tomb. (According to Greek and Roman historians of that time, Marduk's tomb was within the Esagil ziggurat, which was attacked by the Persian king Xerxes in 482 B.C.; ZS has therefore concluded that Marduk died in 484 B.C.). In seeking supremacy, Marduk did not introduce monotheism; once he won the Rank of Fifty, he invited the other gods (Enlilites included) to reside in Babylon's sacred precinct, ordering the building of residential shrines for them; indeed, being Supreme required the existence and recognition of other deities. *See* Akkadian Prophecies, Alexander, Amon, Aries, Babylon, Enki, Fifty, Great Pyramid of Giza, Nabu, Nibiru, Ptah, Pyramid Wars, Ra, Tower of Babel, Yahweh.

▸ *Marduk*: In Babylonian astronomy, the home planet of the Anunnaki, Nibiru, that the Babylonians renamed 'Marduk'. First millennium B.C. astronomical tablets, listed and quoted by ZS in *The End of Days,* recorded the reappearance of the planetary 'Marduk' in the zodiacal Age of Aries.

▸ Mari: An Amorite/Sumerian capital city in the mid-Euphrates region which thrived in the 3rd and early 2nd millennia B.C. Its remains (excavated in the 1930s) included a huge palace with hundreds of rooms, many of them decorated with colorful murals depicting the goddess Inanna/ Ishtar. The palace library had more than 20,000 inscribed clay tablets whose subjects ranged from economy and trade to military and religious matters. Numerous statues, many carved of basaltic stone, depicted male and female Mari dignitaries, often identified by name or title in beautiful Sumerian cuneiform script. The statuary included a lifesize statue of Inanna equipped as an astronaut. Mari was duplicitously attacked and destroyed in 1760 B.C. by the Babylonian king Hammurabi. A visit to the site is described by ZS in *The Earth Chronicles Expeditions*.

▸ Mars: The current name (after the Roman god of war) for the planet called **Lahmu** in the Epic of Creation and **Apin** in Sumerian astronomical texts. It was pictorially depicted on cylinder seals as a six-rayed planet, indicating (per ZS) that the Anunnaki counted it as the sixth planet as they entered the solar system from way out. ZS has shown that it served as a 'Way Station' for the Anunnaki in their space journeys between Nibiru and Earth, and suggested that it was the principal base for the shuttling **Igi.gi** astronauts. While that was considered impossible when *The 12th Planet* was published (in 1976) because Mars was deemed an uninhabitable planet, subsequent multiple studies of the planet by NASA and European nations has shown that Mars in fact once had an atmosphere, lakes, rivers and flowing waters, and was habitable. NASA photographs from Mars also show what appear to be remains of artificial structures; but they have not been pursued by NASA's subsequent orbiters and rovers. (Tests by NASA's Phoenix spacecraft, landed in mid 2008 on the planet's northern part, found that the soil contained ice water and nutrients suitable for growing vegetables.) *See also* Phobos Incident.

▸ Matriarchs: The Bible counts four Matriarchs of the Hebrew people— Sarah, Abraham's wife; Rebecca, Isaac's wife; and the sisters Leah and Rachel, Jacob's wives. Sarah was Abraham's half sister and like him stemmed from Mesopotamia. Rebecca, Leah and Rachel were cousins of their husbands, belonging to Abraham's relatives who had stayed behind in Harran when Abraham left for Canaan. *See* Benjamin, Harran, Laban, Naharin.

▸ Maya, Maya Civilization: The name given to people, linguistically, culturally and religiously distinct, who settled the southern parts of Mesoamerica circa 1000 B.C. and spread from the Pacific Coast northward and eastward—from what is now Guatemala to Mexico's Yucatan peninsula, Honduras, El Salvador and Belize. Famed Mayan cities, such as Chichén Itzá, Uxmal, Palenque, Copan, Tikal and many more, built during a so-called Classic Period (circa 300 B.C. to A.D. 900), were in fact vast sacred ceremonial precincts featuring stepped pyramids, where only royalty and priesthood lived; the people lived in villages in the surrounding countryside. When the Spaniards arrived in the 16th century, they found Mayan books (written on paper made from tree barks) in which the Mayas, in a pictorial-hieroglyphic script, depicted their gods and wrote down their history, legends, and scientific knowledge; except for a few such 'Codices', all were destroyed by Spanish priests as pagan heresy. *See* Chichén Itzá, Balam, Mesoamerica.

▸ Mayan Calendar: Mayan monuments, whose hieroglyphic writing described actual events, frequently bore a date expressed in glyphs of the 'Long Count' adopted from the Olmecs. The glyphs stood for 'Kin' (= a day), 'Uinal' (= 20 days), 'Tun' (= 360 days), 'Ka-tun' (= 20 × 360 = 7,200 days), 'Bak-tun' (= 20 × 20 × 360 = 144,000 days) and so on. Each category was multiplied by a number (represented by dots and bars) next to it; it all added up to a grand total of days that had passed from a Day One (that scholars determined to have been equal to August 13, 3113 B.C.). Accordingly, we are now in the 13th Baktun; and some believe that when it completes its 144,000 days' count, so-called 'Mayan Prophecies' will come into play. *See* Calendars.

▸ Medes: A people who attained control of northern Iran in the 1st millennium B.C. Their kingdom, called *Madai* in the Bible and Media by the Greeks, joined the Achaemenids to their south to form the Persian empire.

▸ Medinet Habu: The location in Upper Egypt, on the Nile's western side, of great temples on whose walls Ramses III depicted battles with invaders called "People of the Sea."

▸ Megalithic Structures: Structures made of huge stones, whether crude boulders erected as found in nature, or of colossal shaped and dressed stone blocks (or combinations of them)—weighing tens and hundreds of tons each, and dating to thousands of years ago—abound both in the Old World and the New World. Some consist just of stones standing in a circle (e.g., Stonehenge in England), some have megaliths in concentric circles (e.g., Gilgal Repha'im on the Golan Heights), some are incorporated in protective walls (as in ancient temples on Malta), some are connected to form rows of multi-angled walls (as on the promontory of Sacsahuaman above Cuzco in Peru), or serve as a foundation (as for the Western Wall of the Temple Mount in Jerusalem). Some, as at Tiahuanacu and Puma Punku near Lake Titicaca in the Andean mountains, are formed into huge chambers or gateways, each one carved out of a single colossal stone; and then there is the unique stone platform and towering structure at Ba'albek in Lebanon, with cut and shaped megaliths weighing more than 1,000 tons each. In all these instances, the stones—in spite of their great weight—were brought to the site from some other distant source, apparently selected for some particular quality. How the feat of transporting, raising and erecting (and sometimes cutting to shape) such colossal weights by the 'primitive' locals was achieved, remains a mystery—unless legendary 'giants', or the gods, were involved. (The unique Giza pyramids are not listed here because their stone blocks, though weighing on the average several tons, are not colossal megaliths.)

▸ *Megiddo*: A mountain fortress situated on a promontory at the eastern end of the Mount Carmel range in Israel that has dominated the ancient north-south "Way of the Sea" along the Mediterranean coast at a vital junction with ancient east-west passages, it was a Canaanite stronghold that the Israelites under Joshua could not capture, but was taken and fortified by King Solomon. The site of decisive battles in antiquity (as recorded by Egypt's 'Napoleon' Thothmes III), it is also the 'Armageddon' (H *Har Megiddo* = 'Mount Megiddo') where, according to the New Testament (Revelation 16:16), the final great world battle will take place. (A similar prophecy is found in the Old Testament—Zechariah 12:11). The significance of an archaeological discovery at Megiddo in which the Sign of the Fishes (for Pisces) is depicted, is discussed by ZS in *The End of Days: Armageddon and Prophecies of the Return*. *See* Armageddon, End of Days.

▸ **Meluḫḫa**: The Sumerian name for the kingdom of Nubia in Africa.

▸ Memphis (Greek from MEN-NEFER, 'The Good Place of Men'): Located centrally where Lower and Upper Egypt meet, it was the capital of ancient Egypt during the Old Kingdom period; called *Moph* or *Noph* by biblical Prophets.

▸ MEN ('Menes' in Greek; also called NAR-MER): The name of the first Pharaoh who reigned when the gods granted civilization and kingship to Egypt, circa 3100 B.C. He established Men-Nefer ('Memphis') as Egypt's first capital.

▸ MENKARA (also MENKAURA; 'Mycerinus' in Greek): The 4th dynasty Pharaoh who, according to Egyptologists, built the third and smallest of the Giza pyramids. ZS, for reasons expounded in *The Stairway to Heaven*, has suggested that it was in fact the first one built by the Anunnaki as a trial scale model for the subsequent much larger two.

▸ Mercury: The current name for the planet called **Mummu** in the Epic of Creation, and **Gu.utu** (= 'The Sun's Lamb') by the Sumerians.

▸ Meroe: The name of an ancient kingdom in Nubia known for its steep-angled narrow pyramids. Alexander the Great went there to consult the Oracle Stone in Meroe's temple to the god Ammon. *See* Nubia, Omphalos.

▸ Mesoamerica: The geographic-cultural zone that encompasses the area from present-day central-south Mexico and the Yucatan peninsula through Guatemala and Belize to parts of Costa Rica, El Salvador, Nicaragua and Honduras, where the pre-Columbian Olmecs, Toltecs, Aztecs and the Mayas (to name the area's principal cultural groups) flourished.

▸ Mesopotamia: Meaning "Between the two rivers" in Greek, the term encompasses not just the geographic area between the Tigris and Euphrates rivers, but also culturally and historically the lands that in antiquity were Sumer & Akkad in the south, Elam in the east, Babylon and Assyria in the north, and Mari and Mitanni in the west. Southern Mesopotamia (where societal settlements have been unearthed going back to the 8th millennium B.C.) is considered the 'Cradle of Civilization' because it was there that the great Sumerian urban civilization burst upon the human scene circa 4000 B.C. Sumerian texts quoted by ZS assert that before the Deluge the area was the **E.din** where the Anunnaki's 'Cities of the gods' were, and that when the land dried sufficiently to enable resettlement after the Deluge, the Anunnaki decided to grant civilization to Mankind, locating Man's cities exactly where their own pre-Diluvial cities had been. *See* Anunnaki, Cities of the gods, Eden, Sumer.

▸ Messiah: A rendering of the Bible's Hebrew word *Mashi'aḥ,* it literally meant 'The anointed one'—one whose selection to serve as priest (viz. Exodus chapters 28, 29) or king (viz. I and II Samuel, re Saul and David) was consecrated by pouring oil on his head. In Mesopotamian texts, it was Sargon of Akkad who claimed to have been "the anointed priest of Anu." In the Bible, the ritual (that was at first also applicable to objects, e.g., when Jacob anointed with oil the stone monument at Beth-El, the "Gateway to Heaven"), evolved to signify a king or king-priest consecrated and chosen by God to carry out His plan (as when Yahweh called the Persian Cyrus "My Anointed One"). As used by the biblical Prophets, the term assumed a connotation of a future savior-redeemer—God's Chosen One who will usher the Messianic Time of the return of Yahweh's glory and the restoration of David's throne in Jerusalem. *See* Apocalypse, David, Prophets, Revelation.

▸ Messianic Clock: A term used by ZS, in *The End of Days*, to trace and predict the periodic rise of messianic expectations throughout human history. He showed that Messianic expectations were linked to Nibiru's orbits, the Nippur Calendar, and the Zodiacal Ages.

▸ Metals, Metallurgy: Man's use of metals began with gold and continued with silver and copper—metals found native in nature. Archaeological evidence indicates that the use of "soft stones" (i.e., metals) by hammering them into useful shapes began in the Near East in the 6th millennium B.C.; use of native metals became Metallurgy with the introduction of the copper-tin alloy called Bronze in the 4th millennium B.C.; and technological advances in the processing of ores ushered the Iron Age in the 2nd millennium B.C. Unlike archaeology, ancient worldwide beliefs in a sequence of Metal Ages (starting with a Golden Age) invariably assigned to those Ages much greater antiquity. The Sumerian tales of the Anunnaki describe their coming to Earth for gold, and of the establishment of Bad-Tibira as a metallurgical center in the Edin, also place those events in pre-Diluvial times. In the Bible too, references are found to metal use before the Deluge—by observing that one of the Rivers of Eden flowed where "the good gold came from," and by noting that Tubal-Cain (of the exiled line of Cain) "was an artificer of gold and copper and iron." According to inscriptions on the temple walls in Edfu in Egypt, the god Horus armed human supporters with weapons of "Divine Iron" that were forged at a foundry he had established there. *See* Anunnaki, Bronze, Copper, Gold, Golden Enclosure, Iron/Iron-Age, Silver.

▸ Metuselah (H *Metushela*ḥ): According to the Bible, the son of Enoch and the grandfather of Noah, who lived the longest of all the pre-Diluvial Patriarchs—969 years.

▸ Mines, Mining: While generally treated as part of the subject of Metals and Metallurgy, mining played a pivotal role in the affairs of the Anunnaki, as clearly described in the 'Atra-Hasis Epic' and other texts cited by ZS. Having been forced to resort to mining to obtain the gold they needed, the Anunnaki assigned to work in the mines mutinied; the mutiny led to the fashioning of a "Primitive Worker"—*Homo sapiens*—to take over the toil. *See* Adam, Anunnaki, Metals/Metallurgy.

▸ Minoan Civilization: The civilization that flourished on the Mediterranean island of Crete from about 2700 B.C. to circa 1500 B.C., so named after the legendary king Minos (who imprisoned the Minotaur in a labyrinth). It was a bridge between the earlier Near Eastern and the subsequent classic Greek civilization. *See* Crete, Mycenaean Civilization.

▸ Mission Control Center: In pre-Diluvial times, the command post of Enlil, which "cast a net over the whole Earth," scanned the heavens, and tracked the comings and goings of the Anunnaki spacecraft, was at Nippur. The Sumerian term for it was **Dur.an.ki** ('Bond Heaven-Earth'). At its heart was a restricted-access chamber, the **Dir.ga** ('Dark

Crownlike Chamber'), where humming and light-emitting equipment was located; it included vital **Me** and the orbital "Tablets of Destinies." Per ZS, in post-Diluvial times Mission Control Center was in Jerusalem, where the Temple was later built. *See* Dur.an.ki, Jerusalem, Jerusalem Temple, Mount Moriah, Nippur, Zu.

▸ Mitanni (= 'Anu's Weapon'): A kingdom that in the 15th/14th centuries B.C. occupied the Upper Euphrates/Tigris region—an area that roughly represents the parts of Turkey, Syria and Iraq settled nowadays by the Kurdish people. Starting in the previous millennium, it was the land of the Hurrians (biblical 'Horites'), people of Indo-European origin who adopted the Sumerian-Akkadian culture and religion but retained god and royal names in a language akin to Sanskrit. Written records from the time, that include correspondence between Mitannian kings and Egyptian Pharaohs, detail how repeated Egyptian forays to capture the upper Euphrates regions—including attacks by Egypt's 'Napoleon' Thothmes III—were blocked by Mitanni both militarily and diplomatically. ZS has suggested that the biblical tale of the events leading to the Exodus, in which the Egyptians feared that the Israelites would become a 'Fifth Column' in a war with enemies in the north, in fact reflects the Egyptian-Mitannian conflict, because the contested upper Euphrates region was settled by the erstwhile relatives of the Hebrew Patriarchs. *See* Harran, Hurrians, Naharin, Nahor, Thothmes.

▸ Moab: A small kingdom on the eastern side of the Dead Sea with which the Hebrew kingdoms of Judea and Israel had variably warring and friendly relations. A stone column (now in the Louvre Museum), inscribed in language and script akin to that of Judea, relates events in the 9th century B.C. concerning Mesha (king of Moab) and Omri (king of Israel) that parallel what is told in 2 Kings 3. According to the Bible, the forefather of the Moabites was a son of Lot, Abraham's nephew; and Ruth, a Moabite, was a foremother of king David. Mount Nebo, where Moses died, was in Moab. A stela (stone column) inscribed by Mesha, a Moabite king, is the only discovered ancient document outside of the Bible in which the divine name YHWH is spelled out.

▶ Moon: The Moon has fascinated Mankind from time immemorial, has been observed since astronomy began, is essential to many calendars, and was associated in antiquity with the god **Su.en** (Akkadian *Sin*). Yet the origin of Earth's sole satellite is still an enigma baffling scientists. The prevailing theory, that it is a part of Earth thrust off as a result of a giant collision with some celestial wanderer, fails to explain its large size relative to Earth, why the Moon's mineral makeup differs from Earth's, and what happened to the impactor. ZS has resolved the enigma by treating the Mesopotamian Epic of Creation as a sophisticated cosmogony. The Moon, he wrote, was **Kingu**, the main satellite of Tiamat; and when the 'celestial battle' with Nibiru/Marduk occurred, it was carried to a new celestial location with the half of Tiamat that became the Earth. *See* Astronomy, Celestial Battle, Earth, Epic of Creation.

▶ Moses (H *Moshe*): According to the Bible, a baby boy who was born in Egypt to parents of the tribe of Levi at a time when the reigning Pharaoh had ordered all newborn Israelite boys killed, ended up as the adopted son of Pharaoh's daughter (who gave him his name). Discovering his true origins, he slew one of his people's oppressors and fled to the wilderness of Sinai; there, God imposed on him the task of leading the Israelites out of bondage in Egypt to their ancestors' land. During the forty years' saga of wanderings, Moses received the Ten Commandments on Mount Sinai, and built a Tabernacle where Yahweh spoke to him from atop the Ark of the Covenant; yet, in the end, he was denied entry to the Promised Land and died on Mount Nebo, on the eastern side of the Jordan River. ZS has shown that if the dating of the Exodus strictly follows the biblical data, it took place in 1433 B.C. and "Pharaoh's Daughter" who adopted Moses was the childless princess Hatshepsut, who belonged to a dynasty in which royal names included the suffix 'MSS' (e.g., RA-MSES). *See* Ark of the Covenant, Exodus.

▶ Mount *Moriah* (= 'Mount of Pointing the Way'): The central of Jerusalem's three mounts, where the Temple was built—and where, per ZS, the post-Diluvial Mission Control Center of the Anunnaki was located.

▶ Mount Olympus: The abode, according to Greek legends, of the twelve Olympian gods, headed by Zeus.

▶ Mount Sinai: The mountain on which, according to the Book of Exodus, Yahweh landed in His *Kavod* in full view of the Israelite people, and where Moses received the tablets with the Ten Commandments. Monks at the St. Katherine monastery in the mountainous southern Sinai call a nearby peak 'Mount Moses' and identify it as the biblical Mount Sinai. Such an identification requires what scholars call a 'Southern Route' for the Exodus. For reasons given in *The Stairway to Heaven* ZS supports the 'Central Route' approach, according to which the real Mount Sinai is located farther north in the flatter part of the peninsula. ZS has also suggested that the Mount was linked to the Anunnaki's post-Diluvial spaceport facilities, and was the "Mount **Mashu**" where Gilgamesh went to be taken aloft. *See* Exodus, Kavod, St. Katherine Monastery.

▶ Mount *Zaphon*: Hebrew for 'Mount of the North'—the biblical name of a mountain peak in northern Canaan; the name could also mean in Hebrew 'Mount of the Hidden Secret'. Because the Canaanite epic tale of Keret describes the mount as "the mount of Ba'al" and his "sacred circuit . . . the circuit of broad span," ZS identified it as the 'Landing Place' of Baalbek in Lebanon. *See* Crest of Zaphon.

▶ **Mu:** A Sumerian term whose interpretation as "Name" ignores its meaning when used in texts describing the aircraft of the Anunnaki (such as the "Divine Black Bird" of Ninurta, the "Heavenly Boat" of Inanna, or the "Supreme Traveler" of Marduk). ZS interpreted it as a technical term for the 'Sky Chamber' itself, and reinforced such understanding with the pictographs that evolved into the cuneiform sign for **Mu**. *See* Aerial Chariots, Shem.

▶ Music, Musical Instruments: Contrary to long held views that Western music had its origin in Greece, discoveries of musical instruments (such as elaborately designed harps), depictions of musicians with their instruments, hymnal texts, words of lullabies, and even cuneiform musical notes—leave no doubt that music was among the many Sumerian Firsts, harmonically in accord with modern music.

▸ Mycenaean Civilization: The civilization that appeared in mainland Greece after 1500 B.C. Together with the earlier Minoan civilization, it formed the basis of classic Greek civilization.

N

▸ **Nabu** ('He Who Speaks [For]'): Marduk's son by his Earthling wife Sarpanit, whose name **En.sag** (= 'Lofty Lord') was changed to the epithet-name **Nabu**, indicating his role as 'Spokesman' for his father in the efforts to gain for Marduk human followers. His epithet-name and role could well be the origin of the biblical term *Nabih*—commonly translated 'prophet', but literally meaning a 'Spokesman' (for God). While his father was in exile, he proselytized for him and converted the people in the Dead Sea area cities to Marduk's side; Mount Nebo on the Jordan's eastern shore, from which Moses saw the Promised Land before he died, is one of the landmarks in that area named after Nabu. After Marduk triumphed, Nabu came annually to Babylon from his 'cult center' Borsippa for the New Year ceremonies, during which Marduk's being buried alive inside the Great Pyramid and triumphant emergence was re-enacted in 'Passion Plays'. Because Nabu was the god's son by his Earthling-wife Sarpanit, the events in the 21st century B.C. evolved to messianic expectations (especially in Egypt) with elements of a Trinity. *See* Akiti, En.sag, Messianic Clock, Marduk, Prophets, Sarpanit, War of the Kings.

▸ *Nabuna'id* (= 'Nabu is exalted'): The son of the High Priestess of the god Sin in Harran who (in 555 B.C.) became Babylon's last king. The unusual circumstances of his ascension to the throne, associated with historic upheavals and the departure of Sin and other Anunnaki gods from Earth, are described on four stelas that archaeologists have discovered in Harran. It was when Nabunaid went into self exile in Arabia and his son Belshazzar reigned as regent in Babylon, that the ominous events described in the Bible's Book of Daniel took place. *See* Adda-Guppi, Babylon, Ehulhul, Harran, Sin.

▶ Nabupolassar (*Nabu-aplu-usur* = '[the god] Nabu his son protects'): A Babylonian king (625–606 B.C.) who for a while re-established Babylonian supremacy by joining the Medians in vanquishing Assyria, then defeating the Egyptian army at Carcemish. He was the father of the famed Nebuchadnezzar.

▶ NAHARIN (= 'The Two Rivers'): The Egyptian name for the Upper Euphrates area. Called *Aram Nahara'yim* (= 'The West of the Two Rivers') in the Bible, it was a region whose heartland centered on the Khabur River where Harran was located; it was where the relatives of the Israelites continued to live after Abraham had left Harran for Canaan. At the start of Egypt's New Kingdom circa 1560 B.C. the area was part of the Hurrian kingdom of Mitanni, and famed Pharaohs of the 18th dynasty persisted in attempts to capture Naharin. ZS, in *The End of Days*, has linked the biblical story of the Exodus to those Egyptian-Mitannian wars, and suggested that the Egyptian reason for oppressing the Israelites ("lest they join our enemies") was fear of an Israelite 'Fifth Column' allied with the Mitannians back in Harran. *See* Exodus, Harran, Hurrians, New Kingdom, Patriarchs, Thothmes.

▶ *Nahash*: (H) for 'Serpent', as in the Bible's tale of Adam and Eve in the Garden of Eden. ZS, suggesting that the tale recorded a second genetic manipulation by Enki and Ningishzida to give the new hybrid the ability to procreate, pointed out that—as in the case of the Sumerian epithet **Buzur** for Enki, the term *Nahash* meant both 'Serpent' and "He who knows/solves mysteries."

▶ *Nahor*: Named in the Bible as one of the two brothers of Abraham; he stayed back in Sumer when their father, Terah, moved with Abraham from Ur to Harran.

▶ Nahuatl: The language of the Aztecs and other tribes in central Mexico.

‣ *Nahum*: A biblical Prophet whose prophecy regarding the fall of Assyria's capital Nineveh when its protective dams would be broken, came exactly true in 612 B.C.

‣ Nakhl: An oasis town in Sinai's central plain at the crossroads of ancient 'Ways' near wadi el-Arish. ZS has suggested that it had been a major Israelite stop during the Exodus and linked the town's name to *Nikhal* (Sumerian **Nin.gal**), spouse of the god *Sin* (the peninsula's probable namesake). *See also* Abraham, Brook of Egypt, Exodus.

‣ **Nam**: A Sumerian term that meant unavoidable 'Destiny'—as Man's destiny to die, no matter what; it was distinguished from **Nam.tar** (which should be correctly translated 'Fate')—a destiny that could be 'bent' (as when a man's free choice to be righteous could earn him a better or longer life, though without escaping his final mortality).

‣ **Nam.tar**: In Sumerian texts, Namtar (in addition to its meaning, of a Destiny that can be 'bent') was the personal name of the Chief Counselor of Ereshkigal, mistress of the Lower World.

‣ **Nannar** (= 'The Bright One'; sometimes shortened to **Nanna**): The Sumerian 'Moon god'—a son, born on Earth, of Enlil and Ninlil. His better-known Akkadian name *Sin* stemmed from his nickname **Su.en** (= 'Multiplying Lord'), for he was the father of the twins Utu/Shamash and Inanna/Ishtar. His 'cult centers' were Ur in Sumer and Harran in Upper Mesopotamia. His numerical rank was 30. Lamentation Texts regarding the nuclear wind that decimated Sumer, assert that Nannar and his spouse delayed their escape from their beloved Ur, and suggest that Nannar was somehow afflicted by the Evil Wind. Later texts dealing with the Day of the Lord and the departure from Earth of the Anunnaki, describe events in Harran that involved the leaving, and then return, of Nannar/Sin and the appointment by him of Babylonia's last king. *See* Adda-Guppi, Harran, Nabuna'id, Sin.

‣ **Nanshe**: A Sumerian goddess of astronomical oracles.

‣ Napoleon Bonaparte: The French emperor who combined a military expedition to Egypt (in 1798) with extensive scientific studies that laid the foundations of modern Egyptology.

▸ *Naram-Sin* (= 'Favored by [the god] Sin'): A grandson of Sargon I, the founder of the Akkadian dynasty, under whose reign (2260–2223 B.C.) Akkad reached its peak. The subject of epic tales and numerous inscriptions (and a famed monument now in the Louvre), he overran other city-states, with the Landing Place in the Cedar Mountain as the ultimate prize. Claiming to have warred "on orders of my gods" (mostly, the goddess Ishtar), his demise was likewise deemed due to campaigns not authorized by the gods; when he died, the Akkadian capital, Agade, was wiped off the face of the Earth, never to be found. *See* Akkad, Akkadians, Sargon.

▸ Narmer: The first Pharaoh. *See* Men.

▸ Navel of the Earth: A term applied to Nippur (before the Deluge) and to Jerusalem (afterward), when they served as Mission Control Center of the Anunnaki. *See relevant entries.*

▸ Naymlap: Local lore in South America about early settlers arriving by boats on the Pacific coast, includes the 'Legend of Naymlap', a leader of a fleet of balsa-reed boats who was guided to a landing place in Ecuador by a green stone through which the god's directions were heard. The legends assert that he did not die, for after accomplishing his mission, he was given wings by the god of the whispering stone, and flew away. *See* Santa Elena.

▸ Nazca, Nazca Lines: The location in southern Peru where images of actual and legendary animals, so huge that their true shape can be realized only from the air, were engraved into the desert soil, alongside miles-long runway-like lines or trapezoid shapes similarly cut into the soil. Attempts to explain the Lines by astronomical orientation have failed, as have attempts to have locals emulate the lines or images by handscraping the soil. ZS has suggested that Nazca is where the Anunnaki had departed from Earth. *See* Adad, End of Days, Tiahuanacu, Viracocha.

▶ Near East: A scholarly term that loosely embraces geographically Western Asia (including Asia Minor), culturally the lands of the ancient civilizations of Mesopotamia, and historically the 'Lands of the Bible'— sometimes including Iran farther east, sometimes sweeping in (though not fully properly) African Egypt.

▶ Nebuchadnezzar II: A major Babylonian king (reigned 605–562 B.C.) who aggrandized Babylon and its empire on behalf of his gods Marduk and Nabu (after whom he was named). He began his career as a general under his father the king Nabupolassar, defeating Assyrian and then Egyptian armies. As king, he expanded Babylonian (and thus the gods' Marduk and Nabu) dominance to the former Sumer & Akkad, to the erstwhile Canaan and Phoenicia, and to the Sinai all the way to Egypt's border. ZS has suggested that the driving motivation was control of the olden space-related sites in anticipation of the imminent return of Nibiru and an expected repeat visit by Anu. Nebuchadnezzar's extensive inscriptions corroborate the Bible's record of his besieging and capturing Jerusalem (598/597 B.C.), when he exiled Judea's leaders and priests (including the Prophet Ezekiel). He returned in 587 B.C. to destroy the Temple (586 B.C.). *See* Baalbek, Carchemish, Jerusalem.

▶ *Nefilim* (H): The term appears in the Bible's description of conditions on Earth before the Deluge (Genesis 6): "The *Nefilim* were upon the Earth in those days [before the Deluge] and thereafter too, when the sons of the *Elohim* cohabited with the daughters of the Adam and they bore children unto them." The beginning of the verse is commonly rendered "there were giants upon the Earth." It was ZS's questioning of his teacher why the word *Nefilim* (literally, "Those who had come down") is wrongly translated 'giants' that started his interest in the subject. The reason for the mistranslation is the biblical explanation (Numbers 13:33) that the *Nefilim* were **Anakim**—a word taken to mean 'giants'. But that, ZS has suggested in his books, was the Hebrew for **Anunnaki**. Sumerian texts, in fact, cite incidents of Anunnaki (specifically, the 300 **Igi.gi**) intermarrying with the "daughters of Man." *See* Anunnaki, Igigi, Marduk.

▸ *Negev* (H = 'The Arid Zone'): Israel's southern and mostly arid part. Bordering the Sinai peninsula, it featured in several biblical events.

▸ Nelson's Chamber: The third up of the compartments, sometimes called 'Relieving Chambers', above the so-called 'King's Chamber' in the Great Pyramid of Giza. It was discovered by Howard Vyse on April 25, 1837, after he had started using gunpowder to blast his way up, naming it 'Nelson's Chamber' after Britain's naval hero. ZS has cast doubt on some of the Vyse claims in *The Stairway to Heaven* and in *Journeys to the Mythical Past*. *See* Great Pyramid of Giza.

▸ Nephtys (Greek for NEBT-HAT = 'Lady of the House'): A major goddess of ancient Egypt, the sister of Isis and the wife of Seth.

▸ Neptune: The Roman god of the seas who (also as the Greek Poseidon) emulated the Sumerian **E.a** ('Whose home is waters'). The planet now called 'Neptune' was likewise associated with Ea/Enki in the Mesopotamian Epic of Creation.

▸ **Ner.gal** (= 'Great Watcher'): A son of Enki who married Ereshkigal (a sister of Inanna/Ishtar) and lorded with her over the Lower World (southern Africa). At first he attempted to be a peacemaker between his ambitious half-brother Marduk and the Enlilites; but in the end he turned against Marduk and carried out the nuclear attack on the 'Sinning Cities' (Sodom, Gomorrah and three others) in the Plain of the 'Sea of Salt'—a deed for which he was given the epithet *Erra* ('The Annihilator'). *See* Erra Epic, Lower World.

▸ New Kingdom: A scholarly term used to distinguish a new, aggressive and eventful era in ancient Egypt from the 'Old Kingdom' and 'Middle Kingdom' periods. It began, after a second 'Intermediate Period', circa 1560 B.C., with the famed 18th dynasty. *See* Exodus, Hatshepsut, Moses, Ramses, Thothmes.

▸ New Year Festival: The central religious event in Mesopotamia was the New Year Festival, celebrated on the first day of spring (calendrically, the first day of the month Nissanu). Called **A.ki.ti** (= 'Build on Earth Life') in Sumer (and *Akitu* in Babylonia), it was replete with symbolic rituals involving the makeup of the solar system, Nibiru and its orbit, and the journey of the Anunnaki from it to Earth. Treated as an opportunity for an affirmation of the Faith, the ceremonies included the public reading of *Enuma elish* (the Epic of Creation) on the fourth night of the twelve-day festival. Part of the steps taken in Babylon to assert the supremacy of Marduk was the revision of the Epic of Creation by calling Nibiru 'Planet Marduk' and claiming for Marduk the creative feats of other gods. *See* Calendars, Marduk, Nabu, Nibiru.

▶ **Nibiru**: The name, in the Epic of Creation, of the planet that invaded the Solar System, and assisted by its seven satellites or moons engaged in a 'Celestial Battle' with a planet called Tiamat. After defeating and cleaving Tiamat, the invader joined the Solar System with an orbit that surpassed those of all the other planets. While the Epic is generally treated as a myth or an allegorical tale, ZS has treated it as a rendering of a sophisticated cosmogony dealing with the makeup of the Solar System and life on Earth. Nibiru (renamed 'Marduk' by the Babylonians), is listed as a planet in Mesopotamian astronomical texts and sky maps, and scholars have argued whether it was just another name for either Jupiter or Mars; but by treating the Epic of Creation as factual astronomy, ZS has concluded that it is the Sumerian name of one more planet in our Solar System that, when nearing the Sun, passed between Jupiter and Mars. The planet's name **Nibiru** meant "Planet of Crossing"—crossing and recrossing the place of the Celestial Battle; and Sumerian depictions signified it by the sign of the Cross. The reappearance of this sign in depictions in the 7th and 6th centuries B.C. served as one of the clues in ZS's book *The End of Days* for deciphering biblical prophecies about the 'Day of the Lord'; many of the Assyrian and Babylonian astronomical texts from that time actually served as guidelines for observing the planet Nibiru as it returned to Earth's vicinity. *See* Ashurbanipal, Astronomy, Celestial Battle, Cross, Day of the Lord, Epic of Creation, Sar, Tiamat.

▶ Nibiru's Orbit: The Sumerian King List measures the lengths of reign by pre-Diluvial Anunnaki rulers in units of **Sar**—a Sumerian term that represents the numeral 3,600. By combining this fact with the zodiacal timing of various key events (such as the Deluge), ZS was able to create a timeline for the periodic return of Nibiru to its perigee (passing closest to the Sun and thus to Earth), and to conclude that—mathematically—Nibiru's great elliptical orbit averaged 3,600 Earth years (but, for the Anunnaki, just one year of their Divine Time). The actual orbital times, especially since the Deluge (as explained in *The End of Days*) digressed from the mathematically perfect Sar. *See* Ages, Astronomy, Day of the Lord, Deluge, Halley's Comet, King Lists, Uranus.

▶ **Nidaba** (Also read **Nisaba**): The Sumerian goddess of writing.

▶ Nile Civilization: A phrase encompassing ancient Egypt and Nubia, termed to match the two other civilizations named after their rivers—the Tigris-Euphrates (Mesopotamia) in the Near East (the First Region of Sumerian texts), and that of the Indus River (the Sumerian Third Region).

▶ Nile River: Africa's longest river, originating in mountainous Uganda and Ethiopia and reaching the Mediterranean Sea in Egypt, more than 4,000 miles in the north. In its southern part it gushes through several gorges and falls (with six main 'cataracts'), but becomes wider and navigable from the city of Aswan (ancient Siena) northward. With hardly any rainfall, Egypt, its agriculture, and indeed civilization, have depended on the Nile and its life-giving waters. Ancient texts ascribed to the god Ptah (= Enki, per ZS) the regulating of the rise and fall of the river's waters by installing sluices near the island of Elephantine in Upper Egypt—where the modern Aswan Dam now performs a similar function. *See* Aswan.

▶ *Nimrod*: The Book of Genesis names the otherwise unidentified 'Nimrod' as the "mighty hunter by the grace of Yahweh" who—after the Deluge—began Kingship in "Babel and Erech and Akkad, all in the Land of Shine'ar; out of that land there emanated Ashur, where Nineveh was built." Nimrod was thus credited in the Bible with starting Man's kingship in Mesopotamia—the lands of Sumer, Akkad, Babylon, and Assyria. Mesopotamian texts credited Ninurta with such a First (in the Sumerian city of Kish). Was 'Nimrod' then a biblical rendering of 'Nini-urta'? It's a good guess: *see* Nineveh, Ninurta.

▸ Nimrud: The name of a site, in what is now northern Iraq, of an Assyrian military center and, on and off, also a royal capital, called Khalhu. In 1988 archaeologists unearthed there, in tombs of three Assyrian queens, a treasure of jewelry and other golden artifacts, known as 'The Nimrud Treasure'. (The Nimrud artifacts were missing from the Iraq National Museum after the fall of Saddam Hussein, and were presumed looted; but were later found intact in the vaults of the Iraq National Bank.)

▸ **Nin.a.gal** (= 'Prince of the Great Waters'): One of Enki's six sons whose domain was in Africa.

▸ Nineveh: An ancient settlement on the eastern shores of the Tigris River (now across the river from Mosul, in the Kurdish region of northern Iraq). Until archaeological excavations in the 19th century began to bring back to light Assyria and its major cities, Nineveh was known only from the Bible, from such tales as the failed siege of Jerusalem by the Assyrian king Sennacherib, or of Jonah and the Whale. When the city was excavated and vast written records were found in its temples and palaces, it emerged as the dazzling royal capital of the three greatest Assyrian kings—Sennacherib, Esarhaddon, and Ashurbanipal (*see relevant entries*). The city's Assyrian name, *Nin-uah*, suggests that it was named after the god Ninurta—whom the Bible might have called Nimrod when it attributed to that 'Divine Hunter' the founding of Assyria's major cities, including Nineveh. *See also* Nimrod, Ninurta.

▸ **Nin.gal** (= 'Great Lady'; *Nikhal* or *Nikkal* in Akkadian): The spouse of Nannar/Sin, mother of the twins Utu/Shamash and Inanna/Ishtar, and of Ereshkigal. *See* Nakhl.

▸ **Nin.girsu**: The epithet by which Gudea called Ninurta in the records of building a new temple in the **Girsu**, the sacred precinct of Lagash. *See* Bau, Girsu, Gudea, Lagash, Ninurta.

▸ **Nin.gish.zi.da** (= 'Princely-Lord of the Tree of Life'; also **Nin.gish.zidda**

= 'Lord of the Artifact of Life'): A god of science, son of Enki, who assisted his father in the second genetic feat that is the theme of the biblical Garden of Eden tale. He provided architectural instructions for the E.Ninnu temple built by Gudea in Lagash, where a splendid vase engraved with the emblem of Ningishzida—a staff with Entwined Serpents on it—was discovered. ZS has identified him as Thoth—the Egyptian god of science, as well as the Mesoamerican god Quetzalcoatl. *See* Eden, Gudea, Ninurta, Resurrection, Quetzalcoatl, Thoth.

▶ **Nin.ḫar.sag** ('Lady/Mistress of the Mountain peak'): A daughter of Anu, she came to Earth as Chief Medical Officer, and helped Enki in the genetic engineering of the 'Primitive Worker'—gaining the epithets **Nin.ti** (= 'Lady who gives Life') and **Mammi** (= 'Mother goddess'). As half-sister of Enki and Enlil, she was desired by both, ended up marrying none, but had a lovechild—Ninurta—by Enlil. By unraveling the complex succession rules of the Anunnaki, ZS has shown how Ninharsag found herself at the center of the rivalries that led to the Pyramid Wars and the peacemaking efforts to end them. Respected by both clans, she was granted dominion over the Fourth Region, the Sinai peninsula. Her rank, 15, her constellation (which we call Virgo, 'The Maiden') and her planet ('Venus') were in time taken over by the ambitious Inanna/Ishtar. The Egyptians too considered Ninharsag 'Mistress of the Sinai', named her ḤAT.ḤOR (= 'Who gave abode to Horus'), but in her old age nicknamed her 'The Cow'.

▶ **Nin.kashi** (= 'Lady of the Straw'): The goddess in charge of beer—an alcoholic beverage that the Sumerians (as many depictions show) drank from a vessel with long individual straws.

▶ **Nin.ki** ('Lady/Mistress of Earth'): The spouse of Enki who came to Earth from Nibiru with their son Marduk. Also known as **Dam.ki.na** (= 'Lady Who to Earth Came').

▶ **Nin.lil** (= 'Lady of the Command'): The title-name granted to **Sud** (= 'Nurse') a young Anunnaki female whom Enlil married after he had date-raped her. Mother of his sons Nannar/Sin and Ishkur/Adad.

▶ **Nin.mah** (= 'Mighty Lady'): The original epithet-name of Ninharsag.

▶ **Nin.sun** (= "Lady Who Irrigates'): The goddess who was the mother of Gilgamesh (the father was the High Priest of Uruk) and other Sumerian demigods.

▶ **Nin.ti** (= 'Lady of Life'): The epithet for Ninharsag in the texts dealing with the creation of Man. *See* Ninharsag.

▶ **Ninurta** (from **Nini.urta** = 'Hunter [and] Ploughman'): The firstborn son of Enlil by Enlil's half-sister Ninharsag, and therefore in line to succeed Enlil and his rank of Fifty, just below that of Anu; his emblem was a double-headed eagle. His feats, that earned him a variety of epithet-names, were recorded in hymns and epics and were the subject of cylinder-seal depictions; they included erecting dams after the Deluge to make Mesopotamia habitable again, and bestowing the plough to Mankind; defeating the evil Zu who had stolen the Tablets of Destinies from Enlil; leading the Enlilites in the Pyramid Wars against Marduk; and joining the god Nergal in the launching of nuclear weapons; it was he, according to the Erra Epic (where he is called *Ishum*, 'The Scorcher'), who nuked the Spaceport in the Sinai. Quoting clay tablet texts, ZS (in *The Wars of Gods and Men*) explained various enigmas concerning inner features in the Great Pyramid of Giza as resulting from Ninurta's attack and entry when Marduk took refuge inside it. Gudea, king of Lagash, described in long inscriptions how he built for Ninurta and his spouse the temple **E.Ninnu** (= 'House/Temple of Fifty'), including a special enclosure for the god's winged aircraft. *See* Aerial Battles, Aerial Chariots, Bau/Gula, E.Ninnu, Erra Epic, Great Pyramid of Giza, Gudea, Kingship, Lagash, Nimrod.

▶ *Nippur*: Akkadian from **Ne.ibru** (= 'The Splendid Place of Crossing'), the pre-Diluvial Mission Control Center of the Anunnaki, where Enlil's **Dur.an.ki** (= 'Bond Heaven-Earth') maintained the link with their planet Nibiru. Also called **Nibru.ki**—translated 'Navel of the Earth' because it was at the center of the landmarks that formed the pre-Diluvial Landing Corridor, and deemed equidistant from "the four corners of the Earth." Rebuilt after the Deluge precisely at its former location, it was Sumer's religious center, site of Enlil's sacred precinct and ziggurat/temple (from which, according to a 'Hymn to Enlil', "his Eye could scan the Earth," his "Lifted beam could penetrate all"). Per ZS, it was the birthplace of Abram/Abraham who called himself an **Ibri** (= 'A Nippurian'). *See* Abraham, Enlil, Landing Corridor, Mission Control Center.

▶ Nippur Calendar: A Sumerian 12 month luni-solar calendar, that periodically adjusted the lunar months to the solar year by adding a 13th month in a leap year. It was adopted by the Babylonians and then by others in the ancient Near East, and still serves as the Jewish calendar to this day, retaining the Akkadian/Babylonian month names and order. Since the Jewish calendar counts the Common Era (A.D.) year 2009 as year 5769, ZS has concluded that the Calendar of Nippur had to begin in 3760 B.C.—soon after the Sumerian civilization began. In Mesopotamia, the New Year began precisely on the day of the Spring Equinox, which was declared the first day of the First Month; called *Nisannu* in Akkadian (Hebrew *Nisan*), it was named in Sumerian the **Ezen** (= 'Festival') month honoring **Anu**. During the Exodus the Israelites were ordered to begin the New Year on the day of the Autumnal Equinox; but the Bible clearly recognized the month, *Tishrei* (Akkadian *Teshritu*) as "the seventh month."

▶ *Nissanu* (= 'Signaling'): The Akkadian name of the first month of the Nippur Calendar (H *Nissan*) that began on the first day of spring. *See* Nippur Calendar.

▶ *Noah* (H = 'Respite'): The biblical hero of the Deluge. In the Bible, it was the same God who decided to have mankind perish, as well as the one who saved it through Noah; in the Mesopotamian versions, it was Enlil who was fed up with mankind, and Enki who saved it through his chosen follower (**Ziusudra** in Sumerian, *Utnapishtim* in Akkadian). *See* Ararat, Deluge, Shuruppak, Yahweh.

▶ Noah's Ark: Built according to the deity's instructions to survive the

Deluge, it is called in the Bible *Tebah* (literally, a box, but translated 'Ark'); in the Akkadian texts it is called *Tebitu* = a boat that is sinkable, and in Sumerian **Ma.gur.gur** = 'a boat that can turn and tumble'—per ZS, a submersible boat that could withstand the avalanche of water.

▸ NTR: The Egyptian term for 'god', akin to the Semitic *NTR* meaning 'Watcher, Guardian'. It was depicted hieroglyphically by an axe with a long handle.

▸ Nubia: An ancient African kingdom to the south of Egypt, today's Sudan (and Ethiopia?), considered part of the greater Nile Civilization. The Egyptians valued it as a source of gold and ivory. *See* Meluhha, Meroe, Omphalos.

▸ Nuclear Weapons: A series of Sumerian texts known as Lamentation Texts ascribe the demise of the Sumerian civilization, at the end of the 3rd millennium B.C., to an "Evil Wind" that brought death to people, animals and flora without destroying any buildings. Cities, houses, stalls, sheepfolds were desolated and emptied; their occupants met a terrible death, "an unseen death," from which there was no escape. The Evil Wind that withered all plants and made the waters "bitter" came blowing from the west. It was, the texts repeatedly stated, "a calamity unknown to man, one that had never been seen before." While the prevalent scholarly guess has been that the texts describe a climate change, ZS has placed the occurrence in the context (and dating) of the mounting conflict between the Anunnaki clans, and linked the unique calamity to the detailed description in the Erra Epic of the decision to use seven hidden "Awesome Weapons" to thwart Marduk's ambitions. In 2024 B.C., ZS has concluded, nuclear weapons were used to wipe out the Spaceport in the Sinai and the nearby five "sinning cities" south of the Dead Sea—the 'upheavaling' of Sodom and Gomorrah as described in the Bible. The unintended consequence was the blowing of the nuclear cloud eastward to bring death to Sumer. *See* Erra Epic, Nabu, Nergal, Ninurta.

▸ **Nudimmud** (= 'He Who Fashions Artifacts' or 'The Artful Creator'): An epithet for Enki, paralleled by his Egyptian name PTAH (= 'He Who Fashions/Develops'). *See* Ea/Enki.

▸ **Nusku**: A Divine Emissary who was Enlil's 'chamberlain' or 'chief of staff', and in later times served as an aide to Nannar/Sin in Harran.

▸ NUT (= 'Sky'): A primeval goddess of Egypt who symbolized the heavens.

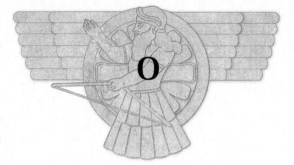

O

- Oannes: Berossus, the Babylonian 3rd century B.C. historian, ascribed the grant of civilization to Mankind to a legendary god—a "Being, endowed with reason"—who had come out of the sea which bordered on Babylonia, taught Mankind, and gave it "Kingship." This god, whose name was rendered by subsequent Greek savants as 'Oannes', looked like a fish, but had a human head under the fish's head, had feet like a man under the fish's tail, and "his voice too and language were articulate and human." The image of the fishman-god is known from Mesopotamian depictions of Ea/Enki priests, and there is general agreement that the Berossus reference is to Ea, who (according to his own autobiography) splashed down in the waters of the Persian Gulf and waded ashore where civilization was later granted to Mankind. *See* Ea/Enki, Eridu.

- Oaxaca: A Mexican archaeological site, named after the southwestern state and its capital city, where a pre-Aztec monument with the oldest-discovered inscription referring to the Sacred Round of 52 years was found. *See* Quetzalcoatl.

- *Obadiah* (H = 'Who worships Yahweh'): A biblical Prophet who, circa 570 B.C., announced that "The Day of the Lord is near." *See* Day of the Lord.

- Obelisks: Monumental stone pillars that taper off to a pyramidlike top that 12th dynasty Pharaohs began to erect in pairs at temple entrances. Called 'Beams of the gods' in ancient Egypt, they were described as 'stone needles' ("obeliscus") by Herodotus, and the name stuck ever since. Most of the obelisks that survived were carted off to Rome and the Vatican, and to world capitals such as London, Paris, Istanbul and New York. ZS viewed them as stone replicas of the gods' rocketships.

▸ Observatories: Structures that served in antiquity as astronomical observatories have been found both in the Old and the New Worlds. Beginning in Sumer (as early as circa 4000 B.C., when Anu and Antu visited Earth) the ziggurats of Mesopotamia—step-pyramids that usually rose in seven stages—served to observe the night skies for planetary phenomena or the zodiacal background at the moment of sunrise. Structures with circular observation chambers (such as the temple built in Lagash by Gudea, the Caracol in Chichén Itzá) served to observe the zodiacal constellations. Other structures, involving stones erected in circles (Gilgal Rephaim on the Golan, Stonehenge in England) were oriented to observe solstices. Twin-towered temples co-oriented with an observation post (such as in the Aztec capital) were built to observe equinoxes; and windows in stone walls (as twice in Machu Picchu) served to observe both equinoxes and solstices. And though not regular observatories, temples from Karnak to Jerusalem to Cuzco were oriented to either the solstices or equinoxes.

▸ Old Testament: A term applied by theologians to the Hebrew Bible, to distinguish it from the later collection of writings concerning Jesus, called the New Testament. *See* TaNaKH.

▸ Ollantaytambu: A mountain site with inexplicable megalithic structures in Peru, some sixty miles northwest of Cuzco. The intricately cut and shaped stone blocks are made of stones that were quarried miles away, on another mountain range across a river valley.

▸ Olmecs: Enigmatic people credited with the earliest or 'Mother' civilization in Mesoamerica who, to judge by their facial and racial features, were black Africans. Their existence came to light when colossal sculpted stone heads (weighing over 20 tons each), depicting helmeted men, began to be found at the end of the 19th century in areas adjoining the Gulf of Mexico—finds followed by the unearthing of major Olmec urban centers now known as Tres Zapotes, La Venta, Izapa, San

Lorenzo and other sites reaching south all the way to the Pacific coast. In those places ceremonial plazas, graves lined with semi-precious jade, concave mirrors made of crystallized iron ore were discovered, as well as hundreds of artistic sculptures of all shapes and sizes, depicting them holding engineering-like tools. The sculpted artifacts also included, per ZS in *The Earth Chronicles Expeditions*, telltale wheeled toys and a toy elephant! Most significantly, Olmec monuments bearing glyph-writing and dates according to the Long Count leave no doubt that it was they who introduced this calendar in Mesoamerica. Most scholars suggest 1400/1500 B.C. as the Olmec starting date, but leave unanswered the Why and How of their coming millennia before Columbus. ZS believes that the start coincided with this calendar's Day One in 3113 B.C. and that the African Olmecs accompanied Thoth (alias Quetzalcoatl = 'The Winged Serpent') when Ra chased him out of Egypt, circa 3100 B.C. The Olmecs faded out of the Mesoamerican scene with the rise of the Mayas, circa 500 B.C. *See* Calendars, Mesoamerica, Quetzalcoatl, Thoth.

▸ Olympian gods: The group of twelve gods, headed by Zeus, who according to Greek lore were based on Mount Olympus.

▸ Omphalos: A short conical stone column rounded at the top that served as an Oracle Stone at certain sacred places, such as Delphi in Greece. Derived from the Latin 'umbilicus' (= 'navel'), Omphalos stones were revered as a means for communicating with the celestial gods—a tradition, per ZS, that harked back to Nippur—the Sumerian 'Navel of the Earth', where the **Dur.an.ki**, a 'Bond'—a virtual 'umbilical cord'— connected Earth with Heaven. A Canaanite text described a "stone that whispers" divine words, that the god Baal used for communicating, at Baalbek. Alexander the Great, seeking confirmation for his demigod status, consulted such oracle stones not only in Delphi, but also at the Siwa oasis in Egypt and one in Nubia.

▸ Osiris (Greek for ASAR): The ancient Egyptian god of death and resurrection. He and his brother Seth were sons of the divine couple GEB and NUT (themselves descended of PTAH and RA). Egyptian texts relate that the two brothers, who married their half-sisters Isis and Nephtys, quarreled about control of the Nile Valley; Seth, by trickery, killed Osiris, cut his body up, and spread the parts far and wide. But Isis managed to retrieve the parts, reassembled and mummified Osiris, and with the help of the god Thoth was impregnated with the semen of Osiris and gave birth to a son, the avenging god Horus. Egyptian Pharaohs expected to journey to an Afterlife by being mummified, to become resurrected like Osiris. *See* Afterlife.

- **Pa.bil** (= 'The Defender'): The Sumerian name for the zodiacal constellation we call Sagittarius (= 'The Archer').

- Pachacamac (= 'Creator of the World'): The principal deity of the central Andean pantheon, for whom a "Vatican City" of pilgrimages was built in pre-Inca times, not far from today's Lima in Peru. The god was also known as 'Rimac', meaning 'The Thunderer', and ZS has wondered whether it was a corruption of 'Raman' (= 'The Thunderer')—one of the epithets, in the ancient Near East, of the god Ishkur/Adad who—in the southern Andes—was called 'Viracocha' ('Creator of All'). *See* Adad, Tiahuanacu, Viracocha.

- Palmyra (= 'The Place of Palms'): An ancient city in what is now eastern Syria, known for monumental ruins from the Graeco-Roman period. The Bible called it *Tadmor* and attributed its development from a desert oasis to a major caravan center on the way from Damascus to Mesopotamia to king Solomon.

- Paradise: What has come to mean the place of optimal and ultimate physical, spiritual and religious attainment, is simply called in the Bible (H) *Gan Eden* ('The Garden/Orchard of Eden')—which ZS has explained as stemming from **E.din** ('Abode of the Righteous Ones'), the pre-Diluvial name given by the Anunnaki to their abode in southern Mesopotamia. *See* Rivers of Paradise.

- Parthenon: The main temple to the goddess Athena (nicknamed 'Parthenos'

= 'The Maiden') in the sacred precinct ('acropolis') of Athens, Greece. It was built to replace an earlier, smaller temple to Athena that was destroyed in the 5th century B.C. during the Persian invasion. By comparing the orientations of the two temples Sir Norman Lockyer laid the foundation of Archaeoastronomy.

▸ Passover (H *Pesaḥ*): The weeklong Jewish holiday, prescribed in the Bible, commemorating the Israelite Exodus from Egypt. Traditionally, Jewish pilgrims gathered in Jerusalem for the holiday, and according to the New Testament Jesus has been so coming to Jerusalem since childhood. *See* Exodus, Jesus, Last Supper.

▸ Patriarchs: The Bible lists ten pre-Diluvial patriarchs of Mankind, beginning with Adam through Noah (but neither counting the first two sons of Adam and Eve, Cain and Abel, nor the descendants of Cain); they are recognized by scholars to parallel the same number of pre-Diluvial Anunnaki 'gods' and demigods named in the Sumerian King Lists. ZS has shown that the 432,000 years assigned to those ten Sumerian pre-Diluvial patriarchs matches the lengths given in the Bible if, under the sexagesimal numbers system, the latter are multiplied by 60. Though the Bible provides in Genesis 10 the post-Diluvial genealogical lines descended from the three sons of Noah, only Abraham (a descendant of Shem), his son Isaac and his grandson Jacob are the "biblical Patriarchs" through whom God has made a Covenant with the Hebrew people.

▸ People of the Sea: Unidentified invaders who beleaguered the Asian and African coasts of the Mediterranean Sea around the middle of the 2nd millennium B.C. They are depicted in sea-battle scenes on a temple built by Ramses III (at Medinet Habu, Egypt) as warriors wearing plumed helmets; ZS, in *The Earth Chronicles Expeditions*, drew attention to the enigma of similar depictions at the Mayan site of Chichén Itzá in the Yucatan, Mexico.

▸ Peopling of the Americas: The established notion that the first human settlers in the Americas came overland, during the last Ice Age, when the ice bridged Alaska to Siberia, has long been sustained by finds at a site in North America called Clovis. ZS, especially in *The Lost Realms* and *When Time Began*, deemed it irrational (and not just impossible) for people to trek thousands of miles during an Ice Age without knowing in advance what lies beyond the ice shelf, and cited, beside local lore, instances of archaeological finds in Chile (Monte Verde), Brazil (Pedra Furada, Pedra Pintada), etc., to support counter-theories of earlier arrivals by sea. Such finds, as often as not suppressed by establishment academics, have been fully vindicated by now.

▸ Pepi I: A 6th dynasty Egyptian king (circa 2300 B.C.), known for the inscriptions in his pyramid that described his Journey to the Afterlife. Taken literally, they indicated (per ZS) a route to the Sinai peninsula. Continued inscriptions and pictorial depictions describe how the Pharaoh would enter there the "Divine Ascender," to be lofted to "the Imperishable Star." The illustrations then showed Pepi and his spouse in the Celestial Paradise, enjoying the life-giving "Plant of Life" and "Waters of Life." *See* Plant of Life, Pyramid Texts.

▸ Persia, Persians: In terms of history as known in the West, 'Persia' (today's Iran) began with the takeover of the plateau east of the Tigris-Euphrates plain by the Achaemenids, after they helped the Medes (biblical *Maddai*) defeat Assyria at the end of the 7th century B.C., and captured Babylon at the start of the 6th century B.C. Under the leadership of Cyrus II and his son Cambyses II they made the Elamite city Susa (biblical *Shushan*) the capital of a fast-expanding empire that embraced even Egypt, and in less than a century crossed from Asia to Europe to challenge Athenian Greece. The counterattack, led by Alexander the Great, put an end to Persian rule and empire in 330 B.C. The Persian religion is called 'Zoroastrian', with a principal deity called *Ahura-Mazda*; monuments depicted this 'God of Truth and Light' with the symbol of the Winged Disc—the olden ubiquitous Mesopotamian and Egyptian symbol for Nibiru. *See* Achaemenids, Alexander, Anshan, Assyria, Cyrus, Elam.

▸ Persian Gulf: Called the 'Lower Sea' in Sumerian and Akkadian texts.

▶ Peru: The South American country that extends along the Pacific coast from fertile Ecuador in the north to Chile's deserts in the south and Lake Titicaca in the southeast, occupying the Andean mountains and the narrow flatlands between the high mountains and the ocean. Deemed the 'Land of the Incas', for it was them whom the Spaniards encountered when they arrived in 1533, it is now known that numerous other coastal cultures preceded the Incas, with impressive archaeological remains that date back to the mid 3rd millennium B.C. ZS has drawn attention to the little known writings of a Spaniard named Montesinos, who recorded local lore about an 'Ancient Empire' in the Andean highlands long before the Incas, attributing to its kings such enigmatic places as Machu Picchu. Peru, where the Spaniards found incredible quantities of gold and golden artifacts, also lies at the core of the Piri Reis map and Nazca Lines puzzles. *See* Cuzco, Gold, Golden Enclosure, Incas, Machu Picchu, Piri Reis, Nazca, Titicaca, Viracocha.

▶ Pharaoh: The term, used as epithet-title for 'king' in ancient Egypt, is first found in the Bible, where the Hebrew word *Phar'oh* is believed to have been a rendering of the Egyptian PER-OH (= 'Big House') = royal palace, and by extension its resident, the king. Manetho, and king lists found by archaeologists, divided the reigning Pharaohs by dynasties, beginning circa 3100 B.C. and ending in Roman times.

▶ Philistines: Identified as *Plishtim* (H = 'Invaders') in the Bible, they were a sea people of Greek origins who settled in the southern Mediterranean coast of Canaan, occupying approximately the area that is nowadays known as the Gaza Strip. The Bible reports almost constant warfare between them and the Israelites, extending to the time of the first kings (Saul and David). The tales of Samson and Delilah and of David and Goliath took place in that context.

▶ Phobos Incident: In July 1988 the Soviet Union launched two identical unmanned spacecraft to Mars. They were named **Phobos 1** and **Phobos 2** because their main mission, after photographing Mars, was to probe the planet's moonlet Phobos, which some experts suspected was an artificial object. Phobos 1 disappeared without sending back any data; Phobos 2 reached Mars in January 1989 and sent back a series of puzzling photographs: They showed the shadow of an elliptical object flying in the planet's skies—the shadow not of Phobos 2 itself, but of another unidentified flying object. Phobos 2 was then commanded from the Soviet Mission Control to change orbit, fly in tandem with the moonlet Phobos, and probe the moonlet with laser beams; whereupon the spacecraft went into a spin and vanished. The last photograph sent by it showed a missile fired at it from the moonlet. ZS managed at the time to obtain the telltale photographs and published them along with other details of the occurrence, which he dubbed 'The Phobos Incident', in his book *Genesis Revisited,* with an update in *The End of Days.* Though officially unexplained to this day, the Incident led to the rushed adoption, in April 1989, of a secret international agreement titled **Declaration of Principles Concerning Activities Following the Detection of Extraterrestrial Intelligence.** *See* Mars.

▸ Phoenicians: A Semitic-speaking people who settled northern Canaan, at coastal cities such as Tyre and Sidon, from the mid 2nd to the mid 1st millenniums B.C. Seafarers and traders, their ships sailed the Mediterranean Sea and beyond; according to the Bible, H̲iram king of Tyre helped king Solomon obtain gold from *Ophir* by circumnavigating Africa. Their western colonies in north Africa, led by *Keret Hadashah* (= 'New City', alias 'Carthage') in time battled Rome for control of the Mediterranean. *See* Carthage.

▸ Piri Re'is Map: A map, kept at the Topkapi palace-museum in Istanbul, that was cartographed in A.D. 1513 for the Turkish admiral Piri Re'is. One of several 'mapas mundi' ('Maps of the World') from that Age of Discovery, it stands out by the sophistication and accuracy of the methods used to project a globe on a flat surface; then, it clearly shows accurately the whole of South America, including the Pacific coast and the Andes mountains—a mystery, since Europeans did not sail there until Pizzaro's voyage in 1530 (17 years *after* the map's date). And, finally, the map shows all of Antarctica—a continent unknown till the 1820s—and shows it without its ice cap!

▸ Pisces: The zodiacal constellation of the Fishes; so called **Sim.mah** and depicted by the Sumerians, who associated it with Enki.

▸ Planets: Extensive astronomical texts, as well as depictions on cylinder seals and varied sculptures, leave no doubt that the Sumerians, and the Babylonians after them, were fully aware of our solar system's makeup. They repeatedly asserted that our Solar System has twelve members— the Sun (which was depicted in the center), the Moon (for reasons given in the Epic of Creation), and ten planets, including Nibiru. They named them, listed them in the correct order and numbered them—from First for Pluto, through Neptune, Uranus, Saturn and Jupiter, to Mars as the 6th, Earth the 7th, Venus 8th, and 9th for Mercury—the order, according to ZS, in which someone (like the Anunnaki) coming into our Solar System from far out (i.e. from Nibiru—the tenth planet and the twelfth member) would count. Generally called **Mul** (= 'Celestial body') in Sumerian (*Kakkabu* in Akkadian), the planets observable from Earth were additionally identified as **Lu.mash** (= 'The familiar Wanderers'). The Sumerian familiarity with our Solar System was such that ZS could predict what NASA would find on Neptune; it even extended to the odd orbit of Pluto, that is sometimes beyond Neptune and sometimes closer than Neptune: It was depicted as a Two Faced planetary god! (To modern astronomers who question whether Pluto should be deemed a planet, ZS has explained why the Sumerians did include it.) *See* Astronomy, Celestial Battle, Nibiru, Pluto.

▸ Planispheres: Literally, representations of spherical data (such as the skies enveloping the Earth) on a flat surface. Such a disklike clay tablet, discovered in the library of the Assyrian king Ashurbanipal (and now on exhibit in the British Museum) depicts in one of its eight segments the route "by the seven planets" that Enlil took (per ZS, from Nibiru to Earth). Two other planispheres, called 'Astrolabes' (literally, 'Takers of stars') that provided observational data about the planet Nibiru/Marduk as it reached its apogee in the 1st millennium B.C., are discussed by ZS in *The End of Days*.

▸ Plant of Life: In the Epic of Gilgamesh, Utnapishtim (the Mesopotamian

'Noah' who was granted long life by Enlil) reveals to Gilgamesh that at the bottom of a well at his abode there grows a plant whose eater gains eternal youth. Gilgamesh succeeded in getting hold of the plant—only to have it stolen from him by a serpent as he slept. References to a "Plant of Life" (and "Waters of Life") are also found in the Pyramid Texts. *See* Pepi I, Pyramid Texts.

▶ Pluto: The outermost known planet before the Space Age, whose odd inclined orbit beyond Neptune sometimes takes it in, closer than Neptune. ZS has identified it with **Ga.ga,** a moon of Saturn that, according to the Epic of Creation, was sent off as a messenger to the other planets, ending up near Neptune. In Sumerian astronomical texts it was called **Ushmu** (= 'He of Two Faces'), and was depicted with two heads—looking this way and the other way. Ushmu, moreover, was the 'vizier' of Ea—the Sumerian god of waters.

▶ Popol Vuh (= 'The Council Book'): The name, in the Nahuatl language, of the Mayan equivalent of a Bible, telling how Sky and Earth were formed, how the Earth was divided into four regions, how the ancestral Fathers and Mothers arrived from across the seas with the help of the gods, leading to civilization and the Mayas.

▶ Poseidon: Greek god of the seas, brother of Zeus (Lord of the gods) and Hades (god of the Lower World)—paralleling the Canaanite *Yam* ('Sea') and his brothers *Ba'al* ('Lord') and *Mot* ('Death'). *See also* Ea, Neptune.

▶ Precession of the Equinoxes ('Precession' for short): The largely unexplained phenomenon in the Earth's orbit around the Sun, whereby the Earth, after a full solar year, falls short of returning to the same previous spot: There is a slight retardation, that accumulates to 1° in 72 years, adding up to a full cycle of 360° in 25,920 years (72 × 360 = 25,920). While scholars used to credit the Greek astronomer Hipparchus (who lived in Asia Minor in the 2nd century B.C.) with being the first to recognize Precession, the fact is that the phenomenon lies at the core of the zodiacal system, with which the Sumerians were already familiar in the 4th millennium B.C. *See* Zodiac, Zodiacal Ages.

▸ Priests, Priesthood: While the Hebrew priestly line began, according to the Bible, with the appointment during the Exodus of Aaron (the brother of Moses) and his sons to serve as "Priests before Yahweh," the very same Bible reported that some four hundred years earlier Egypt's Pharaoh "gave Osnath the daughter of Puty, the priest of Annu, as a wife to Joseph;" and that centuries earlier, after the War of the Kings, Abraham was met and blessed by "Malchizedek, the king of Shalem, who was a priest of the God Most High." Indeed, the institution of priesthood began even earlier, in Sumer, where a demigod named En.me.dur.an.ki was taught by Shamash and Adad "secrets of Heaven and Earth" to become a priest in the temple of Sippar. Priesthood reached a peak in Babylon and Assyria in the first millennium B.C., when hundreds of priests living and serving in Sacred Precincts formed guildlike groups with particular specialties, ranging from cleaning and cooking to sky-watching and omen-solving. The same phenomenon of priests and priesthood arose in both the Mesoamerican and South American civilizations.

▸ Primitive Worker: The translation of the term *lulu amelu* used in the Atra Hasis text to describe the being that the gods decided to fashion, to take over "the back-breaking toil" of the Anunnaki.

▸ Promised Land: A term mostly used nowadays euphemistically rather than literally to describe the territory that, according to the Bible, God promised to Abraham and his descendants, the 'Children of Israel', as "an everlasting heritage" (Exodus 6:4–8): "From the Brook of Egypt" (in the central Sinai) "to the River Euphrates, the great river"; "the whole of the Land of Canaan" (Genesis 15:18, 17:8); "the Western Mount, the Land of Canaan, and Lebanon" (Deuteronomy 1:7); "from the Desert to Lebanon, from the River Euphrates unto the Western Sea" (Deuteronomy 11:24 and Joshua 1:2–4); "the fortified places reaching heavenwards" wherein "the *Anakim* still reside" (Deuteronomy 9:1–2). ZS has pointed out that accordingly, the three then space-related sites— the Spaceport (in the Sinai), the Landing Place (in Lebanon) and Mission Control Center (Jerusalem) were granted as an everlasting legacy to the 'Children of Israel'.

▸ Prophets: The Hebrew Bible renders the oracles, admonitions, pleadings, teachings and prophecies of three 'major' prophets (Isaiah, Jeremiah, Ezekiel) and twelve 'minor' ones, in books bearing their names; but their words were God's words, for *Nabih* (as they were called in Hebrew) meant 'Spokesman'—one who only speaks for, delivers the message of, someone else. The term brings to mind the name and role of the Babylonian god Nabu, and scholars have titled various Babylonian Prediction Texts as "Akkadian Prophecies;" yet nothing has been found in the records of other ancient nations that equals the phenomenon of the Hebrew Prophets, who (from the 8th to the 6th centuries B.C.) were involved in national and international events, preached social justice and called for world peace more than for religious observances. As time went on, they dealt increasingly with events that will come to pass on a nearing 'Day of the Lord' and at a future 'End of Days', asserting and reasserting that "The First Things shall be The Last Things." *See* Day of the Lord, End of Days, Jerusalem.

▸ PTA̲H̲ (= 'He who develops/creates'): The patriarch of ancient Egypt's gods, who (before the Deluge) reigned over the Nile valley for 9,000 years, until his son RA took over. After the Deluge Pta̲h̲ "raised Egypt from under the floodwaters" by erecting sluices at the first cataract. He was also called KHNEMU, the one who fashioned Man out of clay. His name was written hieroglyphically with the symbol of a Double Helix = the Sumerian Entwined Serpents = Ea/Enki, per ZS.

▸ Ptolemy: A general in Alexander's army who seized control of Egypt after Alexander's death, declaring himself king and Pharaoh. His successors, known as the Ptolemaic Dynasty, ruled Egypt and adjoining lands in Africa until Roman takeover in 30 B.C. The Ptolemys vied with the successors of Seleucus, another general of Alexander who took over Alexander's Asian domains, for control of Judea and Syria. *See* Seleucus/Seleucid Dynasty.

▸ Puma Punku: An ancient site near Lake Titicaca, next to Tiahuanacu, that undoubtedly served as the latter's lakeside port. Strewn about the site are stone blocks of varied sizes, all cut with incredible precision with unknown tools, and fashioned into odd shapes with grooves, sharp or odd angles, varied surfaces, circular hollowings and other puzzling features, as though the stones were sophisticated parts of some advanced equipment—or dies for making such parts. There are no standing structures, but some of the remains are undoubtedly of four collapsed side-by-side huge chambers, each cut perfectly out of a single mega-boulder; the physical evidence corroborates Conquistador tales that each such chamber was completely inlaid inside—ceiling, walls and floors—with sheets of gold, held in place with golden nails. Each such chamber was thus a Golden Enclosure. ZS has suggested that the place was erected to accommodate Anu and Antu during their state visit to Earth circa 4000 B.C. *See* An (Anu), Golden Enclosure, Megalithic Structures, Nazca, Tiahuanacu.

▶ Pyramids: Since the term, technically, describes a geometric shape with a square base and four triangular sides that rise at an angle to meet at an apex point, the only true ancient pyramids are in Egypt and Nubia; but the term's general usage encompasses other high-rise monumental structures, such as the ziggurats of Mesopotamia (that rise by stages), step-pyramids in Mesoamerica and South America, and similar structures in other parts of the world—usually with flat tops. Of Egypt's score 'true' pyramids the three in Giza stand out as unique in their perfection, size, inner complexity, and exterior limestone casing; while Egyptologists consider them a 4th dynasty development from lesser prior pyramids, ZS has suggested that on the contrary, they were an Anunnaki-built model that later Pharaohs tried to emulate (with varied degrees of failure). Another issue concerning the Egyptian pyramids is their purpose: contrary to the Egyptologists' theory that each successive Pharaoh built himself a pyramid as his tomb, not a single burial was found inside any Egyptian pyramid. *See* Al Mamoon, Bent Pyramid, Cheops, Dahshur, Giza, Great Pyramid of Giza, Khufu, Landing Corridor, Radedef, Ziggurats, Zoser.

▶ Pyramid Texts: Texts that deal with the Afterlife, believed to be quotations from early sources collectively known as 'The Book of the Dead', found inscribed in various Pharaonic pyramids. *See* Pepi I.

▸ Pyramid Wars: A term coined by ZS to describe wars among Anunnaki clans in which the Giza pyramids were involved. At the center of the first series of such wars was the contending between Horus and Seth; in the second series the Great Pyramid itself was under attack by the Enlilites, because Marduk/Ra had taken refuge in it.

▸ *Qa'aba* (= 'The Cube' in Arabic): The name of the cubic black structure in Mecca, Saudi Arabia, with a black stone (presumably a meteorite) in its northeastern corner, that is the most sacred object in Islam; its veneration precedes Islam, and legends connect it to either Adam or Abraham (or both).

▸ Quechua: The language spoken by the Incas of Peru, which was distinct from the 'Aymara' spoken in the southern highlands.

▸ Queen's Chamber: The name given to an inner chamber within the Great Pyramid of Giza that is located below the so-called 'King's Chamber'. Reached via a long and narrow horizontal corridor, the chamber has a vaulted ceiling, a corbeled niche in the eastern wall, and small squarish apertures in the north and south walls through which narrow shafts (erroneously called "air shafts") lead away from the walls and then upward at an angle. The Chamber, which was found totally empty when first entered, lies precisely on the vertical midline of the Pyramid. In *Journeys to the Mythical Past* ZS disclosed the existence of a tunnel and secret chamber beyond the Niche, and reviewed recent explorations of the horizontal corridor and 'air shafts'—none of which has unveiled the purpose of the 'Queen's Chamber'. *See* Great Pyramid.

▸ Quetzalcoatl (= 'The Plumed/Winged Serpent' in the Nahuatl tongue of the Aztecs): The leading Mesoamerican deity (called Kukulcan by the Mayas), who appeared from across the seas, gave Mankind civilization, and left as he had come, promising to return. The Return was to occur when the 'bundle' that meshed the Haab and Tzulkin calendars returned to its original position once in 52 years. Because the arrival of Cortez—white-faced and bearded, as Quetzalcoatl had been—in 1519 occurred at such a 'bundle' year, the Aztec king Montezuma treated Cortez as the returning god (paying for this error with his life). ZS has suggested that 'Quetzalcoatl' was the Egyptian god Thoth, and pointed out that 52 was the Secret Number of Thoth. *See* Aztecs, Mayas, Ningishzida, Olmecs, Thoth.

▸ Quipos: A set of colored strands that the Incas used to record events, after early writing was abandoned.

R

▶ RA (= 'The Pure One'): The son and successor of PTA<u>H</u> as ancient Egypt's leading deity, who at times was called RA-AMEN (or AMON)—'The Unseen'. He was venerated as a great god "of Heaven and Earth," for he had come to Earth from the 'Planet of Millions of Years' in his 'Ben Ben'—a conical 'celestial barge' which was kept in the Holy of Holies of a special temple in Anu (the later Heliopolis). When expectations of the return of Nibiru into view began, the Unseen Ra/Marduk was also worshipped as the ATEN—the planet of the gods, depicted as a Winged Disc. *See* Aerial Chariots, Enki, Marduk, Pta<u>h</u>.

▶ Rachel (H *Ra<u>h</u>el*): The second and most loved wife of Jacob, mother of Joseph and Benjamin. *See* Harran, Matriarchs, Mitanni, Naharin.

▶ RADEDEF: A 4th dynasty Pharaoh whom Egyptologists prefer not to discuss because his existence and his pyramid defy the theory that three *successive* Pharaohs—KHUFU/Cheops, KHEFRA/Chefren and MENKAURA/Mycerinus built in succession the three Giza pyramids. Khefra (to whom the Second Pyramid is attributed) was not the successor of Khufu—Radedef (sometimes read backwards, Dedefra) was. He was the son of KHUFU/Cheops and reigned as Pharaoh after him; but the pyramid he built (a) is not at Giza but miles away to the north, (b) was primitively built of unhewn stones, and (c) is a pile of rubble.

▶ Ram: *See* Aries, Marduk.

▶ Ramayana (= 'Rama's Journey'): A Hindu epic written in Sanskrit that tells the tale of Prince Rama whose wife was abducted by the king of Lanka (the island of Ceylon), the wars that ensued, and how various gods got involved in the saga—leading to aerial battles among them, in which a variety of fantastic weapons were used. Together with the epic of Mahabharata, these long Sanskrit texts have been a primary source about the ancient Aryan-Hindu pantheon (with its similarities to Greek tales of gods and heroes).

▸ RAMSES (also Ramesses = 'Issue of Ra'): The theophoric name of several Pharaohs of the New Kingdom whose royal names (including AH-MSES/ Ahmose, THOTH-MSES/Tutmose) claimed for the king a demigod status by being the "issue of" this or that god. Most renowned were Ramses II of the 19th dynasty (reigned 1279–1213 B.C.) who some (but not ZS) consider to have been the Pharaoh of the Exodus, and Ramses III of the 20th dynasty (reigned 1182–1151 B.C.) who defended Egypt against the invading People of the Sea. *See* Ahmose, Battle of Kadesh, People of the Sea, Moses.

▸ Rebecca (H *Rivkah*): The wife of Isaac. *See* H̲arran, Matriarchs, Naharin.

▸ Red Pyramid: The second pyramid built by the Pharaoh Sneferu at Dahshur, near the Bent Pyramid.

▸ Red Sea: The long and narrow body of water that separates Africa and Asia, from the Sinai peninsula in the north to the Arabian Sea in the south. Thought for a long time to have been the sea miraculously parted for the Israelites at the start of the Exodus, it is now generally accepted that by *Yam Suff* (literally, 'Sea of Reeds') the Bible referred to the shallower chain of lakes farther north. *See* Exodus.

▸ *Repha'im*: The name, in the Hebrew Bible, of a legendary race of demigods, descendants of the *Nefilim* and the *Anakim* (commonly translated 'giants', but a Hebrew rendering of **Anunnaki** per ZS). The name could mean either 'Healers' or quite the opposite: 'The Weakened Ones.' One of the valleys of ancient Jerusalem is called in the Bible 'the Valley of Repha'im', and an early translation of the Bible into Greek used the term 'Titans' (of Greek myths) for *Repha'im*; most Bible commentators accept that connotation. *See* Anunnaki, Giants, Gilgal Repha'im, Nefilim.

▸ Resurrection: Instances of bringing the dead back to life are found in tales of the gods of ancient nations. The Sumerian text dealing with Inanna's journey to the "Lower World" (the domain of her sister Ereshkigal) describes both how she was put to death and how she was brought back to life by an emissary of Enki. Egyptian tales relate how Horus, having died from a scorpion's sting, was brought back to life by the god Thoth. Canaanite texts assert that Ba'al, having been killed in battle with other gods, was brought back to life by the goddesses Anat and Shepesh. The Bible credits the prophets Elijah and Elisha with reviving a sick person who died; and the prophet Ezekiel had the vision of dry bones reassembling themselves and returning back to life.

▸ Revelation: The New Testament's prophetic book (whose full title is 'The Apocalypse of St. John the Divine') that contains a series of revelations of things to come, most rendered in mystic symbolism. One of its most baffling segments is the referral to "The Beast whose number is 666;" many scholars consider it the numerical code for the name 'Nero Caesar' in Hebrew, which is among the reasons for dating the book to the time of that Roman ruler (first century A.D.). The most apocalyptic prophecy concerns the Final Battle of "Armageddon," which is a rendering in Greek of *Har Megiddo* = Mount Megiddo in Israel. *See* Armageddon, End of Days, Megiddo.

▸ Rider of the Clouds: A nickname-epithet of the god Ba'al in Canaanite texts, as well as of Yahweh in the Hebrew Bible. *See* Aerial Chariots.

▸ Rimac: The site in Peru south of Lima, where the river Rimac reaches the Pacific Ocean, where a huge temple to the god Pachacamac was located. A place of mass pilgrimages, it served as a 'Mecca' in Incan and pre-Incan times. *See* Pachacamac.

▸ Rivers of Paradise: The Bible (Genesis 2) states that the Garden of Eden (the 'Paradise' of lore and myth) was watered by four principal streams, two of which—*Prath* and <u>*Hiddekel*</u>—were unmistakably the Euphrates and Tigris rivers, *Purannu* and *Idiklath* in Akkadian. The 'Garden of Eden' was thus unmistakably the Sumerian **E.din** (Akkadian *Edinnu*)— Mesopotamia. But what about the other two rivers that joined the others at one headwaters? The Bible called them by epithets: *Gihon* ('The Gusher') and *Pishon* ('The One That Rested'), and scholars' suggestions have ranged as far as the Nile in Africa and the Indus in India. The answer occurred to ZS when earth-penetrating radar discovered in 1993 that a river, now dried up, had once run through eastern Arabia to the headwaters of the Persian Gulf—joining there the Euphrates and Tigris. That, ZS suggested, was the Pishon, the river that came to rest. He then guessed that a river (called Kuron) that cascades down from the Zagros mountains on the opposite side of the Gulf, could have been the missing Gihon.

▸ Rocketships: The Sumerian term **Gir**, pictographically depicted as a conical object pointed at its head, has been usually translated 'cutter'. Combined with the term **Din** (= 'Just, Righteous') it was the Sumerian term for 'gods'. Because of astounding pictographic similarity of **Din.Gir** to an Egyptian drawing of a multi-stage spaceship in an underground silo, ZS has concluded that in this context **Gir** stands for the conical upper part of a rocketship. *See also* Aerial Chariots.

▸ Rome, Romans: The city, now the capital of Italy, that gave its name to a country and people that were the mightiest power some two millennia ago. Founded according to legend in the 8th century B.C., it became the capital of a republic (governed by a senate) in the 6th century B.C. Gradually but persistently replacing the Greeks in the eastern Mediterranean, the Roman control of the sea lanes was resisted by the Phoenicians, leading to the Punic Wars (264–146 B.C.) of which Hannibal's march on Rome is best remembered. By the first century B.C. Rome, ruled by an emperor, grew to become an imperial city, deeply involved, through conquest and diplomacy, in the lands and peoples of the olden great civilizations of Egypt, Mesopotamia, the eastern Mediterranean, and Judea. In 60 B.C. the emperor Pompey took control of Jerusalem—having stopped first at Baalbek (then called Heliopolis) where the empire's greatest temple to Jupiter/Zeus was built. Within a century thereafter, Roman governors of Judea were involved in the events described in the New Testament; in 70 A.D., suppressing a Jewish revolt, the Romans destroyed the Jerusalem Temple. Rome, whose religion had been an adaptation of the Greek pantheon, adopted Christianity under the emperor Constantine in the fourth century A.D. *See* Baalbek, Herod, Jerusalem, Jerusalem Temple, Jesus, Mediterranean Sea.

▶ Rosetta Stone: A stone tablet (now on display in the British Museum) discovered at the village of Rosetta in Egypt by one of Napoleon's men in 1799. It was inscribed with the same decree by Alexander's successor Ptolemy V in 196 B.C. in three languages (his own Greek, ancient hieroglyphic, and late 'Demotic' script); it enabled scholars to begin deciphering the hieroglyphic writing of ancient Egypt.

▶ Route of the Exodus: Using the biblical place names, geographic and topographic information, and travel times, it has been the subject of heated debate (and strenuous research) among scholars for the past two centuries. With small variations the three principal alternatives are (a) the Southern Route, requiring Mount Sinai to be located among the high granite peaks near St. Katherine monastery; (b) a Northern Route, following the Mediterranean seashore Way of the Sea; or (c) the Central Route, using one of the time-immemorial passes to enter the central plain, locating Mount Sinai near the caravan stop of Nakhl (Way of the Pilgrims). For a variety of reasons explained in *The Stairway to Heaven* and because of the proximity to the post-Diluvial spaceport there, ZS favors (c). *See* Afterlife, Erra Epos, Exodus, Gilgamesh, Moses, Ningal, Rocketships, Sin, Sinai, Spaceport.

S

▸ Sacsahuaman (= Quechua for 'Falcon's Place'): The Inca name for the promontory above Cuzco. Shaped like a triangle, its base is dominated by huge rock outcroppings that someone somehow cut and shaped into giant steps and platforms and perforated with tunnels, niches and grooves of no obvious purpose. The narrower side of the promontory contains remains of rectangular and circular structures under which passages and tunnels run. Whatever had been on that side has been protected by three parallel zigzagging colossal walls built of huge boulders (weighing between 20 and 300 tons each) cut at numerous angles so as to fit together as a jigsaw puzzle. Except for local lore that all that was built "by the giants," there is no indication of by whom, when and why all that was put up.

▸ Sagittarius (= 'The Archer'): The zodiacal constellation called **Pa.bil** (= 'The Defender') by the Sumerians, and depicted by them as an archer. It was associated with Ninurta.

▸ Sakkara (also Saqqarah = 'The Closed/Hidden Place'): The location, south of Giza, of a step-pyramid built of unhewn stones held together with mud and wood. The crumbling pyramid, which stands in a compound that is surrounded by an artful colonnaded stone wall, is attributed to Zoser, the 2nd Pharaoh of the 3rd dynasty (circa 2650 B.C.). According to Egyptologists, it served the 4th dynasty Pharaohs as a model for the unique Giza pyramids; ZS considered it an attempt to emulate the grandiose and unique Giza pyramids that were built earlier by the Anunnaki. *See* Giza, Pyramids, Radedef, Zoser.

▸ St. Katherine Monastery: A fortlike monastery in the mountainous southern part of the Sinai peninsula, whose origins go back to Roman times when early converts to Christianity in Egypt sought refuge in the desolate area. Named after a martyr, Santa Katarina (purportedly buried on an adjacent mount by angels), the monastery was enlarged and given special status by the emperor Constantine (when he adopted Christianity) because it is located next to a "Mount Mussa"—'Mount Moses'—which the monks claim to be the Mount Sinai of the Exodus. The claim forms the basis for accepting a 'Southern Route' as the Route of the Exodus. Reviewing two centuries of debate and research on the subject, ZS concluded that the monks' tradition is untenable. His on-site evidence for a central Sinai location for Mount Sinai is given in *The Stairway to Heaven* and *The Earth Chronicles Expeditions*. *See* Exodus, Mount Sinai, Sinai Peninsula.

▸ Samuel (*Shmu'el* = 'Named by God'): A biblical prophet and high priest, in charge of the Ark of the Covenant in Shiloh (before it was moved to Jerusalem), who anointed Saul as Israel's first king, and then David. The story of his birth, divine assignment, life and times is told in two books of the Bible, I Samuel and II Samuel. *See* Ark of the Covenant, David.

▸ San Agustin: An archaeological site of the Mochica people in northern Peru, where stone statues portraying giants, sometimes holding tools or weapons, have been found.

▸ San Lorenzo: An important Olmec site in Mexico, where five colossal stone heads depicting Olmec leaders have been found.

▸ Sanskrit: The Indo-Aryan or Indo-European language of ancient India from which Hurrian and Hittite in antiquity and then a variety of European languages have evolved. *See* Hindu Traditions.

▸ Santa Elena: The name of a cape on the Pacific coast of Ecuador where, according to local lore, a group of settlers, worshippers of twelve gods, arrived from across the ocean in a fleet of balsa boats. Their leader, Naymlap, was guided by a god via a divine green stone. *See* Naymlap.

▸ **Sar**: The Sumerian term for the number 3,600. Berossus used it as the time unit for the reign periods of the pre-Diluvial commanders, as do the discovered clay tablets known as the Sumerian King Lists. ZS has concluded that the Sar was an Anunnaki Year, equaling one Nibiru orbit. *See* Divine Time.

▸ *Sarah*: The first of the four Hebrew Matriarchs. The wife of Abraham whose original Sumerian name was **Sarai** (= 'Princess'). She accompanied him from Ur to Harran to Canaan; her beauty was such that on two occasions Abraham feared that he would be killed by a Pharaoh or a Philistine king to be free to take Sarah into their harems. Being a half-sister of Abraham, her son Isaac was the Legal Heir though his brother Ishmael (son of the handmaiden Hagar) was the Firstborn. *See* Abraham, Harran, Hebron, Isaac.

▸ Sargon (*Sharru-kin* = 'Trustworthy King') of Akkad: The Semitic founder of the Akkadian dynasty that assumed control over Sumer circa 2360 B.C., forming a unified 'Sumer & Akkad'. A text known as 'The Legend of Sargon' described him as a foundling, not unlike the biblical Moses. A protégé of Inanna/Ishtar, he ruled from a new capital (*Agade*/Akkad) and carried out military campaigns on her behalf. The atrocities committed by his grandson Naram-Sin led the other gods to wipe Agade off the face of the Earth. *See* Akkad, Akkadians.

▸ Sargon (*Sharru-kin*) of Assyria: A royal name adopted by two Assyrian kings, in an effort to reclaim the fame and status of Sargon of Akkad— one in the 19th century B.C. and the other (who is known from the Bible) in the 8th century B.C. The latter ('Sargon II') built a grand new capital, *Dur-Sharru-kin*, with walls whose length in Assyrian cubits equaled the numerical value of the king's name. Located not far from today's Mosul in northern Iraq, it was discovered by French archaeologists in the 19th century.

▸ Sarmizegetusa: An archaeological site in Romania, where the Danube River reaches the Black Sea. There, a series of right-angled structures, marked by rows of wooden poles, gave the place the nickname 'Calendar City'; one of three circular structures has been dubbed 'the Stonehenge of the Black Sea'. ZS, in *When Time Began,* has joined the speculation regarding the site.

▸ *Sarpanit* (in the absence of a consonant for 'ts' in English, sometimes rendered Zarpanit): The Earthling wife of Marduk; mother of his son Nabu. A Sumerian text quoted by ZS suggests that Marduk's defiant choice served as a 'green light' for **Igigi** astronauts to do likewise—an episode recalled in Genesis 6. *See* Igigi, Nabu, Nefilim.

▸ Saturn: The planet called **An.shar** (= 'Foremost of the Heavens') in the Epic of Creation, and **Shul.pa.e** in Mesopotamian astronomical texts. According to the Sumerian cosmogony, the planet we call Pluto was at one time a moon of Saturn. *See* Epic of Creation, Pluto.

▸ Scales of Fate: In the Egyptian 'Book of the Dead', the scales on which a heart was weighed by the gods to determine whether the deceased (usually a Pharaoh) was worthy of an Afterlife. ZS has compared it to the Sumerian concept underlying the zodiacal Constellation of the Scales (= Libra), which was called **Zi.ba.anna** (= 'Life-decision in the heavens').

▸ Seafaring: Legendary, textual, pictorial and even physical evidence indicate that seafaring began much earlier than usually assumed. Enki, texts tell, liked to sail in a **Ma.gur** (= 'Boat for turning about') in the marshlands while his "crewmen sang in unison." Boats were used by the Anunnaki to transport gold ores for smelting and refining in the **E.din**. Mankind did not completely perish in the Deluge because Noah/Ziusudra/ Utnapishtim built a submersible boat following Enki's instructions. According to the Sumerian King List, after the Deluge, the demigod king of Uruk "Mes-kiag-gasher, went into the sea and came out from it to the mountains." Legends, such as that of Naymlap, recorded the arrival of settlers in boats on the Pacific coast of South America, and of Aztec predecessors arriving in Mexico in boats. Early petroglyphs in Egypt depicted gods arriving by boat from UR-TA (= 'The Ancient Place'). Egyptian Pharaohs battled 'The Sea Peoples' whose plume-headed warriors are also depicted in the Yucatan. The African Olmecs reached Mexico's Gulf Coast circa 3100 B.C. Stone anchors of the same type have been found in the Mediterranean and in the Atlantic tropics. The Phoenicians reached the British Isles, and under king Hiram their ships circumnavigated Africa to bring the gold of Ophir for the Temple in Jerusalem. The list, that can go on and on, affirms the conclusion that gods and men sailed the seas and rivers almost from time immemorial.

▸ Seleucus, Seleucid Dynasty: One of the officers in the army of Alexander the great who fought among themselves for their leader's empire, ending up in control of Asia Minor, the Levant, and Asian lands as far as India. Renaming himself Seleucus Nicator (= 'The Victorious'), he started the Seleucid Dynasty that reigned from Syria until the Roman takeover in the 1st century B.C. Successors of Seleucus Nicator included Antiochus IV Epiphanes (175–164 B.C.) whose oppressive rule in Judea and defiling of the Temple in Jerusalem triggered a Jewish revolt. *See* Hasmoneans, Jerusalem Temple.

▸ Semites: Near Eastern peoples descended (according to the Bible) from Noah's son *Shem*, identified by common languages (including Hebrew, Babylonian, Assyrian, Canaanite, Phoenician, etc. and now Arabic) that all stemmed from Akkadian, the Semitic 'Mother Tongue'. *See* Shem, Table of Nations.

▸ Sennacherib (*Sin-ahe-erib* = '[The god] Sin raised his brother'): The son and successor of Sargon II as king of Assyria in the 8th century B.C. His military campaigns included a failed attempt to capture Jerusalem during the time of king Hezekiah—an event mentioned as a partial success in the Assyrian annals, but detailed as a major and miraculous Assyrian defeat in the Bible (II Kings 18 and 19). *See* Hezekiah, Jerusalem.

▸ Septuagint (= 'That of the 70'): The earliest translation into Greek of the Hebrew Bible, carried out by a group of seventy (or, actually, 72) savants in Alexandria, Egypt, in the 3rd century B.C. by order of king Ptolemy Philadelphus.

▸ Serpent: While the Bible, right in the tale of Adam and Eve in the Garden of Eden, deemed "The Serpent" a cunning, evil and accursed creature, in the Sumerian culture and beliefs "serpent" was both an honorific term and an ignominious one (it stole the Plant of Eternal Youth from Gilgamesh); and in ancient Egypt it was a sign of lordship. A clue to understanding these differences, according to ZS, lies in the Hebrew term *Naḥash* used in the biblical text; though translated 'serpent', it can also mean "He who knows/solves mysteries" and comes from the same root as the Hebrew word for copper. In the Sumerian origin of the Garden of Eden story, Enki's epithet **Buzur** meant both "Solver of Secrets" and "Serpent;" the Bible (siding with Enlil?) chose 'Serpent'. But then the biblical Exodus tale reports that Moses stopped a plague with a Copper Serpent (Enki's epithet). In the Sumerian 'Garden of Eden' tale, Enki engaged in genetic engineering with Ningishzida's help (to enable 'Eve' to procreate. Entwined Serpents—double-helix DNA—were Ningishzida's emblem in Sumer, the hieroglyph for PTAH (= Enki) in Egypt, and the serpent emblem (called Uraeus) was depicted on the headdress of Pharaohs. In Egypt (where Ningishzida was known as Thoth) he was also the Winged Serpent of the Pyramid Texts— translated 'Quetzalcoatl' in Mesoamerica. *See* DNA, Enki, Eden, Ningishzida, Quetzalcoatl, Thoth.

▸ SET (also SETH, SETEKH): According to Egyptian tales of the gods, the son of the divine couple GEB and NUT, whose spouse was his half-sister the goddess NEPHTYS. Quarreling with his brother OSIRIS over the domination of Egypt, he killed and dismembered Osiris. He was then challenged by HORUS, the son of Osiris; their widespread wars ended with an aerial battle over the Sinai peninsula in which Set was defeated.

▸ Seth (H *Shet* = 'Foundation'): The third son of Adam and Eve, born after the killing of Able and the exile of Cain.

▸ Seven, Seventh: The importance and sanctity of the number seem to be universal, present not only in Old World (e.g., the identification of Enlil with 7, the 'seven gods who judge', the seven tablets of the Epic of Creation; the biblical Sabbath right at Creation, the Jubilee after 7 × 7 years, the seventh month chosen by the biblical God as the start of a New Year;

Thoth's calendar of seven-day weeks, seven cows and seven wheat heads in the Pharaoh's dreams, the seven oracle Hathors in Egypt)—but also in New World civilizations (Aztec ancestors coming from seven caves, seven-player teams in Toltec and Mayan sacred ball games, etc.). ZS has attributed that to Earth being the seventh planet as the Anunnaki journeyed past Pluto inwards, leading to seven-stage ziggurat-temples for observing the heavens.

▸ Sexagesimal System: The 'Base 60' mathematical system of the Sumerians, that progressed by continuing to multiply 6 by 10 by 6 by 10 and so on. ZS has suggested that it was devised by the Anunnaki when they sought a workable mathematical ratio between the 3,600 Sar (= Nibiru's mathematical orbital period) and Earth's very short orbital period, using the phenomenon of Precession to create the Zodiacal Ages of 2,160 years—obtaining the Golden Ratio 10:6. *See* Celestial Time, Nibiru's Orbit, Zodiacal Constellations.

▸ *Shalem*: (= 'Complete'): A divine epithet, probably for Utu/Shamash, from which the early name of Jerusalem, *Ur-Shalem* (= 'City of Shalem') probably originated.

▸ Shalmaneser III: An Assyrian king (858–824 B.C.) who boasted in his annals that his god Ashur, on whose command he launched military campaigns, had given him a "weapon of brilliance" that overwhelmed the enemy. On one of his stelas, the famous 'Black Obelisk', he depicted the Israelite king Jehu bowing to him and offering tribute.

▸ *Shamash*: (Akk. 'Sun'): *See* Utu.

▸ **Shara** (= 'Prince'): The only known son of the unmarried Inanna/Ishtar, fathered by an early king of Uruk called **Lugal.banda**.

▸ Sheba: The legendary land whose queen, hearing of Solomon's great wisdom, paid him a royal visit in Jerusalem. Contrary to persistent beliefs, 'Sheba' was not Ethiopia in Africa, but a kingdom in southern Arabia.

▸ *Shem*: The name, in the Bible, of the eldest of the three sons of Noah, forefather of the peoples called Semites. As a noun, *Shem* in Hebrew is usually taken to mean 'Name'; but some scholars have argued that in certain biblical passages the term describes an object—and ZS has suggested that, as its Sumerian counterpart **Mu**, it could refer to a divine 'Sky Chamber'. *See* Aerial Chariots.

▸ *Shin'ar*: The ancient Hebrew name for Sumer, first used in Genesis 11 as the Bible began the tale of Man's first civilization after the Deluge.

▸ SHU (= 'Dryness'): Per Manetho, the third pre-Diluvial divine ruler of Egypt (after PTA<u>H</u> and RA) who reigned for 700 years. With his sister-wife TEFNUT (= 'Moisture') they gave birth to the next divine couple, their son GEB (= 'Piled up Earth') and daughter NUT (= 'The Firmament/Sky').

▸ **Shulgi**: The second king of the famed Third Dynasty of Ur who claimed "divine birth auspices" because the god Nannar/Sin himself arranged the union between his father, king Ur-Nammu, and the High Priestess of the temple of Sin. He started his long reign (2095–2048 B.C.) with fervent temple building and a grand tour of the Sumerian empire, and ended as a lover of the goddess Inanna/Ishtar, overseeing decline, uprisings and invasions. Royal annals called 'Date Formulas', listing the main event or undertaking in any named year of reign, reveal that Shulgi undertook the building of the "Great West Wall" that ran across the country's north, in an attempt to prevent the invasion of Sumer by 'Westerners', followers of Marduk. *See* Ur.

▸ **Shuruppak**: The fifth of the first five cities of the Anunnaki as they settled in the **E.din**, allocated to their chief medical officer Ninmah/Ninharsag. According to Mesopotamian texts, it was in Shuruppak that the Sumerian 'Noah' lived and built the salvaging Ark. Rebuilt after the Deluge, the city served as Sumer's medical center.

▸ **Shu-Sin**: The fourth king of Sumer's Third Dynasty, whose short reign (2038–2030 B.C.) was devoted to defending Sumer against increasing attacks from followers of Marduk.

▸ **Sidon**: One of the two principal Phoenician city-states on the Mediterranean coast (the other was Tyre).

▶ **Siduri**: The "Ale Woman" or innkeeper at whose inn the exhausted Gilgamesh was refreshed and told how to cross the nearby Sea of Death on his way to the Land of Missiles. The location suggests Jericho and Siduri brings to mind the biblical Rahab.

▶ Silbury Hill: An artificial cone-shaped hill, precisely circular and 520 feet in diameter, in the vicinity of Stonehenge in England.

▶ Silver (**Ku.babbar** = 'Shiny Bright'): The first metal used as a monetary means of exchange by being cast in units of a certain weight (= '*Shekel*'), the forerunner of coins. *See* Metallurgy.

▶ **Sim.ma̲h** (= 'Fishes'), the Sumerian name for the zodiacal constellation we call Pisces; it was associated with Enki.

▶ *Sin* (from **Su.en**): The Mesopotamian 'Moon god'; see **Nannar.**

▶ Sinai: The name of the triangle-shaped Peninsula wedged between Asia and Africa, bordered on the north by the Mediterranean Sea, on the west by Egypt and the Red Sea, on the northeast by Canaan, and on the southeast by the Gulf of Eilat. Called **Til.mun** (= 'Land of the Missiles') in Sumerian times, it was the 'Fourth Region' of the Anunnaki where their post-Diluvial spaceport was located—a destination, per ZS, of Gilgamesh to become immortal and of Egyptian Pharaohs in their Afterlife journey. It (and its skies) often served as an Anunnaki battlefield, culminating with the use of nuclear weapons at the time of Abraham. Six hundred years later it was the locale of the events of the Exodus, including the greatest mass theophany on record—Yahweh's landing on Mount Sinai in His *Kabod*. The current name, *Sinai*, stems from the Bible; when and why its apparent association with the god Sin began, is not clear. *See* Afterlife, Exodus, Gilgamesh, Moses, Nin.gal, Spaceport, Tilmun.

▶ **Sippar** (= 'Eagle City'): The fourth city of the Anunnaki and the location of their spaceport in the pre-Diluvial **E.din**; in time placed under the command of Utu/Shamash. According to Berossus, it was there that "every available writing was concealed" to be saved from the Deluge; it was from there that the gods lifted off in rocketships to escape the avalanche of water. Rebuilt after the Deluge precisely at the same location, it served as the 'cult center' of Utu/Shamash and the seat of Sumer's equivalent of a Supreme Court. *See* Landing Corridor, Spaceport.

▸ Siwa: An oasis in Egypt's Western Desert, to which Alexander the Great hurried after he defeated the Persians, to consult the famed oracle there about the veracity of his rumored semi-divinity.

▸ SNEFERU: Considered the first king of Egypt's 4th dynasty (and thus predecessor of Khufu/Cheops), he is credited with attempting to build a 52° pyramid that collapsed at Maidum, then hurriedly (as some including ZS believe) reduced the size and steepness of another pyramid, resulting in the Bent Pyramid.

▸ Sodom: One of five cities that were located, according to the Bible, in the plain south of the Dead Sea, a fertile area of Canaan that Lot, the nephew of Abraham, chose to dwell in. It was later upheavaled, together with the other cities there (including Gomorrah). It was, per ZS, the punishing of the 'Evil Cities' recorded in the Erra Epic when the Sinai spaceport nearby was 'upheavaled' with nuclear weapons. Read literally, the text suggests that the explosion breached the Dead Sea's southern barrier, flooding the plain. *See* Bela, Dead Sea, Gomorrah.

▸ Solar Disk: A misnomer for the Egyptian emblem of the Winged Disk, which like its counterparts throughout the ancient Near East represented not the Sun but Nibiru.

▸ Solar System: In *The 12th Planet* and subsequent books, ZS presented massive textual and pictorial evidence for Sumerian familiarity with our complete Solar System, with the Sun in the center, all the planets we know of including the outermost, plus one more—Nibiru—that together with our Moon made up a twelve-member Solar System. The textual evidence begins with the Epic of Creation, leads through a zodiacal system of twelve 'stations' and a twelve month calendar, and culminates in recorded astronomical observations ranging from the 4th millennium B.C. into the first millennium B.C. The pictorial evidence includes cylinder seal VA/243 (Berlin Museum) that ZS has made famous, plus carvings on statues, boundary stones, etc. *See* Asteroid Belt, Astronomy, Epic of Creation, Nibiru, Planets.

▸ Solomon (H *Shlomo* = 'The Complete/Peaceful One'): The son and successor of David as king in Jerusalem, whose reign (circa 967 to 927 B.C.) was, unlike his father's, a time of peace and prosperity, enabling the construction of the Temple to Yahweh in Jerusalem. As a reward from God, he chose Wisdom—a trait for which he was internationally renowned. Under his rule the Judean kingdom extended northward and eastward, including *Beth-Shemesh* (= Baal'bek) in Lebanon and *Tadmor* (= Palmyra) in Syria—not through warfare, but through commerce, diplomacy, and intermarriage. He has been credited with the authorship of several books of the Bible, including the Song of Songs, Proverbs, and Ecclesiastes.

▸ Solstice (from Latin, 'Sun standstill'): The farthest point north or south as the Sun appears to move northward and back southward during a year, where it seems to hesitate, stop, then move back. In antiquity, many temples (both in the Old and the New Worlds)—or even special structures, such as Stonehenge or Gilgal Repha'im—were oriented to either the summer or the winter solstice. The phenomena (occurring June 20/21 and December 21/22) are caused by the Earth's tilt relative to the plain of its orbit around the Sun. The tilt, now about 23.5°, fluctuates up and down in a millennia-long cycle; archaeoastronomy therefore enables determining the date of such temples by their orientation at the time of construction. *See* Archaeoastronomy, Gilgal Repha'im, Stonehenge, Temples.

▸ Spaceport: The pre-Diluvial one was located at Sippar in the **E.din**; it was destroyed by the Deluge. The post-Diluvial one was located, per ZS, in the Sinai peninsula and was destroyed with nuclear weapons in 2024 B.C. *See* Abraham, Erra Epos, Gilgamesh, Landing Corridor, Pharaohs, Ninharsag, Sinai, Sippar, Utu, War of the Kings.

▸ Spaceships: Interplanetary spacecraft (**Gir**), distinct from the gods' 'aerial-chambers' for flying in Earth's skies. Gilgamesh, who saw one launched, described it as a rocketship. In the Pyramid Texts describing the Pharaoh's 'Journey to the Afterlife', the vehicle was called a 'Divine Ascender'; in the tomb of an Egyptian governor of the Sinai, one was depicted as a multi-stage rocketship in an underground silo. According to the autobiographical text of Enki, there were fifty astronauts with him in his spaceship when he journeyed to Earth. *See* Afterlife, Ben-Ben, Rocketships, Spaceport.

▸ Sphinx: The Greek-origin name for a huge (more than 240 ft. long, 65 ft. high) sculpture of a crouching lion with a human head, carved out of the natural limestone bedrock, in Giza, Egypt. Whom does the face represent is just one of the riddles of Who, When, By whom, How and Why, questions that, like the desert sands that have often buried it up to its neck, swirl about the Great Sphinx. Because a causeway connects its site to the Second Pyramid, Egyptologists attribute it to Khefra/Chefren, and continue to do so even though inscriptions by Khufu/Cheops (who preceded Khefra) already mention the Sphinx. Indeed, as ZS has submitted in *The Stairway to Heaven*, those inscriptions (such as the Inventory Stela) indicate even earlier dates, and pictorial depictions already show the Sphinx in pre-dynastic times. In a chapter titled "The Gaze of the Sphinx" ZS attached great significance to the fact that the Sphinx is located precisely on the 30th parallel north and gazes east—precisely toward the Spaceport in the Sinai. ZS has concluded that the Sphinx was built by the Anunnaki as part of the Giza/Spaceport complex circa 10500 B.C. Recent research by non-Egyptologists, studying erosion patterns and other data, have arrived at a similar date. *See* Giza, Pharaohs, Pyramids, Spaceport.

▸ Sphinxes, Ram-headed: The avenue leading to the great temple of Ra-Amon in Karnak (Upper Egypt) is flanked by facing rows of ram-headed sphinxes. ZS has suggested that it had to do with the expectations of Ra/Marduk to attain supremacy as the Age of the Ram (= Aries) was nearing.

▸ Spring Equinox: The day, in the Sumerian and Babylonian calendars, of the start of a new year—the first day of the month Nissan. *See* Astronomy, Equinoxes.

▸ Stars: From the very beginning of ancient astronomy in Sumer, the heavens enveloping the Earth were divided into three 'Ways', each occupying 60 degrees (i.e. one third) of the celestial arc. The central and most important band was the 'Way of Anu; it extended (in the heavens) from the 30th parallel north to the 30th parallel south, with the Celestial equator in the middle, and the lists of stars in it included all those grouped into the twelve zodiacal constellations. The northern band was called the 'Way of Enlil'; the southern one, the 'Way of Ea' (= Enki). Cuneiform star and constellation lists for the Way of Enlil contain virtually all the constellation-stars known today; the list for the Way of Ea, whose southernmost part was unobservable from Mesopotamia, is not that complete. Though the Sumerian term **Mul** (*Kakkabu* in Akkadian) applied to all celestial bodies (stars, constellations, planets), the Sumerians did sometimes distinguish planets by the term **Lu.bad**. *See* Astronomy, Planets, Solar System.

▸ Storm God: A term frequently used by translators from Hittite when the name of the leading Hittite deity, Teshub, is in the inscription. *See* Adad, Teshub.

▸ Stonehenge: The famed monument in England known for its megaliths that stand in an oval or 'horse-shoe' within megalithic circles. It is believed to have been built in several stages involving ditches, corner markers, 'horseshoe' and rectangular arrangements, an avenue, special viewline stones, etc. starting in the mid 3rd millennium B.C. and attaining their present shape (more or less) circa 2160 B.C. But who actually had conceived and carried out these constructions, and why were its most important stones brought over from distant places, remains an enigma. What seems to be certain, however, is that in its final shape Stonehenge served as an observatory for determining the zodiacal age by observing sunrise on summer solstice day. ZS, in *The End of Days*, associated Stonehenge with a global effort to show Mankind that it was still the Age of the Bull, that the Age of the Ram (of Marduk) had not yet arrived. *See* Astronomy, E.Ninnu, Solstice, Zodiac.

▸ Succession Rules: A clue provided in the Bible has enabled ZS to decipher the Succession Rules that lay at the root of rifts among Anunnaki half-brothers and the struggle for supremacy on Earth between Marduk and Ninurta. The ruler's successor was the Firstborn son, whether mothered by a wife or a concubine; but if at any time later the ruler had a son by a half-sister (whether a spouse or not), that son was the Legal Heir with the Succession Right. Often, to avoid future conflicts (since rulers, like Anu, had numerous concubines), the king (or Patriarch) preferred to marry a half-sister to begin with. That half-sister, as Abraham explained after he had introduced Sarah as his sister, could be "the daughter of my father but not of my mother." That was the reason that Enlil, though Enki was the Firstborn, was Anu's Legal Heir, and why Enlil's son Ninurta (by his half-sister Ninmah) was the dynastic successor, rather than Marduk. The preference for a half-sister as wife was also practiced in Egypt—and, interestingly, also among Inca royalty in South America.

▶ **Sud**: A term meaning 'One who gives succor' in Sumerian, applied to Ninmah/Ninharsag as an epithet when she arrived on Earth, and as a personal name for the young nurse who became Enlil's wife.

▶ **Su<u>h</u>ur.mash** (= 'Goat-fish'): The Sumerian name for the zodiacal constellation we call Capricorn.

▶ Sumer (Akk. *Shumeru* = 'Land of the Guardians'): Called **Ki.en.gi** ('Land of Earth's Lords') in Sumerian, it was the post-Diluvial land where the Anunnaki's **E.din** had been before the Deluge. After the layers of mud sufficiently dried, settlers from the mountain ranges to the east began to arrive; the Bible records their arrival in "the Land of *Shin'ar*" and the start of cities built with mud bricks—a milestone turning point in human history—in chapter 11 of Genesis. Mesopotamian texts assert that Mankind was granted 'kingship'—an urban civilization—by a decision of the Anunnaki leadership, taken in their council, during Anu's state visit to Earth circa 4000 B.C.; and indeed, all excavations of Sumer's earliest cities show no date earlier than that (ZS has suggested that the Calendar of Nippur, still used by Jews as their calendar, that began in 3760 B.C., serves as a good starting-time indicator). It is such a deliberate decision by the advanced Anunnaki to grant some of their knowledge to Mankind that can explain the sudden and unprecedented rise of a high civilization in that part of the world, with its myriad 'firsts'—the first urban centers, first writing, first wheel, first kiln, first kings and a social organization, first musical notes and poetry, first schools and homework, first doctors, first religion (with a pantheon and priesthood), first mathematical system, first taxes, first law codes, first high rise buildings, first observatories, first calendar, etc. etc. Sumer's demise, vividly described in Lamentation Texts, came about as a result of an "Evil Wind"—per ZS, a deathly nuclear cloud blowing over the land from the nuclear explosion in the Sinai in 2024 B.C. Sumerian remnants formed the first recorded human Diaspora, traceable to the Far East as well as to enclaves in Europe. Sumer's legacy lives on in virtually every aspect of modern civilizations, not the least in the continuing Nippur Calendar. *See* Anunnaki, Edin, Mesopotamia.

▸ Susa: The capital of Elam, then of the Achaemenid/Persians, called *Shushan* in the Bible; the locale of the events told in the Book of Esther. *See* Elam, Persia.

▸ Syene: *See* Aswan.

▸ Syria: The current political entity that extends from the Euphrates River westward to the Mediterranean Sea was, in antiquity, primarily the land of the Semitic Amorites (= 'Westerners', biblical *Aramites*). It was over the millennia and centuries since the 3rd millennium B.C. the arena of various kingdoms and city-states (e.g., Aram, Ebla, Mari, Mitanni, Palmyra, Ugarit) as well as of major battles between the imperial powers in antiquity. Its current capital, Damascus, is one of the oldest continuously inhabited cities in the world, and was already mentioned in the Bible's tales of Abraham.

▶ Tabernacle: The portable tent built by Moses, in accordance with God's detailed instructions, to house the Ark of the Covenant during the Exodus.

▶ Table of Nations: The scholarly term applied to chapter 10 of Genesis, in which the Bible lists the spread of humanity on Earth after the Deluge, starting with the three sons of Noah, then listing their descendants and offsprings through the generations, using the individual names as nation-lands names.

▶ Tablets of Destinies: Objects that were used in Enlil's Mission Control Center in Nippur to track planetary orbits and control space travel. When the evil **Zu** stealthily removed them, and "took them away in his hands," the Mission Control Center's hum fell silent, the blueish aura fell dark, and the **Me** (usually translated 'Divine Formulas') "were suspended." *See* Divine Formulas, Mission Control Center, Zu.

▶ *Tammuz*: *See* Dumuzi.

▶ Tampu-Tucco: An earlier name for Machu Picchu. Some of the legends about the place relate to the existence there of a wall with three windows.

▶ *TaNaKh*: A term referring to the whole Hebrew Bible—the initials of the Bible's three parts: *Torah* (= 'Teachings'), *Neviyim* (= 'Prophets'), *Khetuvim* (= 'Writings').

▸ Tanis: The Greek name for the city TANIS in Lower Egypt (the biblical *Zo'an*), a city dedicated to the god Horus where he settled the "Metal People"—followers of his whom he had taught to forge metal weapons.

▸ Taurus: The zodiacal constellation of the Bull, **Gu.anna** (= 'Heavenly Bull') in Sumerian; the constellation associated with Enlil. *See* Bull of Heaven.

▸ Taurus Mountains: A mountain range in Asia Minor (today's Turkey) that runs east-west along a great part of the country's south, with peaks rising to 10,000–12,000 feet; the Euphrates and Tigris rivers and their tributaries originate in those mountains. The Hittites and other Anatolian peoples mined silver and then tin in those mountains; ZS has suggested that after the Deluge, the god Teshub/Adad brought over mining experts from Anatolia to obtain gold and tin in the Lake Titicaca region in South America. *See* Adad, Metallurgy, Teshub, Titicaca.

▸ *Tell Ghassul* (= 'Mound of the Messenger'): An ancient site east of the Jordan River, near the Dead Sea, where archaeologists of the Vatican's Pontifical Biblical Institute found wall murals depicting bulbous spacecraft with round 'eye' openings and extended legs. ZS has associated the site with the biblical tale of the heavenward ascent of the Prophet Elijah "in a whirlwind'.

▸ Temple: The Sumerian term that is translated 'temple' is the cuneiform sign read '**E**', which means 'House/Abode/Residence'—for, distinct from a mere shrine honoring this or that god or goddess, the temple was deemed to be the actual place of residence of an actual god. Thus, Enlil (and his spouse Ninlil) were deemed to actually reside in the **E.kur** (= 'House which is like a mountain'), their ziggurat-temple in Nippur; Marduk actually resided and granted kingships in his magnificent ziggurat **E.temen.an.ki** (= 'The Heaven-Earth Foundation House'), and was served there by a complex retinue of priests; when Gudea completed building the new temple **E.Ninnu** (= 'House of Fifty') in Lagash, Ninurta and his spouse Bau took up residence in it amid ceremonial festivities. The temple to Yahweh that Solomon built was also called

Beit Mikdash (= 'Consecrated House'), except that only God's 'Spirit' or 'Glory' were to make it their home, for "Yahweh's abode was in the heavens." In post-Sumerian times, temples that were not ziggurats were usually rectangular structures, divided into three sections—an entrance hall, a main large hall for rituals and worship, and an innermost Holy of Holies. There is no indication that Egyptian temples were intended as physical godly residences—in the innermost Holy of Holies, only effigies of gods were found. The Canaanite texts held that the head of the pantheon, *El* (with his spouse *Asherah*) lived somewhere in retirement, and that the active *Ba'al* (= 'Lord') resided in the 'Secret Place of the North' (Ba'albek per ZS). Aztec, Maya and Inca temples seem to have emulated the Egyptian model, serving mostly as glorified shrines.

▸ Temple Mount: Mount *Moriah* (= 'Mount of Directing'), the middle mount of Jerusalem's three, situated between Mount *Zophim* (= 'Mount of Observers') to the north and Mount *Zion* (= 'Mount of the Signal') to the south. It is so called because it was on its platform that the Temple to Yahweh was built. Surrounded by a wall, the elevated platform contains the sacred *Even Shatit* (= 'Foundation Stone') where, tradition and archaeological studies indicate, the Temple's Holy of Holies was (now, encompassed by the Dome of the Rock, it is a Moslem shrine). On the west, the ancient platform is supported by the Western Wall, a relic from Temple times whose foundations reach native bedrock. Remains from the time of Jesus indicate that the public access to the Temple was via a ceremonial staircase and gates in the south wall. *See* David, Jerusalem Temple, Solomon.

▸ Temple Orientations: From the very beginning, the celestial orientation of temples was a most important aspect of their construction. Square ziggurats had their corners pointed precisely to the four cardinal points. In rectangular temples, the long axis ran either precisely east-west, or was aligned with one of the solstices; Sir Norman Lockyer, the father of archaeoastronomy, called the former (as Solomon's Temple in Jerusalem) Equinoctial or Eternal Temples, and the latter (such as those in Egypt or the Americas) Solstitial Temples whose orientation could help date them. Gudea received divine help in orienting the E.Ninnu temple in Lagash; Egyptian depictions showed gods indicating where the corner stone of a temple should be laid.

▸ Ten Commandments: The term applied to the ten religious and ethical principles of the Covenant made between God and the people of Israel at Mount Sinai, as stated in Exodus 20:2–17 and reiterated in Deuteronomy 5:6–18. The first three state the religious principles of a monotheism centered on following Yahweh; the fourth commands keeping the seventh day as the Sabbath; the fifth instructs respect for one's parents; the other five, beginning with the words "thou shalt not," direct social and moral behavior. In establishing monotheism and prohibiting graven images, the Commandments were unique in the prevailing polytheism involving worship of many gods represented by their statues; in its social and ethical instructions, the Commandments differed from the law codes of other nations that (like Hammurabi's in Babylon) were lists of crimes and their punishments. The Commandments (literally, 'Sayings' in Hebrew), were inscribed on two stone tablets that Moses was given on Mount Sinai; they were the only objects kept in the Ark of the Covenant.

▸ Tenochtitlan (= 'City of Tenoch'): The Aztec name for their capital, established in the midst of a lake by following legendary guidelines. When the Spaniards arrived, they were astounded to find a bustling metropolis, crisscrossed by canals, with twin-towered temples and great palaces. ZS has wondered whether the name might be understood as the 'City of *Enoch*'—because according to the Bible the outcast Cain built a city "in the Land of Wandering" and called it by the name of his son, Enoch. Mexico City was built by the Spaniards over the destroyed Aztec capital; recent archaeological excavations in Mexico City's main square have exposed some remains (and many artifacts) from Aztec times.

▸ Teotihuacan (= 'Place of the gods'): A huge ancient site northwest of Mexico City, known primarily for its 'Pyramid of the Moon', 'Pyramid of the Sun', and a wide 2.5-mile-long 'Avenue of the Dead' along which the step-pyramids and many other sacred structures, including a tem-

ple to Quetzalcoatl, are situated. Legend has it that the pyramids commemorate a Time of Darkness, when the Sun failed to rise. The gods
gathered at Teotihuacan to discuss what to do. After two gods sacrificed
themselves, the Wind God blew at the Sun and it resumed its motion.
Archaeological evidence suggests that the site's first builders were the
Olmecs; carbon dating suggests a date of circa 1400 B.C. for the two
pyramids. All that has induced ZS to relate the delayed sunrise (that
is also mentioned in South American lore) to the 'Day the Sun stood
still'—did not set for twenty hours—on the other side of the world at
the time of Joshua—also circa 1400 B.C.

▸ *Tera<u>h</u>*: The father of Abraham who moved from Ur in Sumer to <u>H</u>arran
in northern Mesopotamia with his family, including his sons Abram and
Nahor and their wives. Based on literal readings of the Hebrew text,
ZS has concluded that the family originated in Nippur, and that *Terah*
comes from the Sumerian **Tirhu** (= 'Oracle Speaker'), suggesting that
Terah was an Oracle Priest.

▸ Teshub: The head of the Hittite pantheon, so-called 'Storm God'. *See*
Adad, Hittites, Ishkur.

▸ Thebes: The name, from the Greek Thebai, of the southern capital of
ancient Egypt, on the Nile's eastern bank, during the Middle and
New Kingdoms. It is mentioned in the Bible as *Noh Amon*, matching
its Egyptian name NEUT-AMON (= 'The pleasant city of [the god]
Amon'). The great temples of Karnak and Luxor, a major tourist attraction, were part of ancient Thebes.

▸ Third Pyramid: Usually a reference to the smaller of the three pyramids in
Giza; attributed by Egyptologists to the Pharaoh Menkara. ZS, who has
attributed all three to the Anunnaki, has suggested that this pyramid
was in fact the first one—built by the Anunnaki as a scale model, to test
the incline and other features that were subsequently incorporated in the
larger two.

▸ Third Region: The Indus Valley, chosen by the Anunnaki as the third
region for giving Mankind civilization; put under the aegis of Inanna.

▸ Thirtieth Parallel: Per ZS, just as the heavens around the Earth were divided into segments at the 30th parallels north and south (*see* Stars), so was the Earth itself divided by the Anunnaki. The 30th parallel north was the most important one: It ran through the heart of the Giza complex, with the Sphinx gazing precisely east along this parallel, toward the Spaceport in the Sinai, which was located on the 30th parallel (north); so was Eridu (Enki's city, the first Anunnaki settlement in the Edin); and farther east—Harappa of the Indus Valley civilization. All focal points of the Four Regions—the Anuunnaki's in Giza/Sinai, the three first civilizations—were thus located on this parallel. So were the centers of subsequent civilizations: Persepolis (the Persian capital), then Lhasa (the sacred center of Tibet).

▸ Thoth: A major god of ancient Egypt whose attributes included that of Divine Architect (and thus his Egyptian name TEHUTI = 'Drawer of the Cord' = the Divine Measurer); the Divine Scribe, who recorded the decisions of the gods or the deeds of men when their fate was weighed; god of secret knowledge, god of mathematics, numbers and the calendar; god of magic who could resurrect the dead. He was usually depicted with the head of an Ibis bird (meaning 'Wisdom'). According to Manetho, Thoth was descended of Ptah, and reigned for 1,560 years when gods alone ruled over Egypt; but in time, having quarreled with his half-brother the god RA, had to go into exile (according to ZS, Ptah, Ra and Thoth were the gods Enki, Marduk and Ningishzida in Sumer). In Egypt, Hieroglyphic texts known as 'Tales of the Magicians' revealed that the 'Secret Number of Thoth' was 52; it was expressed in the 52 x 7-day weeks calendar (and in his reign of 52 x 30 = 1,560). That was one of the clues suggesting to ZS that in Mesoamerica Quetzalcoatl was Thoth, for there 52 was the 'Sacred Number' of the Haab and Tzolkin calendars, when they meshed back to the same spot, linked to the promised return of Quetzalcoatl. ZS has thus suggested that in 3113 B.C. Thoth, expelled by Ra/Marduk from Egypt, took along a group of African followers to Mesoamerica, where he was called Quetzalcoatl. *See* Calendars, Mesoamerica, Ningishzida, Olmecs, Quetzalcoatl.

▶ Thothmes (also Thothmose, Tuthmosis) = 'Issue of Thoth': The name given to several Pharaohs of the 18th dynasty, the most famous of whom was Thothmes III (1504–1450 B.C.) who greatly extended Egypt's domains in Africa and Asia, launched campaigns to capture the Landing Place and Naharin, and controlled Canaan up to the Hittite border after a great battle at Megiddo. Thothmes IV is mostly remembered for his encounter, when still a prince, with the Sphinx. As recorded on a stela erected between the paws of the Sphinx, the Sphinx at that time was covered by the desert sands up to its neck. Tired after a hunt, the prince fell asleep there and in a dream the Sphinx spoke to him, asking to be freed of the sand, promising the prince future kingship if he would. The prince did, and in time became king. *See* Ahmose, Hatshepsut, Mitanni, Moses, Sphinx.

▶ Tiahuanacu (also Tiwanaku): A major site near the southern shores of Lake Titicaca (now in Bolivia) where—according to any one of several legends—the Creator God Viracocha had arrived in great antiquity, and from which human settlement of South America began. Surprisingly, explorers and archaeologists had to reach corroborating conclusions. Spanish chroniclers declared the place "the oldest in the world." The 19th century explorer E. G. Squier called it "the Baalbec of the New World;" and its most famous and dedicated explorer in the 20th century, Arthur Posnansy, calling Tiahuanacu "The Cradle of American Man," determined it to be more than 10,000 years old. The principal monuments at the site corroborate its great age, and per ZS hold clues to the identity of its builders and their reasons for creating a megalithic city amidst barren mountains some 2.5 miles above sea level. Of the three principal monuments, the most picturesque is the ***Gate of the Sun***, a colossal stand-alone gateway whose large doorway, decorated arch, jambs, lintels, niches and false windows are all cut and shaped from a single huge stone block weighing over one hundred tons. Intricate carvings on the archway depict the god Viracocha as a central figure dominating three rows of winged beings—an arrangement with calendrical meaning. ZS has shown that the depiction of Viracocha, holding a scepter and a lightning, is similar to the way the Hittites of Anatolia depicted their principal deity Teshub/Adad, and the winged beings emulate similar Hittite depictions.

This and other facts led ZS to suggest that, when in the aftermath of the Deluge the Anunnaki shifted the gold obtaining operations to South America, the metal savvy Hittites led by Teshub were brought over. That Tiahuanacu was a metallurgical center—for gold as well as for tin—is further attested by the second prominent monument, the *Akapana*: an artificial hill that was thought to be the remains of a pyramid; but excavations revealed in its interior a series of channels and chambers connected by conduits and equipped with sluices that suggest that it was a facility for metallurgical processing—the obtainment of tin from its Cassiterite ore, per ZS. Conclusive to determining the site's age is the third prominent monument; called the *Kalasasaya*, it is a rectangular enclosure of about 400 × 450 feet that included a sunken court and was delineated by a series of standing stone pillars. The east-west orientation, and the number of pillars and their positions, suggest an astronomical function relating to both equinoxes and solstices. The angle (or 'obliquity') for the solstices conforms to a construction date of either circa 10000 B.C. or 4000 B.C.—the former (per ZS) coinciding with the post-Diluvial activities of the Anunnaki, the latter matching Anu's state visit to Earth. *See* Akapana, Anu, Gate of the Sun, Kalasasaya, Megalithic Structures, Metallurgy, Puma Punku, Solstices, Tin.

▸ **Ti.amat** (= 'Mother of Life'): According to the Epic of Creation—taken as a sophisticated cosmogony by ZS—an early planet in our Solar System, with eleven satellites (moons), with which an invading planet (called Nibiru/Marduk) collided. As a result of that 'Celestial Battle', Tiamat broke up into two parts—one smashed to bits and pieces to become the 'Heavenly Bracelet' (the Asteroid belt) and the other, thrust to a different orbit, becoming planet Earth, carrying with it Tiamat's main satellite to become Earth's Moon. *See* Asteroid Belt, Celestial Battle, Earth, Epic of Creation, Kingu, Marduk, Nibiru, Planets, Solar System.

▸ Tiglat Pileser III: An Assyrian king (745–727 B.C.) who extracted tribute from the Kingdom of Israel. He was the first Assyrian king to legitimize Assyria's sway over Babylon by paying obeisance to Marduk.

▸ Tigris River: The second great river of Mesopotamia (= 'The Land Between the Rivers') that runs north-south parallel to the Euphrates River, though its sources begin much more to the east; listed in the biblical tale of the Rivers of Eden as *Hidekel* (from the Akkadian *Idiglat*, Sumerian **Idilbat**), it is correctly described as the river "which floweth towards the east of Assyria." *See* Edin, Mesopotamia, Rivers of Paradise.

▸ **Tilmun** (= 'Place/Land of the Missiles'; sometimes rendered Dilmun): A Sumerian name for the Sinai peninsula (or that part of the Peninsula) where the spaceport of the Anunnaki was located. According to the Epic of Gilgamesh, Tilmun, "where the rocketships were raised up," was one of the destinations in his search for immortality; it was there that he encountered Ziusudra/Utnapishtim, the survivor of the Deluge who was granted (together with his wife) Long Life and sent to dwell in Tilmun, the sacred region of the gods. *See* Deluge, Gilgamesh, Ziusudra.

▸ Time: ZS has suggested that faced with an immense difference in time cycles (starting with the planets' orbital periods) between their home planet Nibiru and the Earth—which he named Divine Time and Earthly Time—the Anunnaki created the median of Zodiacal Time. Due to the phenomenon of Precession, Earth's retardation accumulates to one Zodiacal House of 30° every 2,160 years—a number which gave the Anunnaki the 10:6 ratio with Nibiru's 3,600 (Earth)-years orbit (3,600:2,160 = 10:6). It also explains, per ZS, the mathematical basis for the sexagesimal system.

▸ Tin: A metal that, unlike gold, silver or copper, is extremely rare in pure form in nature. It is mostly found oxidized in the form of an ore called Cassiterite, from which the tin is obtained by smelting in furnaces at very high temperatures in a multi-stage process that requires recovery after recombining with carbon. Its usefulness lies in the fact that when added to copper in a small proportion (just over 10%), the resulting alloy—Bronze—gains extraordinary strength. In spite of all the complex metallurgical processes that lead from Cassiterite to Bronze, the 'Bronze Age' was launched in Sumer (where tin was called **An.na** = 'Heavenly stone') as early as 3600 B.C., spreading within several centuries throughout the Near East. The Sumerian achievement was even more remarkable in view of the fact that while copper was available from nearby Near Eastern sources (such as Cyprus, Crete), the tin-bearing ores were far away—either in the Indian subcontinent and the Far East, in the British Isles (Cornwall), or in South America (the environs of Lake Titicaca). ZS, in *The Lost Realms*, quotes a Sumerian text in which Inanna speaks of her domain in the Indus Valley as a source of tin, and provides evidence that the Anunnaki obtained tin at Tiahuanacu in Bolivia—where the world's leading source of tin still is. ZS has even wondered whether the center's name may come from the Akkadian word for tin—*Anaku*—making *Ti-anaku* literally mean 'Tin City'! *See* Bronze, Puma Punku, Tiahuanacu, Titicaca.

▸ Titicaca: The large freshwater lake in the Andes mountains—at the highest elevation on Earth—that is now divided between Peru and Bolivia. The important ruins of Tiahuanacu and Puma Punku, now not far from the lake but originally on its southern shore, served, per ZS, as the metallurgical source of gold and tin of the Anunnaki after the Deluge. The Lake's name, ZS has pointed out, could be understood as 'Rock of Tin' in the native Aymara tongue—matching a legend that the god Viracocha obtained for Mankind tin from an island in the midst of the lake. *See* An (Anu), Bolivia, Bronze, Gold, Megalithic Structures, Puma Punku, Tiahuanacu, Tin.

▸ Tlaloc: The god of waters and rains of ancient Mesoamerica. His spouse was named Chlchiuhthicue, which meant 'Lady of Waters'.

▸ Tollan: *See* Tula.

▸ Toltecs: A people who were the dominant tribe in north-central Mexico before the Aztecs, known for their advanced artisanship and building skills. The proximity of their capital Tula (also known as Tollan) to Teotihuacan led many scholars to believe that the Toltecs inhabited

Teotihuacan either before or after Tula became their capital, circa 200 B.C. Due to some internal rifts of an unclear nature, the Toltecs one day (maybe circa A.D. 800) packed up and left; some went as far as the Yucatan peninsula, where they took part in designing and building the Mayan Chichén Itzá. *See* Tula.

▸ Torreon (= 'The Tower'): A semi-circular structure in Machu Picchu, Peru, built of perfectly cut, shaped and dressed ashlar stones. Part of a rectangular enclosure reached by seven steps, it stands atop the Sacred Rock of Machu Picchu.

▸ Tower of Babel: According to Genesis 11, it was after men settled in Sumer, when "the whole Earth was of one language and of one kind of words" that the people schemed to "build a city with a tower whose head will reach the heavens," so that they could obtain a *Shem*—a term commonly translated 'Name'. Yahweh got concerned and suggested to unnamed colleagues to foil Mankind's plot by confusing its languages: The Bible draws the city's name, *Babel* (= Babylon) from the Hebrew verb *BLL* (= 'Mix up, confuse'). While the notion that at one time Mankind had only one language is found in varied Sumerian texts as well as in the writings of Berossus, ZS connected the tale to Marduk's first attempt to build a Launch Tower in Babylon, his city in Mesopotamia, and dated the event to 3460 B.C.—a chaotic period when Ra/Marduk was away from Egypt. ZS based his interpretation on a "Tower of Babylon" tale in a clay tablet (K. 3657) found in the library of Ashurbanipal, and on his suggestion that, in certain contexts, *Shem* means a rocketship. *See* Babylon, Confusion of Languages, Marduk, Shem.

▸ Tree of Knowledge: According to Genesis 2:9, two special trees were growing in the Garden of Eden, the "Tree of the Life" and the "Tree of Knowing good and evil;" it was of the latter's fruit that God forbade The Adam to eat. A female companion, Eve, was then fashioned; and it was she who was persuaded by the Serpent to eat and share with Adam the fruit of the Tree of Knowing—a transgression for which the couple was expelled from the Garden of Eden. While the biblical term is usually rendered 'Tree of Knowledge', ZS has suggested translating 'Tree of

Knowing', "knowing" being the term used in the Bible to mean having sex in order to procreate. The tale, per ZS, deals with a second genetic manipulation—by the 'serpent' Enki—to enable the infertile hybrid to procreate. *See* Eden, Enki, Serpent.

▶ Tree of Life: In the biblical tale of Adam and Eve in the Garden of Eden, the Tree of Life "grew in the midst of the Garden." It was after the couple ate the fruit of the Tree of Knowing that Yahweh expressed (to unnamed colleagues) his concern lest they would also eat of the Tree of Life "and live forever;" so Adam and Eve were driven out of the Garden of Eden, and Cherubim were placed "to guard the way to the Tree of Life." Egyptian texts refer to the "Tree in the Land of Living;" Mesopotamian texts refer to a "Plant of Life." Depictions in both civilizations show the tree as a Date Palm; in Mesopotamian art (and especially so Assyrian) the Tree of Life is often shown flanked by divine beings. *See* Date Palm, Plant of Life.

▶ Tres Zapotes: A leading Olmec site in Mexico, where the first sculpted giant Olmec stone head was discovered (at the end of the 19th century).

▶ Trilithon: The name applied to three colossal stone blocks, each weighing more than 1,100 tons, emplaced in the western retaining wall of the platform at Ba'albek. *See* Ba'albek.

▶ Tubal-Cain: A descendant of the exiled Cain who, according to the Bible, "was the master of all smiths."

▶ Tula: The erstwhile Toltec capital on the banks of the Tula River in north-central Mexico, also known as Tollan (= 'City of great many people'). It was completely abandoned by its inhabitants circa A.D. 800; but its pyramids, monumental buildings, and other features of its vast sacred plaza still amaze and thrill visitors to this day. Best known and most enigmatic are the 'Atlantes'—gigantic statues of humanlike warriors, armed with weapons that include a kind of 'ray guns', but whose facial features are unlike any known people on Earth; they stand arrayed on the flat top of one of the step-pyramids. *See* Atlantes, Toltecs.

▶ Tunnel of Hezekiah: A secret subterranean tunnel cut through bedrock by king Hezekiah to supply Jerusalem with water during an anticipated siege by the Assyrian king Sennacherib. Explorers found in the 19th century an inscription, in royal Hebrew script, carved into the tunnel's wall where the diggers, working from both ends, met. The wall segment with the inscription is now in the Istanbul Museum in Turkey. *See* Hezekiah.

▶ Turin Papyrus: A major archaeological find, now kept in the Egyptian Museum in Turin, Italy, that lists Egypt's ancient rulers arranged by dynasties, starting with the divine dynasty of the gods.

▶ Turquoise: A semi-precious blue-green stone that was cherished by the ancient Egyptians, and was mined by them in the Sinai.

▶ Twelve: Alongside the number Seven but perhaps of longer lasting significance was the number Twelve—12 months in a year, 12 zodiacal houses, 12 double-hours in a day, 12 Great Gods of Sumer & Akkad, a pantheon of 12 'Olympians', 12 sons of Jacob, 12 tribes of Israel, 12 apostles of Jesus, etc. ZS has suggested that this significance stems from the Sumerian repeated statements that the Solar System has 12 members: the Sun, the Moon, and ten planets—the 10th being Nibiru. (Correctly, the title of ZS's first book, *The 12th Planet*, should have been 'The Planet which is the 12th member of the Solar System'.)

▶ Typhon: In Greek tales of the gods, Typhoeus (Typhon) was a monstrous Titan whom Zeus defeated with thunderbolts in aerial battles. The Greek historian Herodotus, in rendering the Egyptian tale of the contending of Horus and Seth, equated Seth with Typhon. The final battle in both tales took place in the skies of the Sinai peninsula.

▶ Tyre (H *Tzor*): One of the two principal Phoenician city-states in biblical times. Its king Hiram provided Solomon with cedars of Lebanon for the building of the Temple in Jerusalem, and Hiram's ships circumnavigated Africa to bring gold from Ophir. *See* Phoenicia.

▶ Tzolkin: The Aztec/Mayan 'Sacred Year' calendar, which was based on

13 rotations of 20 days, to form a 'year' of 260 days; its origin and basis have baffled scholars. It is certain, however, that it was supposed to rotate gearlike with the Mesoamerican Haab calendar, in which 18 rotations of 20 days resulted in a year of 360 days (to which, as in Egypt, 5 special days were added to result in a solar year of 365 days). When the two geared calendars rotated, they repeated the cycle after 52 years—fifty-two being the Secret Number of Thoth. *See* Calendars, Thoth, Quetzalcoatl.

▶ **Ubartutu**: According to the Sumerian King List and the Atra-Hasis Epic, he was a human of divine descent whose son, **Ziusudra** (Akk. *Utnapishtim*), was the hero of the Deluge. *See* Deluge, Lamech, Noah, Utnapishtim, Ziusudra.

▶ Ugarit: A major 2nd millennium B.C. Canaanite city, unearthed in the 1930s at a site called Ras Shamra on Syria's Mediterranean coast. The finds included a hoard of clay tablets, in what had been the royal library, inscribed (in cuneiform script) in a language akin to Hebrew, bringing to light Canaanite tales of gods and heroes. The writings made possible an understanding of Canaanite culture and religion in the context of biblical references.

▶ Upper Sea: The term, in Assyrian and Babylonian texts, for the Mediterranean Sea. *See also* Great Sea.

▶ **Ur** (= 'The City'): The 'cult center' of Nannar/Sin that served three times as the capital of Sumer. The Ur III period (2113–2024 B.C.), considered the most glorious era of the Sumerian civilization, ended with Sumer's demise in the aftermath of the nuclear events of 2024 B.C. At its peak, Ur was a walled city with a king's palace, administrative buildings, wide streets, schools, workshops, merchant's warehouses, two-storied dwellings, and a sacred precinct with a majestic ziggurat-temple with a monumental stairway for Nannar and his spouse Ningal. Its two harbors, linked by canals to the Euphrates River, enabled its merchants to trade with distant lands, importing metals and raw materials and exporting the garments for which Ur became famous. The Bible states that Abraham came to Harran from "Ur of One Chaldea;" ZS has suggested that he was actually born in Nippur, then grew up and was married in Ur, where his father Terah served as a priest. Some of the most artful artifacts discovered in Sumer were unearthed by Sir Leonard Woolley in what he termed 'The Royal Tombs of Ur'. *See* Abraham, Nannar, Sin, Sumer, Terah.

▶ Uranus: According to the Epic of Creation (when treated as a cosmogony), the twinlike planets we call Uranus and Neptune were formed at the same phase of the Solar System. Its Sumerian name was **En.ti.mash** (= 'Lord of Bright-Greenish Life'); its Akkadian name was *Kakkab Shanamma* (= 'Planet which is the double'), and ZS has used these epithets to predict the main Voyager 2 1986/1989 discoveries at Uranus and Neptune. Uranus is unique in that it lies on its side, its north pole (rather than its equator) facing the Sun—the result, according to NASA, of the planet getting a "big whack" at some time. One of its moons, Miranda, also shows signs of having been 'whacked', and ZS, in *The End of Days*, has suggested that it was all due to a collision with one of Nibiru's moons during a passage that might have coincided with the Deluge on Earth. *See* Deluge, Halley's Comet, Nibiru, Planets.

▶ **Ur.gula** (= 'Lion'): The Sumerian name for the constellation we call Leo (= The Lion). According to Sumerian texts, the Deluge occurred at the start of that zodiacal time, i.e., some 13,000 years ago.

▶ *Uriah*: According to the Bible, a Hittite officer in king David's army who was killed because the king coveted his wife Bathsheva.

▶ **Ur-Nammu** (= 'The Joy of Ur'): The first ruler of the Third Dynasty of Ur whose mother was the goddess Ninsun (the erstwhile mother of Gilgamesh). The transfer of the capital to Ur, under the auspices of Nannar/Sin, and the selection of a man of divine ancestry as the new king (in 2113 B.C.), were intended by the gods—and indeed turned out to be—a new page in Sumer's 2000-year-old history, an attempt to reintroduce the moral codes and "Way of Righteousness" that typified the civilization's beginning. Unfortunately, the Near East was already caught in the mounting Enki'ite-Enlilite conflicts spearheaded by Marduk's lurch for supremacy; and Ur-Nammu, the "Peace King," ended dead on a battlefield in 2096 B.C. *See* Sumer, Ur.

▸ *Ur-Shanabi*: The boatman, in the Epic of Gilgamesh, who ferried Gilgamesh across the "Waters of Death" on his way to the abode of Utnapishtim (the hero of the Deluge in the Akkadian version). *See* Dead Sea, Utnapishtim.

▸ **Ur-Shulim**: The name of a city not far from the Spaceport in the Sinai granted to the god Utu/Shamash, one of whose epithet was **Shulim** (= 'Supreme')—very probably, the origin of *Yeru-Shalem* (= 'The Supreme City'), from which the name of Jerusalem stems.

▸ Uru People: The name of a tribe, now with few remaining members, who settled in the sacred valley of the Urubamba River in Peru at a time "before the Day of Darkness." The similarity of their name to the Sumerian 'Ur', and the fact that many words in their language seem identical to Akkadian, have led to speculation that the Uru indeed represent remnants of Mesopotamians brought over to the Andes in antiquity.

▸ Urubamba River: An important river in Peru whose valley, amidst the Andean mountains, served as the arena of Peru's oldest settlements and megalithic sites, connecting the Inca capital Cuzco with Machu Picchu (the secret capital of the Ancient Empire). *See* Cuzco, Machu Picchu, Ollantaytambu, Uru People.

▸ **Uruk**: One of the first Sumerian cities, begun as a place for Anu and Antu to stay during their state visit to Earth circa 4000 B.C. *See* Erech, Gilgamesh, Inanna.

▸ **Urukagina**: A Sumerian king in Lagash who, circa 2400 B.C., instituted a code of laws based on social justice, prohibiting mistreatment of poor by rich, of the widowed and the disabled by men of power.

▸ **Usmu** (also **Ushmu**): The two-faced 'vizier' or messenger of Enki. ZS has pointed out that Ea/Enki's celestial counterpart was the planet we call

Neptune, whose 'vizier', the planet Pluto, has an odd orbit that at times faces Neptune from the outer side, and at times from the inner side; the Ea-Ushmu relationship thus matches the celestial Neptune-Pluto phenomenon.

▸ *Utnapishtim* (= 'His day is Life'): The name, in the Akkadian renditions, of the hero of the Deluge. *See* Noah, Ziusudra.

▸ **Utu** (= 'The shining one'): The 'Sun god', better known by his Akkadian name *Shamash*; his pantheon rank number was 20. A grandson of Enlil, the twin brother of Inanna. As the second generation born on Earth (after their parents, Nannar/Sin and Ningal/Nikkal), Utu and his sister grew up quickly, and he became at a young age commander of the Eaglemen at the spaceport in Sippar. According to a text quoted by ZS, after the Deluge Utu, nicknamed *Shulim*, was put in charge of Mission Control Center in *Ur-Shulim* (= Jerusalem). In his old age, Utu/Shamash, retired in Sippar, was considered the god of justice and laws. *See* Eaglemen, Sippar, Spaceport.

▸ Uxmal: An important Mayan site in the Yucatan peninsula of Mexico.

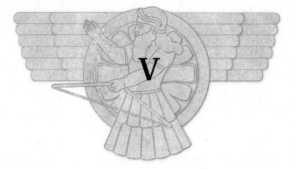

V

▸ Varuna: One of the principal Hindu deities. *See* Adityas.

▸ Vedas: Sacred scriptures of ancient India, consisting of compositions of hymns, sacrificial formulas, spells and 'Sayings' pertaining to the gods—composed, according to Hindu traditions, by the gods themselves at a previous age, then rendered in Sanskrit by sages who arranged the verses in four books. Because the Vedic tales bear surprising resemblances to Greek tales of the gods, it is assumed that they all have a common 'Indo-European' origin from the Caucasus region.

▸ Venus: A name applied to a goddess, a zodiacal constellation, and a planet—both nowadays and in antiquity, starting in Sumerian times: The goddess was the unmarried Inanna/Ishtar (having replaced the unmarried Ninmah/Ninharsag); the constellation (that we call Virgo = 'The Maiden') was called **Ab.Sin** ('Whose father is Sin'); the planet was called *Lahamu* in the Epic of Creation, **Dilibad** or **Dilbat** in Sumerian, and 'Inanna' or 'Ishtar' in later astronomical texts.

▸ Veracruz: The site, on Mexico's Gulf coast, where the Spaniards led by Hernando Cortés landed in 1519. (The house he built there as his head-quarters, though in ruins, still stands there.) The Mexican state that bears this name was a principal realm of the Olmecs. *See* Mesoamerica, Olmecs.

▸ Viracocha: The principal deity of the south Andean peoples in pre-Columbian times whose name meant 'Creator of All'; possibly the

217

same deity worshipped as 'Pachacamac' (= 'Creator of All') in the central Andes. Legends assert that he had come from elsewhere, and in time left, promising to return. His main abode and center of creativity was the southern shore of Lake Titicaca and two islands therein; it is his image that is carved on the 'Gate of the Sun' in Tiahuanacu. It was there that the first human couple, or brother-sister couples, were given by Viracocha a golden wand with which to find the place (later called Cuzco) for starting Andean civilization. ZS has linked these tales to Mesopotamian lore and has identified Viracocha as Enlil's son Ishkur/Adad. *See* Adad, Ayar Brothers, Bay of Paracas, Cuzco, Golden Enclosures, Pachacamac, Tiahuanacu, Titicaca.

▶ Virgo: The zodiacal constellation of 'The Maiden'—**Ab.Sin** in Sumerian. *See* Inanna, Venus.

▶ Vishnu: A principal Hindu deity. *See* Adityas.

▶ Votan: Spanish chroniclers of Mayan Tales of Beginnings recorded the 'Legend of Votan', according to which a leader by that name, whose emblem was the serpent, arrived by boat in the Yucatan peninsula of Mexico and built there the first cities; he was "a descendant of the Guardians, of the race of *Can*, and his place of origin was the land called *Chivim*." This tale was one of the reasons ZS has wondered whether the distant 'Land of Wandering' of the biblical *Cain* might have been Mesoamerica. *See also* Tenochtitlan.

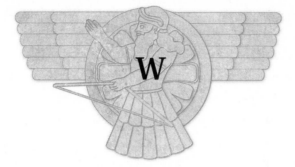

▶ War of the Kings: An international war at the time of Abraham, described
in chapter 14 of Genesis, that pitted four Kings of the East against five
Kings of the West. Most of the names of the kings and their kingdoms
have been easily identified, except for the leader of the eastern alliance,
"Amraphel king of Shin'ar" (i.e. Sumer); ZS has applied to the problem a
body of cuneiform tablets known as The Khedorla'mer Texts, and has suggested that *Amraphel* stands for **Amar.Pal**, also known as **Amar.Sin**—an
Ur III king at the time of Abraham. ZS has also suggested that the
target of the invasion was the Spaceport, which Abraham successfully
defended.

▶ Wars of the gods: The lore of all the ancient civilizations of the Old World
contains references, descriptions and even depictions of fighting between
gods. While the *Enuma elish* ('Epic of Creation') described the celestial
collision between Tiamat and the invading Nibiru as a battle in heaven
between two gods, Tiamat and Marduk, other Sumerian texts dealt with
actual battles between gods on Earth, starting with one on one (Ninurta
against Zu) and expanding to group fights (Enlilites versus Enki'ites).
Hittite texts likewise describe fights between Kumarbi and Ullikummi,
involving in time allies of both. Egyptian tales kept the struggles to one on
one: Seth against Osiris, Horus against Seth (except that Horus is stated
to have been the first god to organize a human army to fight for him).
Canaanite tales focused on the battles between Ba'al and his brothers Yam
and Mot. Greek lore used one-on-one conflicts (Zeus against Typhon) as
the explanation for widening conflicts that included groups of gods (Titans,

Giants, Cyclopes, etc.). Hindu tales, emulating the Greek ones, described one-on-one battles (Indra versus Vritra) but thrilled with descriptions of group battles (sometimes involving fleets of airships). With few exceptions (e.g., Inanna against Marduk to avenge the death of Dumuzi) the fights were about supremacy and control of Earth. *See* Weapons of the gods.

▶ Waters of Life: While in Mesopotamian texts the way for mortals to attain immortality was to partake of the Food (or Fruit) of Life, Egyptian Pyramid Texts depicted the Pharaoh seeking eternal life by drinking the Water of Life (in which a Tree of Life sometimes grew). It is unclear whether (or what) the Anunnaki who had come to Earth required to be supplied from Nibiru to sustain their longevity.

▶ Ways: There were several 'Ways'—major traditional caravan routes—that were used in biblical times in peace and war, and are mentioned in the Bible as well as in cuneiform texts. Two were major north-south ways: One, *Derekh Hamelekh* (= 'The King's Way') ran along a mountain range in what is now Jordan, connecting northeastern Mesopotamia with the Red Sea, the Sinai Peninsula, and Egypt. The other, *Derekh Hayam* (= 'Way of the Sea') ran along the Mediterranean coast, connecting Asia Minor and the Levant with Egypt via the Sinai Peninsula; it was still in use in Roman times as their Via Maris. The Bible mentions in the Patriarchal tales and in connection with the Exodus three Ways for crossing the Sinai Peninsula: The Way of the Sea; a somewhat more southern Way of the Land of the Philistines; and the Way of the Pilgrims that cut diagonally from northwest to southeast, leading to the eastern rather than the western side of the Jordan River. *See* Exodus, Route of the Exodus.

▶ Ways of Heaven: The three segments, each occupying 60° of the celestial arc, into which Mesopotamian astronomy divided the heavenly sphere enveloping the Earth: The Way of Enlil in the north, the Way of Ea/Enki in the south, and the central Way of Anu. *See* Astronomy.

▶ Weapons of the gods: Ancient tales of the gods include references to extraordinarily crafted weapons used by the gods in the numerous struggles between them, or when aiding their favored side in Mankind's wars.

Sumerian texts mention the 'Brilliance' of Enlil, which could "turn the gods opposing him into clay;" in the 'Tale of Zu' who stole the Tablets of Destinies, Ninurta used "seven whirlwinds which stir up the dust" to be able to approach Zu and shoot him down with a missile. Ishkur/Adad was depicted holding a lightning bolt as his weapon (and likewise depicted as Viracocha in South America). Horus shot a 'Harpoon' at his opponent Seth; called the "Weapon of Thirty," it was pictorially depicted with multiple arrowlike warheads. Zeus overwhelmed his opponents with a "Thunder Stone" that fired thunderbolts; Indra shot "flashing thunderbolts" that shook the Earth when they hit the ground; Vritra fought with "sharpened missiles." Hindu depictions of gods invariably showed them holding intricate weapons in each hand. Such tales often mention a 'Craftsman of the gods' who fashioned special weapons (including a magical bow for a Canaanite hero that the goddess Anat wanted for herself). And there was the tale in the Erra Epic about the use of nuclear weapons (the biblical upheavaling of Sodom and Gomorrah). In various royal annals, claims were often made by a king that he was provided by his god with special weapons that overwhelmed the enemy. *See* Adad, Aditi, Ashur, Ba'al, Hephaestus, Horus, Inanna, Indra, Kothar Hasis, Ninurta, Viracocha, Zeus, Zu.

▸ Wellington's Chamber: The name given to the second 'Relieving Chamber" above the 'King's Chamber' in the Great Pyramid in Giza. *See* Great Pyramid.

▸ Western Wall (H *Kotel Ma'aravi* or just *HaKotel*): The western retaining wall of the Temple Mount in Jerusalem, upper parts of which date from the Second Temple and the lower courses from the First Temple. The lower courses, now visible down to bedrock via an Archaeological Tunnel, include three colossal stone blocks—a feature that resembles, on a reduced scale, the Trilithon in Baalbek. *See* Baalbek, Jerusalem, Jerusalem Temple.

▸ Winged Beings: Mesopotamian depictions, from Sumer on, frequently showed anthropomorphic beings with wings, often called in translations 'Eaglemen'. Close inspection showed that they were not 'Birdmen'—

creatures half human, half birdlike—for their wings were clearly worn or put on—presumably as part of the uniform of an Anunnaki 'astro-naut'. Utu/Shamash, who commanded the Spaceport, and the flying-about Inanna/Ishtar, were likewise depicted. In Egyptian art (as in the decorations and sculptures in Tut-Ankh-Amen's tomb), such winged divine beings were mostly female. In the Bible, the *Cherubim* atop the Ark of the Covenant and the *Seraphim* (divine beings accompa-nying God's chariot) were described as multi-winged. *See* Cherubim, Eaglemen.

▸ Winged Disc (also Winged Globe): A ubiquitous symbol, found through-out the ancient Near East and Egypt, that was (per ZS) the emblem of the planet Nibiru.

▸ Writing: The recording of objects, a transaction or an event by the use of agreed-upon signs representing a spoken language—as distinct from using mere pictures (such as petroglyphs or cave paintings)—began in Sumer, where scribes using a stylus with a wedge-shaped (= 'Cuneiform') tip impressed signs into wet clay to create a record that others could read and understand. Scholars believe that such writing began in the 4th millennium B.C. as record keeping in temples. Cuneiform writ-ing, in which signs represented spoken syllables (a consonant with a vowel) that could be combined to be read as the spoken word, was adapted to Akkadian, Hittite and other languages and remained in use throughout the ancient Near East until replaced by alphabetic writ-ing at the end of the 2nd millennium B.C.; it differed from Egyptian hieroglyphic writing, which remained essentially a pictographic system until some of its pictographs came to represent consonants. Sumerian texts asserted that when the gods chose **En.mer.dur.anna** to become the first priest, they taught him writing and arithmetic, suggesting that writing was god-inspired; on the other hand, the absence of writing in South America has been explained there by saying that it angered the gods. References in Mesopotamian texts to *Kitab Ilani* (= 'Writing of the gods') and the Bible's assertion that the first set of Tablets given to Moses on Mount Sinai were written by 'the finger of *Elohim*', raise the unresolved issue of what was the language, and thus the 'writing', of the Anunnaki. ZS has suggested that the Alphabet, first encountered in the Sinai at Exodus time, and the structure of Hebrew, reflect the principles underlying DNA. *See* Alphabet, Ashurbanipal, Clay Tablets, Cuneiform Script.

▸ Xerxes: An Achaemenid king of Persia (486–465 B.C.), son of Darius I, who invaded Greece and succeeded in capturing Athens. Most scholars believe that he was the biblical King Ahasuerus, during whose reign the events described in the Book of Esther took place. He is sometimes designated Xerxes I, to differentiate him from his grandson Xerxes II who was murdered as soon as he became king in 424 B.C. *See* Achaemenids.

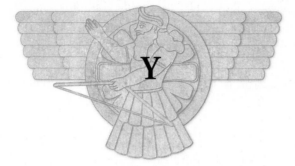

▸ *Yahweh*: A rendering in English of the Tetragrammaton, the four Hebrew letters *Y-H-W-H* that are given in the Bible (Exodus 3:15–16) as God's name; devout Jews avoid pronouncing it, and translators render it 'God' or 'the Lord'. It was revealed by God himself to Moses in the Sinai: When Moses was given the mission to lead the Israelites out of Egypt, he asked for God's name, and at first got the answer "I will be whoever I shall be" (**incorrectly** translated "I am who I am"); but when Moses persisted, he was told to say to them: "YHWH, the God of your fathers, the God of Abraham, the God of Isaac, the God of Jacob hath sent me unto you; this is My eternal name, this is My remembrance from generation to generation." The theological complexities of the subject have been compounded by the use of the name in biblical versions of Mesopotamian tales (e.g., of the Deluge) in which Enlil or Enki are the protagonists: Yahweh is named in the Bible (Genesis 6) where in Mesopotamian texts Enlil sought Mankind's demise, and then is named where in Mesopotamian texts Enki saves Noah. Starting with the assertion that the biblical *Elohim* were the Anunnaki, ZS has explained that the apparent contradiction was no contradiction at all if the true meaning of Yahweh's first answer to Moses is understood. As a cosmic entity, Yahweh acted (on Earth) through physically present emissaries, including various Anunnaki/Elohim; when He was angry with Mankind he was Enlil; when He decided to save Noah, he was Enki. As the Creator of All, he was also the gods' creator—*El Elohim*, the God of the gods, who even reminded them (according to Psalm 82) that they too were mortal as men; only He was God with a capital 'G', eternal and everlasting. ZS has devoted to the subject a chapter in *Divine Encounters*. *See* God/gods.

▶ *Yam* (= 'Ocean, Sea'): In Canaanite tales of the gods, the oldest son and intended successor of *El* (the head of the pantheon), whom the younger son Ba'al challenges and defeats.

▶ Yazilikaya (= 'Inscribed Rock' in Turkish): A sacred Hittite site in north-central Turkey, not far from their ancient capital Hattushas, known for its rock carvings that depict the Hittite gods in procession. The carvings show male deities, organized in companies of twelve (their ranks indicated by garb, weapons and emblems) marching in from the left, and female ones marching in from the right, the two columns meeting at a central panel in which the great god Teshub and his spouse Hebat were depicted in appropriate stance.

▶ *Yeraḥ* (H = 'Moon, Month'): A Semitic epithet for the Moon god Nannar/Sin, from which comes the name of his city in Canaan, *Yeriḥo* ('Jericho').

▶ Yucatan: A large peninsula in eastern Mexico that was the principal land of the Maya peoples. It was one of the early mainland destinations of the Spanish Conquistadors, who sailed there from Cuba in 1511 in search of slave labor—and were astounded to find cities with stone buildings and pyramidal temples. Of some one hundred known Mayan sites—many destroyed by zealous Spanish priests as places of idol worship—several still amaze visitors, at such locations as Chichén Itzá, Dzibilchaltun, Izamal, Mayapan, Oxmal, Tulum. *See* Mayan Civilization.

▶ Yugas: The Hindu name for the Ages that Earth and Mankind have experienced since the beginning of time, in which the key number was 432,000. A Cataryuga ('Great Yuga') was divided into four Yugas whose diminishing lengths were multiples of 432,000, starting with the Fourfold Golden Age (432,000 × 4), then the Threefold Age of Knowledge (432,000 × 3), the Twofold Age of Sacrifice (432,000 × 2), and the present Age of Discord (432,000 years), resulting in a count of 432,000 × 10 = 4,320,000 years for the Cataryuga. A Day of the Lord Brahma—a Kalpa—consisted of 1,000 cycles of Cataryugas = 4,320,000,000 years (which is about the scientifically established age of the Earth). ZS has pointed out that 432,000 was, according to Sumerian texts, the number of years that passed from the arrival of the Anunnaki to the Deluge, equaling 120 orbits of Nibiru (3,600 × 120 = 432,000). *See* Ages.

- Zagros Mountains: The mountain chain forming the eastern boundary of the Mesopotamian plain and marking the beginning of the mountainous plateau where Elam, then Persia, were located.

- *Zaphon* (H = 'North; That which is hidden'): A double meaning applicable both in the Bible and in Canaanite tales of the gods to a site in Lebanon that ZS has identified as the Sumerian 'Landing Place'—Baalbek. *See* Crest of Zaphon, Mount Zaphon.

- Zarpanit: *See* Sarpanit.

- *Zechariah* (H = 'By Yahweh Remembered'): A biblical Prophet who received the word of God "in the second year of Darius"—520 B.C. Unlike earlier prophets whose concern was the nearing Day of the Lord, Zechariah predicted events at the End of Days, suggesting that the Future shall repeat the Past. His messianic oracles regarding a rebuilt Jerusalem included visions that, scholars believe, inspired the author of the New Testament's Book of Revelation.

- *Zephania* (H = 'By God Concealed'): A biblical Prophet who, at the end of the 7th century B.C., proclaimed that "the great Day of the Lord is approaching—it is near." *See* Day of the Lord.

- Zeus: The head of the twelve Olympians of the Greek pantheon, who attained supremacy at the end of long generational wars, after overwhelming his two brothers Hades and Poseidon, and defeating the monstrous Typhon. The Romans renamed him Jupiter (from the Indo-European

Deus-Pitar, 'Father of gods'), and erected the largest-ever temple to him in Baalbek.

▸ **Zi.ba.anna** (= 'Heavenly Scales'): The Sumerian name for the zodiacal constellation we call Libra (= 'The Scales').

▸ Ziggurat (From Akkadian *Ziquratu* = 'That which soars high'): The term used to describe Mesopotamian step-pyramids, built of mud bricks of a specific shape and size, that were the central and tallest structure in a city's sacred precinct; they were a city's most important temple, as well as its astronomical observatory. Begun in Sumer (where they were termed **Esh** = 'Most high'), they were literally ancient skyscrapers, celestially oriented. They usually rose in seven receding stages from a solid first square stage, with the sixth stage serving as a platform for the final houselike seventh stage, the whole structure forming a cube whose height equaled each side of the first stage; the great one in Babylon was a cube of 15 *gar* on each side—about 300 feet; the one in Ur, whose 4,000 year-old remains still dominate the landscape, was somewhat smaller. Studies have shown that the height of the various stages was such that priests, stationed on the various stages, could observe the sequence in which the Moon and planets came into view at night. The houselike seventh stage was no accident either: The ziggurats were intended as actual residences of the gods, each one in his (or her) 'cult center'—as the ziggurats' names, starting with 'E' (= 'House, Abode' in Sumerian) indicated: Enlil's **E.kur**, Ninurta's E.Ninnu, Marduk's E.sag.il, Nannar's E.hul.hul, etc. *See* Gudea, Temples.

▸ **Ziusudra** (= '[His] Life-days Prolonged'): The 'Noah' of the Deluge tale in its original Sumerian version. He was a "man of Shuruppak," the city assigned to Ninmah/Ninharsag, son of the demigod Ubar-Tutu. According to that version, Enki warned him of the coming Deluge, gave him instructions how to build a **Ma.gur.gur** (= 'A boat that can turn and tumble'), and provided him with a navigator to steer the boat to Ararat. Enlil, relenting that he had planned Mankind's demise, then granted to Ziusudra and his wife long life in a land called **Til.mun**, where (millennia later) Gilgamesh managed to reach him. *See* Deluge, Gilgamesh, Noah, Tilmun, Utnapishtim.

▶ *Zo'an*: *See* Tanis.

▶ Zodiac (From the Greek, 'Animal Circle'): The term applied to the twelve star groups (constellations), pictorially representing the 'animals' (bull, lion, ram, fishes, etc.) after which some of them have been called. The significance of dividing the skies around Earth into this central band of twelve stems from a phenomenon called Precession—the retardation in Earth's orbit around the Sun that accumulates to 1° (out of 360°) in 72 years, so that the transition from one zodiacal "House" of 30° requires 2,160 years—the mathematical length of a Zodiacal Age. Though scholars continue to credit 3rd century B.C. Greek astronomers in Asia Minor with the discovery of the zodiacal phenomenon, the undeniable fact is that it was already known in Sumerian times: In *The 12th Planet*, ZS has provided the complete list of the 12 zodiacal constellations, in the Way of Anu, by their Sumerian names and depictions—names, depictions and order used to this day, after some 6,000 years! Calling it 'Celestial Time', ZS asserted that the zodiac was a device invented by the Anunnaki as a workable ratio between their planet's orbit ('Divine Time', averaging 3,600 Earth years) and Earthly Time (Earth's fast 1-year orbit), resulting in a ratio of 10:6 to the 2,160 years of a Zodiacal Age. He has pointed out that the very fact that texts about the Deluge date the event to "the Age of Lion" (that began circa 10860 B.C.) indicate how old the zodiacal device has been. Zodiacal constellations are mentioned in the Bible, where they are called *Mazalot* (from the Akkadian *Manzalu* = 'Stations'). The ZS scenario also explains familiarity with the 12-house zodiac in the Americas, which attributing the zodiac to 3rd century B.C. Greeks fails to explain. Sumerian lists of the zodiacal constellations began with Taurus; Egyptian depictions (among them the one in Denderah) began with Aries. *See* Ages, Ways of Heaven, *and names of individual constellations.*

▶ Zodiacal Ages: The observation, begun in Sumer, of sunrise on the day of the Spring Equinox, to determine (when the starry sky is still observable) which zodiacal constellation is seen in the background. As long as the rising shows, as it was when the Sumerian calendar began, the Constellation of the Bull, one would say it was the 'Age of Taurus'; when the background began to shift to the Constellation of the Ram, we would say that the 'Age of Aries' had begun, and so on. While mathematically a Zodiacal Age lasts 2,160 years (72 × 30 = 2,160), *observationally* the 'Ages' differ in length because the constellations occupy different segments of the sky. In fact, that difference was a paramount issue in the conflicts with Marduk in the 21st century B.C., when the expected changeover from Enlil's Age of the Bull to Marduk's Age of the Ram was delayed. *Mathematically*, this Zodiacal Clock rendered the Ages thus (all dates B.C.): Lion (Leo), 10860 to 8640; Crab (Cancer), 8640 to 6480; Twins (Gemini), 6480 to 4320; Bull (Taurus), 4320 to 2160; Ram (Aries), 2160 to 0; then Fishes (Pisces), 0 to A.D. 2160. According to Berossus, the zodiacal Ages were turning points in the affairs of gods and men—an assertion that has a basis in history, as well as in the fact that Sumerian mathematical tablets were found which listed multiples of 12,960 (= 2,160 × 6) as fractions of the ultimate number 12,960,000 (2,160 × 6,000). *See* Ages, Astronomy, End of Days, Prophecy, Zodiac.

▸ ZOSER: The 2nd Pharaoh of the Third Dynasty (circa 2650 B.C.) whom Egyptologists credit with building the first pyramid in Egypt. The site, called Sakkara or Saqqarah, on the west side of the Nile south of Giza, still staggers visitors with its magnificent stone-walled compound; the pyramid itself—a seven-step structure emulating Sumerian ziggurats— built of crude rocks, wooden logs and mud-mortar—is crumbling. *See* Giza, Pyramids, Sakkara.

▸ **Zu** (from **An.zu** = 'Knower of the heavens'): The evil hero of an epic tale, who misused Enlil's trusting to steal the 'Tablets of Destinies' that were essential to the operations of the Anunnaki; Ninurta succeeded, with great difficulty, to defeat Zu and retrieve the tablets. *See* An.zu, Aerial Battles, Mission Control Center, Nippur, Tablets of Destinies.